My Country, 'Tis of Thee

MY COUNTRY, 'TIS OF THEE

My Faith, My Family, Our Future

KEITH ELLISON

HUNTER

Gallery Books / Karen Hunter Publishing

New York   London   Toronto   Sydney   New Delhi

G

HUNTER

A Division of Simon & Schuster, Inc.	A Division of Suitt-Hunter Enterprises, LLC
1230 Avenue of the Americas	598 Broadway, 3rd Floor
New York, NY 10020	New York, NY 10012

Copyright © 2014 by Congressman Keith Ellison

First Karen Hunter Publishing/Gallery Books trade paperback edition
October 2014

GALLERY BOOKS and colophon are registered trademarks
of Simon & Schuster, Inc.

The excerpt from the speech "The Drum Major Instinct" (on page 63)
is reprinted by arrangement with The Heirs to the Estate of Martin Luther King Jr.,
c/o Writers House as agent for the proprietor, New York, New York.

For information about special discounts for bulk purchases,
please contact Simon & Schuster Special Sales at 1-866-506-1949
or business@simonandschuster.com.

The Simon & Schuster Speakers Bureau can bring authors
to your live event. For more information or to book an event,
contact the Simon & Schuster Speakers Bureau at 1-866-248-3049
or visit our website at www.simonspeakers.com.

Interior design by Aline Pace
Cover design by James Perales
Cover photograph by Carlo Rodrigo Rojas

Manufactured in the United States of America

10 9 8 7 6 5 4 3 2 1

The Library of Congress has cataloged the hardcover edition as follows:

Ellison, Keith, 1963–
    My country, 'tis of thee / Keith Ellison.
        pages cm
    1. Ellison, Keith, 1963–   2. African American legislators—Biography.
3. Legislators—United States—Biography.   4. Muslims—United States—
Biography.   5. United States. Congress. House—Biography.
6. Multiculturalism—United States.   7. United States—Ethnic relations.
8. Social change—United States.   9. United States—Social policy—
1993–   10. United States—Politics and government—2009–   I. Title.
    E901.1.E45A3 2013
    328.73'092—dc23
    [B]   2012051565

ISBN 978-1-4516-6687-8
ISBN 978-1-4516-6688-5 (pbk)
ISBN 978-1-4516-6689-2 (ebook)

To Mom and Dad, Clida and Leonard

CONTENTS

Contents

Introduction

MY COUNTRY

It was a surprisingly cold Tuesday morning on January 20, 2009.

I sat in an area designated for members of Congress, a few feet from the podium where Barack Hussein Obama would be sworn in as America's forty-fourth president. Before he took the oath of office, Aretha Franklin stepped up to the podium to sing "My Country, 'Tis of Thee."

As she began to belt out that song, I forgot the cold.

Maybe I was moved by the solemnity of the moment, or maybe by the rich power of her voice (or maybe my body was numb from the cold), but my mind drifted to another thought.

It occurred to me that maybe I was witnessing America's final step toward actually becoming that "sweet land of liberty."

From the beginning, America was, as President Abraham Lincoln said in the Gettysburg Address, "conceived in Liberty." Yet in 1863 when that speech was delivered, America allowed millions of human beings to be held in bondage.

I thought to myself, here we were at the heart of American liberty—in front of the United States Capitol, built mostly by African American slaves—witnessing a man of African descent being sworn in as president, less than 150 years after the abolition of slavery. If anyone needed further proof of how far we'd come, there I sat: a Muslim by faith, elected to the United States Congress less than ten years after 9/11.

On August 28, 1963, Dr. Martin Luther King Jr. stood at a similar podium on the opposite end of the Mall, on the steps of the Lincoln Memorial. That day he gave his famous "I Have a Dream" speech, marking the end of the March on Washington. Before he proclaimed, "Free at last, free at last, thank God Almighty, we are free at last!" and before he talked about letting freedom ring from the hills of New Hampshire to the Lookout Mountain in Tennessee, he discussed hope and faith.

He said that little black boys and little black girls would be able to join hands with little white boys and little white girls as sisters and brothers. Then he reminded both those gathered before him and all Americans that this hope of his, this faith, was rooted in the promise of America. It was written in our very Constitution.

And he recited the words to this song:

My country, 'tis of thee,
Sweet land of liberty,
Of thee I sing;
Land where my fathers died,
Land of the pilgrims' pride,

From ev'ry mountainside
Let freedom ring!

The lyrics to the familiar song were written in 1832 by Samuel Francis Smith, while a student at Andover-Newton Theological Seminary in Massachusetts. Every American knows this song. It embodies the essential tension of the American ideal. How fitting for Martin Luther King Jr., the great-grandson of slaves, to stand in Washington and recite those words.

And how equally fitting for Aretha Franklin, also a descendant of slaves, to sing of liberty at the swearing-in of America's first black president.

Liberty has had to evolve. It may have been our birthright, but it wasn't always our circumstance. We had to create liberty out of a *hope* for liberty. Liberty needed to be established *after* it was declared.

Just as one relay runner hands the baton to another, we've had signal moments in our history where someone stepped up and took that baton to reach the next runner to get us to the finish line—to that ultimate goal of liberty and justice for all.

In the past, our country has struggled with racial inclusion, and it still does today. We've righted some wrongs, too. Black people have secured full rights as citizens. Racists can try to deny those rights, but the government has laws in place to ensure that liberty is upheld.

Beyond that, it's not socially acceptable for people to make racial comments or be openly racist. In 2007 radio shock jock Don Imus stirred up a tremendous backlash and ultimately was fired for referring to the Rutgers University women's basketball team as a bunch of "nappy-headed hoes." A sports commentator on ESPN was fired in 2012 for referring to the Washington Redskins' quarterback Robert Griffin III as a "cornball brother." And that commentator was black. On the racial front, we as a nation have certainly turned a corner, even if we have many more corners to turn.

Americans have suffered from a wide variety of bigotry. At one time, Catholics were frowned upon by the majority, which is why John F. Kennedy's election as president caused such a stir in 1960. Nor was it easy to be Jewish in America. Throughout the Jim Crow South, signs in front of restaurants, hotels, and theaters would read "No Niggers, No Jews, No Dogs."

Those of us originally from Detroit have an unhappy hometown example. In the 1930s, Father Charles Edward Coughlin was perhaps the most influential and vocal anti-Semite in the country. This was before my time, but if you lived in Michigan, you knew of Father Coughlin. He was a Roman Catholic priest at the National Shrine of the Little Flower in Royal Oak, just outside Detroit. His Sunday afternoon radio show, *The Hour of Power*, carried over the CBS network, was one of the first to command a huge national audience, estimated at forty million listeners. Coughlin was the Rush Limbaugh of the Great Depression. He appealed to "the common man"—the white working class—railing against "the Jews" and defending the rise of Adolf Hitler and the Nazis in Germany. The radio priest's hateful philosophy was spreading like a plague, but a few courageous leaders shone a light on his hatred, providing a beacon for good, decent Americans.

My adopted hometown, Minneapolis, was once a very anti-Semitic place, but Mayor Hubert H. Humphrey stood firmly against bigotry. He fought to get Jews admitted to Anglo-Saxon clubs, declared that discrimination was wrong, and passed the first municipal civil rights ordinance in the nation.

Over the years, courageous people have died fighting for the rights of all our people, but in time the cause of liberty has won out for more Americans.

Our new national stain is hatred of Muslims. As has happened many times, we have both a short memory and a sense of detachment—that it's not a problem as long as it's not happening to us. That is not the American way.

I can't begin to list how many American Muslims have told me stories of how they were humiliated, snatched off airplanes, harassed on their jobs, or fired because of their faith. Mosques have been burned, vandalized, and picketed. The law says that you can have a house of worship anywhere in America, but in places like Lower Manhattan and Sheepshead Bay, Brooklyn, and Murfreesboro, Tennessee, the law is deemed irrelevant.

People have been beaten, had their rights violated, and have been killed simply for "looking like" they might be Muslim. People and congregations have been spied on, not just by their fellow citizens but also by law enforcement authorities. You might think that this was a post-9/11 backlash, yet if you compare statistics on Muslim harassment and cases of assault right after 9/11 with those for today, the numbers have continued to rise. Why?

Groups exist in the country whose purpose, in my opinion, is to spread anti-Muslim hate. They stoke the flames of fear and keep them burning. These groups are urged on by conservative bloggers such as Pam Geller and Robert Spencer. Even some members of Congress have chimed in. These individuals have an agenda, and they spread their stereotypes and politics of fear in the public debate.

We need people who are willing to stand up to them and say, "You do not represent America." Every American is entitled to liberty.

In 2013 a colleague of mine, Representative Walter Jones, who represents the Third Congressional District of North Carolina, stated that he didn't want a local community college library to have books on Muslim culture. When he was challenged for being anti-Muslim, he said, "I don't hate Muslims. Representative Keith Ellison is my friend." To that I responded, "Walter Jones is a friend of mine, but on this he is wrong."

Former representative Tom Tancredo of Colorado's Sixth Congressional District said that if another terrorist attack were launched on America, we should bomb Mecca in Saudi Arabia, the cradle of Islam. This sort of blanket condemnation makes no sense. He basically said that 1.5 billion people are all the same, think the same, and behave the same; if one of them does anything harmful, all should pay. In fact, Muslims throughout the world are incredibly diverse.

Just because you're a member of a religion doesn't mean that you subscribe to the views of its most extreme believers. Even before Osama bin Laden was killed in 2011, he spoke for very few Muslims.

I'm an African American with an English name, so I'm not obviously in the target group. I'm a Muslim and I could get a "pass," but I choose not to. When hate is allowed to go unchecked it persists.

I'm reminded of a quote attributed to the German pastor Martin Niemöller:

> *First they came for the Communists, and I didn't speak out because I wasn't a Communist.*
> *Then they came for the Socialists, and I didn't speak out because I wasn't a Socialist.*
> *Then they came for the trade unionists, and I didn't speak out because I wasn't a trade unionist.*

*Then they came for the Jews, and I didn't speak out because I
wasn't a Jew.*

*Then they came for the Catholics, and I didn't speak out because
I wasn't a Catholic.*

Then they came for me, and there was no one left to speak for me.

If hatred runs rampant, there is only one result. Americans,
while having their issues with hate, have always eventually risen
above it. I'm hopeful that we will do so toward Muslims. Look
how far we've come on race. I can see the tide turning on religion
as it relates to Muslims. For example, I might have been the first
Muslim elected to Congress, but I am not the last.

In 2008 Representative André Carson was elected in the Seventh Congressional District of Indiana. His grandmother Representative Julia Carson was the first woman and the first African
American elected to Congress from her district. He won in a special election, and he's been a great addition to our body.

That's progress.

In April 2011 Terry Jones, pastor of a small church in Florida,
decided to hold a Quran-burning rally in Dearborn, Michigan, a
city of about one hundred thousand, including one of the largest
Muslim populations in America. This boneheaded move was akin
to a Chicago neo-Nazi group's threat in 1977 to march through
Skokie, Illinois, which had a large Jewish population—seven thousand of them Holocaust survivors.

Jones wanted to agitate in the heart of a Muslim area. And
guess what? The people of Dearborn stood up against him. Christians, Jews, atheists, and Muslims came together to let him know
that bigotry and hate weren't welcome. The people of Dearborn
outnumbered Jones's group by five to one. There was an outpour-
ing of protest against hate.

I was invited to attend the anti-Jones rally, but first I reached out to one of my colleagues, Congressman John Dingell, who represents Michigan's Twelfth Congressional District, which includes Dearborn. He told me, "If you want to make Terry Jones irrelevant, then don't go. If you want to add to the circus and give Terry Jones a larger platform, then go and make the most fiery speech you can." The advice made a lot of sense. I called the leaders in Dearborn and told them I wasn't coming. They held their vigil peacefully and showed the haters that love conquers all. Jones ended up bringing people together—for all the right reasons.

The community of Dearborn is a shining example of the hope and promise of America, and not just because it stands against people like Jones. The community has an active sports scene, and many Muslim athletes play on the local high school teams. One year preseason practice fell during the holy month of Ramadan, a time when Muslims fast during the daytime, abstaining from food and water. In the heat of August, players would certainly pass out without water, so the coach of Fordson High School decided to hold his double sessions after sundown, when the fast ends. This action was a beautiful expression of interfaith solidarity.

When Americans are challenged, we generally rise to the occasion. When we're fearful, we generally become divided. When we're courageous and have good leadership, we unite.

This nation was founded on the notion of religious freedom, yet in the wake of 9/11, we somehow forgot our way. The 2001 Patriot Act, enacted just six weeks after the attacks of 9/11, and similar local laws adopted since, have been abused in some cases to deny American citizens our rights. Some of these measures have been passed out of fear rather than justice. Now it's time to be rooted in our strengths and act with courage, hope, and faith.

Yet we have clearly begun to achieve a measure of racial equality and liberty.

))))➤

After Aretha finished singing, and Barack Obama came to the podium with his family to be sworn in by Chief Justice John Roberts, I understood this as the fulfillment of our promise. But we still have more to do. What we accomplished on January 20, 2009, was an unmistakable sign of evolution and growth. But on a deeper level, we still face challenges surrounding race, gender, sexual orientation, and religious diversity.

America is still a land of contrasts.

I learned at an early age alternate words to "My Country, 'Tis of Thee." This was an abolitionist version, penned in 1843 by A. G. Duncan. He wrote:

> *My country, 'tis of thee*
> *Stronghold of slavery, of thee I sing;*
> *Land where my fathers died,*
> *Where men man's rights deride,*
> *From every mountainside, thy deeds shall ring!*

> *My native country, thee,*
> *Where all men are born free, if white's their skin;*
> *I love thy hills and dales,*
> *Thy mounts and pleasant vales;*
> *But hate thy negro sales, as foulest sin.*

And it ends with this:

Trump of glad jubilee!
Echo o'er land and sea, freedom for all.
Let the glad tidings fly,
And every tribe reply,
"Glory to God on high!" at Slavery's fall.

Both versions are patriotic. Both indicate love of country. One smooths over the ugliness of slavery, and the other sees only that ugliness. The first lifts us up as a nation, but the second keeps us firmly grounded, facing the tough realities that we must overcome to be that land of liberty. It is not unpatriotic to acknowledge America's flaws. No country is perfect. All nations have blood on their hands. But our country promised liberty. We have been making progress toward it, albeit inconsistent and choppy. Setbacks, and advances made by imperfect people, still represent progress, especially when we look back across the decades. This is why I love both versions of this song.

Like the first version, I am hopelessly optimistic. But like the second, I am aware of America's unkept promises and its yet-untapped potential for advancing humanity to greater heights. We can't reach the top of the mountain if we don't work together to confront injustice.

I was reflecting on all of this while Aretha Franklin sang. This great-granddaughter of slaves, this daughter of the civil rights icon Rev. C. L. Franklin. This daughter of America. I'm sure her father couldn't have imagined that day. Barack Obama's father couldn't have imagined it, and I know that my maternal grandfather, Frank

Martinez, a civil rights worker in rural Louisiana in the 1950s, would have been dumbfounded.

But what did it mean? Nirvana? Heaven on earth? No. Just more struggles. More challenges. But since we have ascended past hills, we know we can climb the ones before us.

Two years before Barack Obama took his oath to serve our country, I stood before Nancy Pelosi—the first woman Speaker of the House—for the symbolic swearing-in to the 110th US Congress. I felt humbled, awestruck, inspired, and grateful to be there. Among my family in attendance were my mother, a devout Catholic, and my older brother Brian, a Baptist minister who'd donated to George W. Bush's campaign.

The ceremony took place in the Rayburn Room of the US Capitol building. I was the first among the newly elected congressional members to take the oath. I had attracted so much national attention, I guess they wanted me to go first and get it out of the way.

I raised my right hand and placed my left on the Quran, which was being held by members of my family. Suddenly I was blinded by a cascade of camera flashes.

My swearing-in caused so much controversy because of that Quran.

What started out as a simple question posed to me on a late-night Somali-language public access cable TV station turned into a national debate over whether a Muslim should serve in Congress and whether that Muslim should be allowed to swear on anything other than a Bible.

I believe that my oath taken on the Quran was truly an *American* moment. It was a fulfillment of all of those words written in the Constitution by Benjamin Franklin, James Madison, Thomas

Jefferson, and the other framers about their vision for this nation. I'm sure they never could have imagined an African American Muslim from the state of Minnesota serving in Congress, but they created a Constitution that would make it possible.

The Quran on which I chose to lay my hand belonged to Thomas Jefferson, one of the most complex figures in our history. His lofty vision did not align with the way he lived, on a plantation with slaves, but it's our ideals that distinguish us, leading us through the everyday process of redefining this nation and what it means to be American.

What *does* define an American? It's not race. It's not religion. It's not culture. You can go to most neighborhoods and find Chinese takeout or an Italian restaurant. You can buy black hair care products from a place run by Koreans or milk from a corner store run by folks from Central America, the Middle East, or India.

So what's an American?

An American is defined by an attitude. An ethos.

America operates under the notion of equality before the law. Basic fairness is an article of faith. We may not all agree on everything all of the time, but we select our leaders together. The people who lead us are of us. *We* send them to office, and *we* can send them home. America proves that people can govern themselves.

Before the United States was founded, most believed that an elite class was needed to govern because the people were too ignorant. We were the first to succeed at this experiment in self-governance. We can't forget that. We can't forget who we are. As Lincoln said a century and a half ago, "We are engaged in a great civil war, testing whether that nation, or any nation so conceived and so dedicated, can long endure."

And we should never turn back.

What other nation has our history? Barack Obama has no

equivalent in ancient Rome or Greece—or in any modern-day nation, for that matter. Can you imagine a black man being president of China? I'm sure that an African college student somewhere has had a baby with a Chinese woman. Could that child grow up to one day lead China? Very doubtful, perhaps impossible. But in America, it's not only possible, it's been done. I've traveled to many countries in Europe, and I can't imagine a nonwhite person being elected the leader in any of them. France has black leaders in its French Socialist Party, and Poland has a Nigerian-born man in the Parliament. But would Poland or France ever elect a black person as its president or prime minister? If you look beyond European countries, the chances appear slimmer. In countries such as Saudi Arabia, it is very difficult to even become a citizen if you aren't born there. I met a woman recently who was born of Sudanese parents in the United Arab Emirates. She had never set foot in Sudan, but she could never be a citizen of the UAE because her parents were Sudanese. Not here. If you're born in America or legally naturalized, then you're as American as the president. I believe in the greatness of the people in each of these countries, but it is clear that America is a unique place, even exceptional.

In 2010 Tim Scott was elected to represent the predominantly white First Congressional District of South Carolina. He was the first black Republican to represent South Carolina in Congress since 1897. He is a Tea Party–backed Conservative, in a district where Civil War reenactments are held regularly. Many of his constituents have roots in the Confederacy and bemoan the outcome of the Civil War. In fact, one of our congressional colleagues from neighboring Georgia referred to the American Civil War as the "Great War of Yankee Aggression." Whatever.

Yet Representative Scott represented Charleston, where probably more slaves arrived than anywhere else in the country. Now Senator Scott represents the entire state of South Carolina. There is irony in this story: in 2013 he was appointed to the US Senate by South Carolina's governor, Nikki Haley, whose parents immigrated from India.

Only in America!

What do I make of it? I believe that America is a country that is fundamentally fair. If you stick with it, you will not be permanently locked out. But you will need to stick with it, and organize.

Slavery in this country began in 1619, when the first African slaves arrived by ship in Jamestown, Virginia, and it didn't end until 1865. Slavery was permitted in America for nearly 250 years. Blacks were enslaved longer than they have been free. During the period of freedom, however, we've had a black secretary of state, a black secretary of defense, black Supreme Court justices, a black president, several black CEOs of companies such as American Express, Time Warner, and Merrill Lynch, and a few black billionaires.

This movement toward inclusion has not been easy or linear. It took a Civil War and a civil rights movement. Now we see other countries, such as those in the Arab world, fighting for their rights and their identity. But we have led the way.

That's why everyone has an opinion about the United States. I've run into many types of people in my life, but there are two types that I find frustrating. The first are those who have nothing good to say about America. Some of our own citizens, who live under a flag that guarantees their freedom, won't acknowledge that America has made world-leading strides in the cause of human freedom. Then there are those who believe that America is perfect, has always been perfect, and needs no fixing. They will deny the atrocities committed against Native Americans, African Americans, women, and Japanese Americans.

Both of these views are wrong, just as both versions of "America" are correct.

Despite our history and our individual differences, we abide by an awesome promise of liberty and justice for all. It's our job to fulfill it. In order to form a more perfect union, we must continue to extend our promise to everyone.

That's our duty. That's our charge. That's our America.

1

From the Black Bottom to Cane River

I have lived my adult life in Minneapolis, Minnesota, but I was born in Detroit, Michigan. My American journey actually began long before that. My story is best told through the people who raised me, because their history shaped the man I have become. Both of my parents grew up in a Jim Crow America where opportunities for people of color were limited. Both of them managed to fight through adversity to build success, but their paths were quite different.

My mother was nurtured and even cosseted by a strong family unit that provided the opportunity for her to grow. In fact, her nickname was Pet. My dad, however, had to fight a culture, a city, a nation, and sometimes his own family. His constant battles made him tough and callused enough to forge ahead to success but, at the same time, left him altered by the experience.

Leonard Ellison Sr. was born in Detroit in 1928. Today it is one of the most complex cities in the United States, filled with both great pride and serious challenges. It has some of the most culturally diverse neighborhoods in the country and also some of the most racially polarized. It has some of the most beautiful architecture surrounded by some of our most dilapidated communities. It is the original home of Motown Records and General Motors. It brought the world everyone from Eminem to Madonna, from Dr. Ben Carson to Charles A. Lindbergh, from Henry Ford to Berry Gordy.

Though we were both born in Detroit, my dad and I grew up in different times and in different cities. I was raised on the West Side, which was relatively affluent and safe. It's where my father wanted to live as an adult.

The Detroit of his childhood was best known for the Black Bottom, made famous in August Wilson's play *Ma Rainey's Black Bottom*. Many people think that the area got its name from the color of the people who settled there, but the real reason was its black soil.

Before World War I, the area was predominantly Jewish, but after the Great Migration of black Americans from the rural South to the northern industrial cities like Detroit, the color of its inhabitants began to match its soil. The Black Bottom evolved into Detroit's central community of black-owned businesses, lodges, churches, and nightclubs. It became renowned for music and entertainment: blues, swing, and jazz.

Every major urban area has a center of black culture, and certain streets have an iconic status. In Detroit, it was Hastings Street, which was to the Black Bottom what Bourbon Street is to New Orleans, Beale Street is to Memphis, and 125th Street is to Harlem.

My dad loved to regale my brothers and me with stories about Paradise Valley, another name for the Black Bottom. As a teen, he would sneak into the nightclubs on Hastings to see Duke Ellington, Count Basie, Billy Eckstine, and Pearl Bailey. Aretha Franklin started her singing career in her father's church, New Bethel Baptist, also on that street. By the time I was growing up in the 1970s, most of Hastings Street had long since been bulldozed to create the Chrysler Freeway segment of Interstate 75. But my father talked with pride about the hustlers who displayed such class and cachet that they almost had celebrity status on the streets. He made the era sound so thrilling and exciting that I could vividly imagine it.

This was my dad's world during the height of segregation—segregation northern style. There were no Whites Only signs per se, but you knew where you could and could not go. Blacks everywhere faced structural isolation and denial. The silver lining of this oppression was social cohesion. The doctors, undertakers, and lawyers, as well as the pimps and the hustlers, all lived in the same segregated community and contributed to the tapestry of the Black Bottom. My dad was exposed not only to the greatest entertainers and most successful professionals but also to the worst of the criminal element, and he was influenced by it all. The Black Bottom contributed to my father's character and soul as much as his unique upbringing.

My father was the son of a farmer turned factory worker turned entrepreneur. My grandfather Zollie Crawford Ellison, born in 1896, was a part of America's Great Migration, detailed in Isabel Wilkerson's *The Warmth of Other Suns*. He originally hailed from a farm near Sardis, in Burke County, Georgia. His father, Crawford Ellison, was born into slavery in 1862. And his grandfather Jacob Ellison lived and died a slave.

We knew all this family history because my father and his only brother, Uncle Bob, would sit around and talk about these men. They drilled those names and their stories into my four brothers and me. They gave us a sense of belonging and meaning and purpose. We knew we had a slave heritage, but it wasn't given to us with shame. My dad always exuded pride and strength. For him, that heritage was a source of pride, a mark of perseverance, of survival over terrible odds.

As a young man, Grandpa Zollie left the farm and "went north" to work in Detroit's factories. He wasn't educated—not in a classroom—but he was a genius when it came to understanding how to succeed in this world. Grandpa Zollie was smart and industrious. In addition to working in the factory, he also saved his money and acquired several residential rental properties and opened a neighborhood store.

My grandfather was a driven man and not someone to mess with. I will never forget jumping in the car with my dad to check on Grandpa Zollie after we got a call that some guy had tried to rob his store. My grandpa, who stood just five foot four inches, had thrown the would-be robber through the display window.

"A strong farm boy," my dad joked, shaking his head as we stood surveying the broken glass on the sidewalk. Grandpa Zollie had a few scratches on his knuckles but otherwise was none the worse for wear.

I spent a lot of time with my grandfather. He would take my brother Brian and me to our Little League baseball practice, and to see the Detroit Tigers play at Tiger Stadium. We'd sit in the senior citizen seats for just fifty cents. On the weekends and during the summers, my brothers and I used to help cut the grass at his rental properties. He would ask us to make out the rent receipts while we were there.

"I can't find my glasses," he would say by way of an excuse for not doing it himself.

"But, Grandpa, your glasses are on your head," I would point out.

"Boy, just fill out the receipts!" he'd fuss.

One day, after cutting the grass, as I was rummaging through the kitchen for something to eat, I asked my mother, "How come Grandpa always tells us to write out the rent receipts?"

My mother, who was usually mild mannered and patient, shot me a stern look. "What did you say to him?" she asked.

"Nothing, really. He said something about not being able to see, and I told him his glasses were on his head."

"Don't you ever embarrass your grandfather like that!" she said angrily.

"What?" I was confused. I didn't think I had embarrassed Grandpa.

"You know Grandpa never had a chance to go to school like you."

It had never occurred to me that my grandfather couldn't read. He was one of the smartest men I knew. He seemed to know everything. Plus, everyone else in my family was educated. My father was a doctor: a psychiatrist. Uncle Bob was a dentist. My mother had her degree. My mother's deceased father had been college educated, as was her mother. I just assumed that everyone knew how to read. I couldn't imagine the times in which my grandfather was raised in Georgia, just a generation removed from slavery.

))➤

In such a hostile environment, choices were limited, especially for women. My paternal grandmother, Marian, married Grandpa Zollie when she was just nineteen and he was thirty. I never knew whether they fell in love or if they joined forces for convenience. Whatever the case, their marriage didn't last long. You know it had to be bad, because hardly anyone got divorced back then.

After his parents split, my dad and his brother were raised by their grandmother, Marian's mother. Grandpa Zollie had to work, and to the best of my knowledge, Grandma Marian started a new life.

My dad's grandmother died when he was about ten. After that, he and Uncle Bob lived briefly with their mother, but that didn't last long. My father was headstrong, willful, and boisterous. I imagine he was resentful about his broken family as well, although we've never talked about it. In any case, his mother couldn't manage him, and he was sent to live with Grandpa Zollie's sister, Carrie, who had moved up to Detroit and, like Grandpa Zollie, was quite enterprising. Aunt Carrie, according to family legend, operated an after-hours establishment.

My father recalled that he liked staying with Aunt Carrie. For a while, he made good money on tips, bussing tables and getting cigarettes or drinks for Aunt Carrie's guests.

Someone finally decided that it wasn't a good idea for a teenage boy to be living in that kind of situation, so my dad moved in with Grandpa Zollie, who had remarried. That arrangement didn't work out for very long, either. The new wife didn't take to my dad, and at this point, my father wasn't trying to accommodate anyone.

So, at fifteen, near the end of World War II, my father finagled his way into the United States Army. He was stationed in Hawaii and remembered that he spent a lot of time in the library, but he didn't talk much about his army time. The rampant segregation must have made his stint very lonely and difficult.

When he was discharged, he came back to Detroit, finished high school, and enrolled in college. The GI Bill gave him the start he needed. He joined Uncle Bob at Wayne University (now known as Wayne State U), majoring in pharmacy science. He was on his way to graduation and a better life when he ran out of money and had to drop out. But he went to work in one of Detroit's auto factories and saved up enough to go back to college. When he finished at Wayne, he was a little older than the other grads, but he made it.

With a background like that, my dad never made any excuses. His mantra was, "There are no handouts or handups." So guess what? None of his sons would have any excuses either. If he could make his own way in the world, so could we. Period. End of discussion. And believe me, no one gave my father any back talk.

He had lived what some would call a rather rough life. He had to work for everything he got. He had watched his own dad build a business by the sweat of his brow, with no help and no educational foundation, so he knew that the effort would pay off.

My father knew what so many Americans believe: that if you put your mind to something and are willing to work hard, you can achieve your goals. My dad wanted to be a doctor. He wanted to see *Dr.* in front of his name. After graduating from Wayne State, he enrolled at the University of Michigan Medical School and got his medical degree with a specialty in psychiatry.

While at Michigan, he met my mom, Clida. She was, on paper, his polar opposite. But she provided just the balance he needed in his life. She had the right kind of strength to match his fire.

So I was raised by two very different but equally strong-willed personalities.

My mom is ten years younger than my dad. She was born in Cane River, Natchitoches Parish, Louisiana, in 1938. It is an isolated, self-contained place on the banks of Cane River Lake—a tributary of the Red River that got cut off long ago—where the inhabitants survive on farming. A distant ancestor of my mother, Augustin Metoyer, the patriarch of a set of interrelated families who populated the area hundreds of years ago, built the Saint Augustine Catholic Church, in Melrose, around 1829. His portrait hangs in Saint Augustine Church to this day.

My mother's father, Frank Martinez, was the product of a Spanish father (from Seville) and a black mother. People often mistook him for something other than black. My mother's mother, Doris Balthazar Martinez, was the distant granddaughter of a French merchant, Thomas Pierre Metoyer, and Marie Therese, known as Coincoin (pronounced "KO-kwe"), a slave. Metoyer freed Coincoin and gave her several acres. My mother was born on one of those plots of land.

My mom, an only child, was raised with a ton of love and support on a farm with a host of aunts and uncles, her grandmother, and chickens, pigs, dogs, and horses. Mother describes her childhood as wonderful and smiles when she recalls her horse, Pocketbook. Growing up like that must have been fun.

She worked on the farm alongside everyone else, but mostly she attended school. She was sent to Holy Rosary Institute, a boarding school in Lafayette, Louisiana, because my grandparents wanted to protect her. Grandpa Frank, you see, was a civil rights activist, fighting for civil rights and voting rights, and the Ku Klux Klan used to harass him. My mom tells the story of how one time they set up a burning cross outside her family's home on Lee Street (which is now Martin Luther King Jr. Drive). After high school, she went to New Orleans to attend Xavier University of Louisiana, where she graduated with a degree in medical technology. Education was a priority in my mother's home. My grandma Doris, whom everyone called Dot, taught the neighboring farm kids reading, writing, and arithmetic in a one-room schoolhouse. Children of many different ages gathered in that classroom, some attending only sporadically, but she managed to make sure they learned the basics. Grandma Doris's father was also a teacher, specializing in industrial arts.

As I mentioned, Doris was the distant granddaughter of Coincoin, who was a medicine woman, trained in pharmacology and nursing—skills that she passed along to her children. Both of Coincoin's parents were straight off the boat from Africa, and I'm sure they handed down some old-country knowledge to her. We know that she was from the Ewe (pronounced "EE-vay") people who inhabit the coastal nation of Togo.

I didn't know the impact my grandmother had on the community until her funeral. I stood there with my mother at Saint Augustine Church on Cane River as person after person came up to her.

"Your mama would be there day after day and made sure us children got our lessons," one said, clutching my mother's hands.

"Some of us never had no schooling 'cept what your mama gave us," another said, tears in her eyes. "I really thank your mama."

My mother was so proud of Doris. My mom also clearly adored her father too. He died in 1957 when a tractor overturned on him. His brother-in-law, my great-uncle Boo (Carroll Balthazar), tried to lift the tractor off him, but it was too heavy. Uncle Boo sat there holding my grandfather's hand until he took his last breath. Uncle Boo, my mother's uncle, was a farmer and industrial arts teacher like my grandfather. He was such a loving and supportive figure in our lives, I wonder if he thought of himself as looking out for his dead friend's grandchildren. He was so awesome, I kind of think so.

My mom always talked wistfully of her dad. Besides being an activist, he was also a skilled mechanic. He trained black soldiers to fix airplanes during World War II. After the war, he continued to teach young black men how to fix trucks, cars, and planes.

She was very much a daddy's girl and also a bit of a tomboy. Probably because she was his only child, he taught her all the things he would have wanted a son to know. So while she learned to take care of a home, she also could build things and work around the farm. My mother was raised to be confident, resourceful, and self-reliant, and I am trying to raise my daughter, Amirah, the same way.

I remember the day my mother got it into her head that she wanted her children to have a sandbox. She was tired of packing us up and trekking to the local park when we had a perfectly nice-sized backyard to play in.

She decided that she would build this sandbox herself. The only problem was that she couldn't haul the materials in her own car. So she took my dad's brand-new white Cadillac convertible with red leather interior (and whitewall tires, of course) and headed to the local hardware store. With the top open, the Cadillac was perfect.

It was a running joke in the neighborhood that my dad had all of these nice cars—including a Ferrari and even a Rolls-Royce at one time—and my mom drove around in these old, modest cars. But if you knew my parents, that was perfectly normal. My father was a flashy, over-the-top personality. He wore tailored suits and was opinionated. A real character. My mother was down-to-earth. She was no wallflower, but she was never loud or boisterous. She was levelheaded and even-keeled. The only time she would really show a lot of passion was when it came to her kids. If we needed something or she decided she wanted us to have something, nothing was going to stop her.

That day, she put us all in the front, so she could load up the backseat of Dad's convertible. She put down plastic to protect the precious interior from the bags of sand, pieces of wood, nails, and fasteners. Once we got back home, she built us that sandbox. I was about five years old, but I still remember her determination to get it built. And I remember the fun my brothers and I had in it.

My father, who worked fourteen-hour days at his practice and didn't drive the Cadillac convertible except on weekends—his get-around car was a Pontiac Sunbird—didn't get home until late. You can imagine the argument that erupted when he noticed sand on the precious red leather of his baby. Apparently the plastic my mother had put down didn't protect against all of the sand.

She heard him out but wasn't fazed by his anger, and she wasn't apologetic. She'd done what she had to do. She was taking care of her children.

This fierce desire to protect us played out a number of times while we were growing up. The year before, we had moved into a mixed neighborhood in Detroit, and a rash of robberies occurred shortly after we arrived. One of our neighbors who lived across the street started telling everyone to "watch out for those Ellison boys." He claimed we were the ones committing the robberies.

When my mother caught wind of this, she gathered us all up and said, "Come with me!" We didn't know what was up, but we all stopped what we were doing and followed her. She marched across the street with us trailing behind, went up to this man's house, and knocked on his door. When he came to the door, he looked shocked.

"Sir, these are my boys," she said firmly. "They are not doing anything to your property or anyone else's. Before you start saying what the Ellison boys are up to, you should know what you're talking about."

She then turned and walked back across the street with us following, leaving that man standing there with his mouth open. She had made her point. My oldest brother, Leonard, was only nine. I was six. In other words, we were all little kids. There was no way that we were the menaces this man was claiming, and my mother wasn't having anyone talking badly about her boys. We all thought it was funny: "Man! Mom is *tough*! Ha-ha."

My mother usually worked outside of the home, but she was involved in the PTA and the neighborhood watch, she came to our various sports games, and she was very active in the community.

When we were all old enough to go to school, she went to work at my father's practice, running his office. But she was always home in time to cook us dinner. She was the one who made sure that we had lunch packed for school, did our homework, and got to bed on time. She was a disciplinarian, but her biggest threat when we misbehaved was "I'm going to tell your father." None of us wanted that. We were all scared of that. We didn't want her telling him anything.

We kept in line—all five boys—primarily because our mom instilled in us a sense of right and wrong. We didn't get into much trouble, because to have done so would have reflected poorly on her.

I believe she was the right woman to raise five boys because she had the right father to raise her. My grandfather may have died before we came along, but my mom made sure we knew about him. She embodied a lot of his strength and wisdom. His picture hangs in my home as a reminder. And I'm certain that it's the spirit of

Frank Martinez that enabled my mom to bring up five boys. She knew exactly how to handle each of us.

While my father showed us valuable lessons through example—getting up every day and going to work, working hard, demanding excellence from himself and everyone around him, and carrying himself with immense pride—my mother was more hands-on in teaching us values, humanity, and what it meant to love one another. Together they raised five men who by society's standards have done well. Because of our parents, my brothers and I had a chance to live the American dream. I can speak for them when I say that we all, in our own ways, work to extend it to everyone.

2

No Mercy for the Weak

As I reflect on my upbringing and the way in which I raise my own four children, I am struck by how we as a nation care for our children. According to the US Centers for Disease Control and Prevention (CDC), ours may be the first generation not to outlive their parents, as a result of obesity and other controllable factors. We are also lagging behind our parents in income and achievement. As a nation, America is trailing in education—we are eighteenth among industrialized nations. More than one in five children live below the poverty line. Programs serving children in poverty, such as Food Stamps (now called the Supplemental Nutrition Assistance Program) and Project Head Start, face the budget ax in this age of austerity, while loopholes for Big Oil and Big Coal go unclosed.

The quality of our children's lives has eroded. Today's kids face so much more violence, crime, and tragedy than my generation and even my parents' generation encountered. And that's saying a lot, considering that both of my parents were raised during a time of discrimination against people of color. But what they had that we don't seem to have today was a sense of community. While signs may have banned them from certain public places, they had at least one place where they absolutely belonged. There was also a sense that if the world was going to deny them rights, they were just simply going to work so hard that they would make their own way.

That was my dad's philosophy. Work hard. Excel. No excuses.

I was raised, as the middle child of five boys, by a man who thrived on pushing the limits. My mom had a major hand in our rearing—she provided the love and balance—but my father set the tone.

He had a saying: "No mercy for the weak." It meant that either you performed and excelled, or you would be left behind. We would get no babying, no coddling, no hand-holding.

My father was never a strict individualist, though. He was grateful for the GI Bill, which helped him earn a college degree. He also attended public schools before college. He understood that no one does it alone; however, he was all about individual responsibility and effort.

In our home it was survival of the fittest. Competition at its highest. My father believed you have to give people something to reach for. You don't want anyone feeling comfortable with mediocrity. The herd is going to run, and you have to keep up. He was always referring to nature.

"If you watch the wildebeest running around the Serengeti, you see they got to keep up or get eaten by a lion," he would say.

I didn't really appreciate it at the time, but as I got older, I understood that my mom and dad were raising five male children in the city of Detroit, in a nation that stacked the deck against blacks, and if we were going to survive *and* succeed, we would have to learn some tough lessons at an early age.

To my dad, competition bred excellence, and he demanded it from his sons.

"Let's see who can do the most push-ups" was one of his favorites. We'd drop our homework assignments and start puffing away. Each evening around the dinner table, my dad was the source of much indigestion because that's where he liked to conduct his daily interrogations.

"Your brother got a good report card. What are you doing?" he would say to us. There would be long silences and a lot of hemming and hawing. I knew what was coming, and I remember never wanting to be the weak link or the one doing the worst. So I made sure I kept my grades up, because it felt terrible to be the one who got chewed out for doing poorly. My dad would even skip you altogether while going around the table, which to me was worse than being called out, because it meant you didn't matter. We all wanted to matter.

This atmosphere of competition sometimes spilled over into household brawls. The fights were unending. We would fight over dumb stuff, like who ate the last Pop-Tart. (It was usually Brian, by the way. He was the hungry one. He would eat cereal out of a mixing bowl. During certain stretches, he used to go through half a box of cereal a day.)

The competition at home paid off outside. The Ellison boys were successful both on the playing field and usually in the classroom. Although we're all close, our father promoted so much competition among us that there was conflict, too.

Leonard, my father's namesake, is the oldest. Although only three years separate us, he was definitely the big brother of our clan. He was the big brother of the whole neighborhood. All the younger guys admired him. He was the talker, the schmoozer, a great negotiator. He also was very good at talking tough, hoping the other person would back down, which they usually did.

Brian, the next oldest, was the biggest and toughest. He was a very good person to have on your side. As you might expect, with two brothers so close in age, Leonard was highly verbal, whereas Brian didn't talk much, which is ironic given that today Brian is a Baptist preacher *and* a lawyer. He and I are only eleven months apart, and we shared a bedroom. Brian was also an independent agent. He never had a bunch of friends hanging around, and he didn't care about being popular, but he was also not to be toyed with. Brian was built like a refrigerator. He weighed 150 pounds in seventh grade, no fat. He weighed 215 by the time he got to high school. He was just a brick of a dude. He played offensive guard and linebacker, and, boy, could he hit. People were scared of him. Brian was also very quiet, which made him even more forbidding. He was pretty serious, definitely not someone to pull pranks, chase girls, or act rambunctious. He declared his love of Jesus at eighteen and ended up becoming a minister.

Brian was the best baseball and football player among us. I was okay with that. I was a pretty good player, too, but in school I felt more comfortable hanging out with friends or reading. In my household, you had to find your place. I got decent grades without much effort. Brian was good in baseball without much effort and was an all-star at twelve. (In an all-star game at Palmer Park Baseball Field, he actually hit a home run out of the park.) Leonard was really good at track and field. Our younger brothers also participated in baseball, football, basketball, and track. They didn't have a choice. In my home, you had to win at something. The pressure was enormous, and I don't believe the competition it bred among us boys was all healthy.

Looking back, I will allow that my dad's method was effective—in theory. Four of us are lawyers and one is a doctor. Would we all have chosen those paths if we'd actually had a choice? I don't know. I do know that I liked going to law school and loved practicing law. Being a lawyer definitely enriched my life. It was the foundation to pursue a career as a public servant. But I didn't really have much of a choice in the matter. My father decreed that I was going to law school or medical school. Period.

Unfortunately, many children are forced into careers that they hate. As kids, they sit around the dinner table and every night are pressured into a profession in which they have no interest or aptitude. I see that happen a lot. Those children are miserable.

So the question as a parent is: Should you pressure your children into being successful, or should you just let them grow into their own interests? Or should there be a reasonable balance? I didn't raise my kids exactly the way I was raised. My ex-wife, Kim, and I, had high expectations, but our inclination was to let them find their own way.

For instance, my daughter, Amirah, wanted to be a dancer at a young age. So we enrolled her in dance classes. After two sessions, she decided she didn't want to go anymore.

"Why don't you want to go, honey?" I asked her.

"I just don't want to," she said, folding her arms and pouting.

I spoke to the dance teacher, and she suggested that we leave Amirah in the class—don't force her to dance, but don't let her just quit, either. During the next class, and the one after that, she sat and watched and was mad. By the third class, she was back on that dance floor.

The difference between the way I handled my daughter and the way my dad would have is that I talked to Amirah lovingly. I didn't raise my voice or pressure her. I simply told her she wasn't allowed to quit. I didn't want her to get in the habit of quitting something because it appeared to be too difficult. She had to learn to push through.

The other difference was that I didn't demand that any of my kids be the best. But they did have to finish. Participating and completing was important. I also never compared them with their siblings or other kids.

I also never believed I had to pit my kids against one another. Any parent knows that you don't have to encourage competition among siblings. They are going to ask one another how he or she did on the test. They are going to compare and compete without parents doing anything. Cain and Abel were brothers, and you can see what competition did for them.

With my kids I tried to soften the blow of losing, but I never wanted to shield them from the experience. Experience has shown me that you will eventually lose at something, so you should learn to face adversity with some dignity and detachment, and learn from that loss.

Kim and I taught our kids that if you participate and try your hardest, you're a winner. The only loser is someone who doesn't try or who quits. None of my kids was a world-class athlete, but all of them played two sports: football or wrestling or basketball in the winter and track in the spring.

Their mother and I kept them in sports year-round not for the medals and the trophies but for lifelong health. We told them, "When you're our age, you want to be able to go up and down stairs without huffing and puffing."

We told them they weren't going to sit around the house playing video games and watching TV. They were going to be out doing something. Fitness was their incentive. So they learned about winning and losing, and because their motivation for participation wasn't rooted in winning and losing, they also got to have fun. And they had a blast.

We used athletics as a way of bringing the family together, not tearing it apart in crazed competition. Their mom and I tried to go to all of their games and matches.

Isaiah, Jeremiah, and Elijah all played football from the age of seven to eighteen. Amirah plays girls' rugby at Minneapolis South High. None of them missed a season, and they were all good. Isaiah, five foot five but tough as nails, went on to play college football at Drake University in Des Moines, Iowa. He was a state champion sprinter and was also on the swim team. Jeremiah and Elijah were wrestlers.

In the spring, track and field was an Ellison family treat. I have loved track since I was a kid, and I loved it as a parent because we could go to a meet and see all of our kids compete in their different age brackets. Amirah and Isaiah were on the same team, wearing the same uniform.

I actually coached track. It was time we could spend together doing something healthy and constructive. At home I taught my kids how to pass a baton, how to come out of the blocks, and other running techniques. Then I started coaching the other kids. While most parents wanted to coach the older kids who were sprinters, I preferred to coach the little kids, who weren't very good. You don't have to motivate a high schooler who is fast and eyeing a college scholarship, but you really have to work with a seven- or eight-year-old who is still finding his or her way to keep them interested. I loved seeing it catch on with them.

I also enjoyed working with the discus throwers and the

shot-putters—even though I'd never competed in those events. On our sprint-heavy team, these bigger kids, the throwers, weren't exactly doing the cool thing, not like the 100-meter or 200-meter sprinters. So I liked showing them some attention. There was one eleven-year-old girl, five foot eight and about 250 pounds, who was very sweet and had an infectious smile. Because of her weight, though, she was having a difficult time, and some of the other kids would tease her. She wasn't going to be a sprinter, so I taught her the shot put.

She struggled at first because even with the shot put, you need speed and coordination. She had only power. Yet by the summer track season, all of the work in the spring had come together. Guess what? She won the gold in her age bracket. I can still remember that smile as she pranced around with her medal. She was a champion.

In that instance, winning mattered, because it changed the way this kid felt about herself and the way other kids saw her. No one believed she could do it, but she did it. She didn't quit, and she found out that hard work brings results.

I know that working with her and figuring out what she might be good at mattered. I haven't seen her in years. She's a young adult now, but I am sure that she remembers winning that medal. That's why it was important for me to not just encourage my kids but also try to put real time into them. I made sure my work schedule was coordinated with my kids' activities.

I didn't start my work in the state legislature until 2003. By then, the kids were into their high school sports and had paid coaches—usually teachers, not sports dads. I would still watch their games, cheering from the stands. I also loved attending Amirah's dance recitals. We could see her looking for us in the audience. Amirah is still dancing, and she has grown to be quite good at it.

There are several formulas to raising successful children. My dad had one approach; my mother had another. I have tried to combine the two: high expectations along with nurturing and support. It seems to be working.

What I know *does not* work is to ignore your children—sit them in front of a computer or a video game or a television and let them entertain themselves. Kids need guidelines and boundaries. They need to know that you care.

When kids are pushed to do well, the family also needs a balance. While my dad was all grit and push, my mom was there with the hugs. She came to our games to cheer us on, and she made sure each of us got the time we needed to grow into the adults we would become.

Together they fostered the notion of hard work. That was not just the expectation, it was the rule, and it was accompanied by discipline. There were no time-outs in my home: we got good old-fashioned butt whuppings. Yet even though my mom would warn us, "Wait until your father comes home," we didn't get many whuppings. The threat was usually enough. When he came home, he mostly reasoned with us. He would use the Socratic method. He was, after all, a psychiatrist.

His approach was sometimes over-the-top, but that's him. My father, who didn't realize his dream to become a doctor until he was thirty-three, wanted it all. He went overboard with everything: education, life, you name it. He didn't just eat pork and beef, he ate it to excess. He never worked out, and he smoked regularly. He believed in doing things all the way and doing exactly what he wanted. That attitude eventually caught up with his health, but there were definite benefits to his outlook.

My father, growing up in a world where he bumped up against a lot of nos and a whole lot of obstacles, wanted to make sure that his children knew how to navigate obstacles in their world.

While we all pretty much followed my dad's blueprint for success, we all grew up to be independent-minded people. Our home was a breeding ground for independent thought. That's probably why my family includes a Muslim, a Baptist, a couple of Catholics, and an agnostic, and still we all love and respect one another.

My oldest brother, Leonard, is a physician. Brian, as you know, is a lawyer and a preacher. I, too, practiced law for sixteen years before going into politics. Tony, who is four years younger than I am, is our third attorney, and the youngest, Eric, is lawyer number four, but he also has a real estate business and is probably the wealthiest among us.

My parents are five for five: all of their sons have graduate degrees and are gainfully employed. We are all relatively successful men. Coincidence?

After we all grew up, the dynamics in my childhood household changed. My mom already had a degree in medical technology, and when my father suffered a stroke, she went back to get her master's in social work, and then went to work for the county. Today she's in her seventies and doesn't seem to want to slow down.

Why would she? She lives by the same rules she taught her five sons.

3

IDENTITY CRISIS

My brothers and I had to straddle two worlds growing up in Detroit in the 1970s and 1980s. In the world created by our parents, we were expected to achieve in the classroom, at home with chores, and on the playing field. Yet on a daily basis, we had to navigate the other world of the streets.

We were Catholic schoolboys whose father was a doctor. I guess we were definitely upper middle class, but there was no way we could behave as such on the streets. You just couldn't project weakness in our neighborhood. We were all known for standing our ground. My father insisted on it. Thanks to Brian, who was the toughest among us, not backing down to anyone was the rule. And while not all fights were fair, if you got licked, you took it without a tear.

We would say, "Leonard Ellison didn't raise any punks." He taught us all how not to back down, starting with one another. He also reinforced those lessons with fear. He told us, "If your brother comes home beat up and you're not beat up, I'll whup both of you!" In the house, we fought regularly, but out on the streets, we stuck together: all-for-one, one-for-all. That's the way it was. The problem was, if we got into trouble in school for fighting, we would get a whupping. My father didn't tolerate hoodlum behavior in his house. So we had to find a balance between how we behaved in school and how we behaved on the streets. I got suspended in the sixth grade for fighting in school, and believe me, that was my last school fight. I made sure it never happened again.

I had to learn to adapt to multiple situations. At home I was the kid who did his homework, got good grades, cleaned up after myself. On the streets I had to show no fear. I wore an Afro and carried an Afro pick (the one with a little black-power fist on the end) in my back pocket and walked with confidence. I had some trouble reconciling this behavior with what took place around the dining table at home. My dad wouldn't allow us to wear Afros. Imagine growing up in the 1970s and not being able to sport a 'fro! I got around this restriction by patting down my hair and staying out of his way for months. By the time he got home from work, I would already be in my room on most nights. He was gone before we got up for school.

On days when I couldn't avoid my father, I used to wear a cap. Because I played sports, that was acceptable. The hat also helped pack my hair down so that the Afro wasn't too noticeable. On my way to school, I would pick out my hair. I didn't have the biggest Afro in the world, but I had one. It was my declaration of independence.

It was also a form of self-protection. In Detroit, as in other cities, you have to keep your eyes open. People are just on edge—ready for anything. My father used to say, "If you *stay* ready, you don't have to *get* ready."

We lived on the northwest side of Detroit, which was probably one of the nicest parts of the city. But it was still Detroit. We frequently had to walk through rougher areas to reach our neighborhood, which meant we needed to always be ready. While kids were not shooting one another when I was growing up, you could certainly get jumped.

One time Leonard and I were walking home, and some tough guys from the neighborhood stopped us.

"Give us whatever money you got in your pockets!" the biggest one demanded.

"I'm not giving you anything," Leonard said, and took off running. Remember, he was a track star. I wasn't a track star, but I knew I'd better keep up, so I went running right behind him.

"You better not come back here tomorrow!" they shouted after us as we left them in the dust.

We had to figure out a new route home for the rest of the year.

Once I grew up and moved away, I forgot how tense Detroit could be. Then I returned home for Christmas one time after living in Minnesota for a few years. By then, I was married and had kids. I decided to go to the Charles H. Wright Museum of African American History as part of our Kwanzaa celebrations. We wanted to give our children a good cultural experience while in Detroit, and we did. We had a wonderful time at the Kwanzaa observance. As we left, we were talking about how great the event was, and how we wished there was an African American museum and cultural center in Minneapolis. But then I got a wake-up call.

As we were driving down Woodward Avenue toward my mother's home, a guy pulled in front of us and jammed on his brakes, stopping dangerously short.

We tried to turn to get around him, but the driver jumped out of the car and shouted, "I don't give a fuck! You cut me off, you better be prepared to die!"

Really? Was what I did *that* serious? My wife and kids were shaken up. And I had spent so much time away from Detroit that I wasn't prepared for that kind of behavior, either. I hadn't realized how dramatically I had let my guard down. My degree of "being ready" had diminished since moving to Minnesota. I immediately remembered that the kind of stress I had experienced growing up in Detroit—even on the so-called good side of town—was significant.

That's why, even though we were raised in a middle-class home, we had to stay street-smart. The pressure grew worse when I reached adolescence, and one time I even contributed to it. When I was fifteen, some friends and I went to the annual Michigan State Fair on Woodward and Eight Mile Road. (Sadly, the fair, the nation's oldest, shut down in 2010 after 160 years.) To get in, we jumped the fence. We had decided that we weren't paying the $3. It wasn't so much that we didn't have the money; we just wanted to see what we could get away with.

One of my friends planned to meet up with a girl he liked. The two of us were bouncing along, when I spotted an ex-girlfriend of mine with her. Some guy was talking to my ex, so I walked up on the three of them in high-jerk mode.

"What's up, Honeys?" I said, real cocky. "What are y'all doing with this loser?"

I can't really say what made me do it. This fellow hadn't done anything to me. I guess I was just showing off. But he, like me, was "ready."

"What!?" he growled, and got in my face.

The girls, being the grown-ups, got between us.

"I came here to have fun," my ex-girlfriend said, and pulled him away.

I had to have the last word, though. "You're just lucky you got those girls to protect you," I called after him as they were walking away.

A few weeks later, I was with my boys, riding our bicycles around Palmer Park. It was a hot, sunny summer day, and folks were polishing their cars, radios blaring, and driving real slow, showing them off. The park was packed. As we rode past a group of boys, one of them hollered at me to come over.

I figured it was someone trying to sell us marijuana. I didn't smoke weed, so I was going to say, "No, man. No, thanks."

When I got closer, I recognized the kid from the state fair.

"You remember calling me a loser?" he said, and then he turned to his crew. "This is the muthafucka who called me a loser."

Never one to run from a fight, I told one of my buddies to hold my bike. As I handed it over, I felt someone grab me from behind as this guy took a swing. Just in time, I ducked, and he ended up hitting the guy who was holding me from behind.

Some of the adults in the park ran over and broke up the fight before it got out of hand. I was relieved. I was woefully outnumbered, and I knew it wasn't going to end well for me. Plus, I felt ashamed that I'd started this mess with this guy just to look bold in the eyes of my old girlfriend. My pride would not allow me to apologize, nor would it allow me to run. I *wasn't* going to run.

That was the machismo of the streets, and it's still prevalent today. Except that these days, kids don't fight only with their fists. The prevalence of guns has transformed confrontations between teenage boys from an affair involving a bloody lip or swollen cheek into a deadly encounter.

I dropped that whole macho-guy thing when I graduated from high school in 1981. By that time, it dawned on me that it wasn't worth the risk. It was mostly useless and perhaps dangerous. It conflicted with my emerging idea of being a responsible person— a contributor. My mother's voice of calm was making more sense, and I was moving on to be someone that my father would respect. The lessons my parents taught all their kids, though, about not backing down, standing up for your convictions, were deeply ingrained in us all.

As a kid, I didn't quite understand all the different forces that drove my dad. For example, on the one hand, he was a doctor, a professional who made a good living; but on the other, he forced us to work. He did not believe in spending money on fashionable clothes, the latest toys, or video games for us. We didn't get many new things, so we learned to take care of what we had. I would use a toothbrush to clean my tennis shoes if they got dirty or scuffed, because a new pair of sneakers would not be on the horizon unless I bought them myself.

"When you get a job, then you can buy what you want," my dad used to tell us.

Without saying it, my dad didn't think being dressed to the nines benefitted our characters, unless we could do it on our own power. He wasn't handing out the latest and the greatest for free.

"Go rake some leaves and cut some grass if you want that stuff," he would say.

I did. We all did. Leonard spent his money on clothes. He was a pretty snappy dresser and, unlike me, had a talent for accumulating money (and still does).

I shoveled a lot of snow. At one point, roller skating was big, and I bought some pretty expensive roller skates with my haul. I tended to save my earnings, but I did splurge on a leather jacket one time. By that point, I didn't want to have to ask my parents for anything, so I was okay with working and making my own money.

One of my father's favorite expressions was that he wasn't a bank. If one of us asked him for money, he'd snap, "What do I look like, NBD?" (NBD stood for National Bank of Detroit, which merged with another bank long ago and doesn't exist anymore.) Then came the lecture.

"I put a roof over your head. I feed you. That's not enough?" he would start. "This is *my* house. I let you stay here . . ."

We heard that about a thousand times: how we should be grateful, because many kids didn't have a roof over their heads. We had clothes, just not the latest styles. Every one of us but Leonard Jr. suffered through hand-me-downs.

The irony was that my father liked to buy fancy things for himself. I understand his reasoning now. He believed that if things came too easy for us we would never appreciate the hard work it took to acquire them. But that still doesn't explain his taste for fancy stuff, a taste I never picked up. He grew up in a time when black people weren't supposed to own nice things. I think buying things he couldn't have imagined affording as a kid gave him a sense of accomplishment. For my father, those things signaled to the rest of the world that he was a man of achievement to be respected. His wealth, his purchase of high-ticket items, was an assertion of personal worth and importance. They sent a message to the establishment: I am just as good as you are. He was saying, "I can buy anything *you* can buy. Now what?"

I remember watching some old footage from 1968 of the striking Memphis garbage workers, whom Martin Luther King Jr. was supporting when he was assassinated there. They held placards proclaiming "I Am a Man!" I thought of my father.

I'll never forget the Saturday afternoon he came bursting through the door with a huge smile on his face—a rarity, to say the least.

"Fellas, I bought a boat!" he announced. I was about eight years old, and I became very excited. I was also a little embarrassed. I didn't know anyone who had a boat. Nor did my father buy just *any* boat: it was a thirty-six-foot sailboat, big enough for us all to sleep on. I am pretty sure my father didn't know how to sail a boat when he bought it.

A couple of years after that, he bought an expensive Italian sports car. He hardly ever drove it. It sat in the garage for so long, a family of squirrels made a home inside it. After he won the prize, maybe it lost some allure.

My dad's excesses sometimes made me uncomfortable. But that was my dad: flamboyant, showy, and over the top. I admired him then, as I do now. But now I understand him a little better, in the context of today's sensibilities. There was a time when a black person owning a new car, a freshly painted porch, or even having a piano in the home might cause some whites to consider him to be "uppity" or "getting out of his place." There is a scene in the 1997 movie *Rosewood*, directed by John Singleton, where Don Cheadle's character incenses his white neighbors when they see that he owns a piano. As they are leaving, one of them says to the other, "Why does that nigger have a piano when I don't?" The other one says, "You can't play a piano!" And the first one says, "That ain't the point! The point is, he got one and I ain't!" This was the climate and mentality that led this predominantly black town of Rosewood, Florida, to be burned to the ground—killing many residents—when a white woman falsely accused a black man of attacking her. The film is based on a true story.

Maybe my dad's sailboat was his piano, but in his case, no one ever tried to kill him because he had the temerity to get one. My dad didn't grow up sailing. At best, he might have fished from a dock as a kid. But I'm sure he would have sat on that dock and looked out on the Detroit River with its sailboats and said to himself, "One of these days, *I'm* going to own one of those."

My dad and I are quite different in this respect. I really don't care for fancy stuff. I drive a 2009 Pontiac G6. I live in a modest home. I don't own any fancy jewelry or pricey stuff, and I don't want to. It doesn't bother me in the least if someone else has these things. In fact, I see these material things as a burden. To each his own. But maybe I don't have this attachment to stuff because my father and his generation provided me with everything I needed, including a modern society where anyone of any color can have anything he can afford. I owe him for clearing that path for me. As much as my dad's generation reduced some racial barriers, we still have a very real challenge of helping more people pay for what they need.

Now, my dad wouldn't be satisfied with just *owning* a sailboat. Being the kind of guy he is, he took it a step further. Every year since the early 1920s, the Bayview Yacht Club has sponsored the Port Huron to Mackinac Island sailboat race. It is one of the longest freshwater races in the world, and for people in Detroit, it's a pretty big deal. But the race had never had a black participant. My father bought that boat to enter that race. My dad was never a civil rights activist—you wouldn't catch him out marching or holding signs—but if *he* wanted to do something, he was going to do it.

He wanted to enter that race, so he did. I was about seven years old.

Many people in the black community hailed it as a historic event. But my dad simply wanted the freedom to enter that race for himself.

We had some good times on the boat. My dad would invite the kids from the neighborhood to come sailing with us. Of course, my dad found a way to turn it into work for us. He would have us swab the deck and all that seafaring stuff. We used to joke that he was Captain Bligh, barking commands at us.

As we got away from shore, we would see some of his harshness melt away. He would become a little more relaxed. These were some of the few times we'd see our dad lighten up.

Even though my dad liked to challenge racial barriers, he never had any intention of forgetting who he was. If you wanted to know where to get the best barbecue in Detroit, you asked him. He loves to eat watermelon and fried chicken, chitlins, neck bones, pickled pig feet—but usually at home around Christmastime. Actually, when he had my mother cook chitlins for him, the awful smell ran us out of the house, and there was no way any of us would eat any of it. "No, thanks, Dad. It's all for you." My dad loves jazz bands and quartets; Count Basie and Miles Davis are among his favorites. Dad loved to argue with friends and relatives about how best to end racism and inequality, and he read about the black experience constantly. His medical practice saw mostly black patients, and he thought a lot about how racism affected the mental health of those patients. I remember him talking about how African Americans needed to address stress, depression, and illnesses associated with the black condition. He was particularly concerned about hypertension. In fact, he handed me my first copy of *Black Rage*, a famous 1968 text on the psychological trauma of racism by two black psychiatrists, William H. Grier and Price M. Cobbs. But even though he knew the debilitating effects of racism on black people, he would not allow his sons to offer racism as an excuse for failure. He would not allow it to be an impediment for himself.

As I look back, it makes me wonder how this reaction to oppression fits into the larger scheme of what it means to be black in America. What my father thought was freedom, I thought was excessive. But was he wrong to react that way? Was I right? Who can say? What does it mean when you've moved beyond the Jim Crow segregation to this new era? Are we postracial now? That's one question a lot of people are asking today. Where, exactly, do we go from here?

4

THE COLOR LINE IN
THE TWENTY-FIRST CENTURY

In *The Souls of Black Folks* (1903), W. E. B. Du Bois, a pioneering scholar of sociology and Harvard University's first black PhD, wrote that the "problem of the twentieth century will be the problem of the color line." But wait a minute: Isn't it now the twenty-first century? Still, much of our identity, and the way that opportunity is distributed in this country, are tied to superficial distinctions—of neighborhood, country of origin, and race.

Race, for this current generation, is no longer as much of a burden as it was for my generation, which is nothing compared to what my parents' generation experienced. Still, we face stereotypical attitudes and conflicts that must be eradicated so that we can continue to move forward successfully as a nation. Seemingly intractable racial disparities involving the criminal justice system, education, and the economy linger.

Race is largely a political, social, and cultural construct, and has very little to do with one's biological makeup, yet it is such a powerful component of our nation's history that it has, in many ways, defined America. Though founded in liberty, the United States tolerated a population living in slavery for over two centuries because of race. Americans fought a bloody Civil War and then experienced a momentous civil rights movement all because of race. The lessons of these struggles have helped us to arrive where we are today, as a relatively more inclusive and accepting nation.

If this were apartheid South Africa, Barack Obama, Lenny Kravitz, and Halle Berry would be considered "colored." But Will.i.am, Viola Davis, and Danny Glover would be "black." The late Adam Clayton Powell Jr. would be white, along with the rock guitarist Slash and the actress Maya Rudolph. In America, we're all black. So being black is malleable and transitory. So is being white. Today Italians and Irish are considered white, but that wasn't always the case. Arab Americans have a floating and highly situational racial status. But what is racial identity, and why is it so important in modern America? My own background has caused me to wonder.

When I was in high school, I was making a point at the family dinner table about "black people this" and "black people that," expressing curiosity and opinions about black people. My mother said, "Wouldn't you be surprised to know about your French ancestry, and your Croatian ancestry, and your Spanish ancestry?" Of course, I wasn't surprised. My mother had talked about her family history before.

At the time, my understanding of American history and politics was embryonic, and I was just starting to grasp something of black pride, wearing my Afro, my pick jammed into my back pocket. But my mother, as she so often does, challenged me to think a little deeper. Maybe because my skin is a little lighter, I'd felt the need to show my "blackness" and to push my authenticity a little harder. But as I learned from my mother, racial identity is very complex.

My mother is a Creole from Louisiana. Many people believe that being Creole means you're mixed—French with black—but it simply means that you were born in the colonies. Louisiana has white Creoles and Creoles of color, like my mother. She is the product of an institution known as *placage*. During slavery, when a white man had a child with a slave in Louisiana, the issue was handled differently from the rest of the states, where, according to law, that child would automatically be a slave. In Louisiana the child was still considered a slave legally, but elevated in conditions and treatment. A white man could claim the child as his own—not equal to any white children but not a common slave.

These children might be given a chance at a better life. Their father-master could connect them with other offspring of *placage* relationships and, in doing so, create a different culture. Sometimes they would free them, and a whole new class was born: the *gens de couleur libres,* or "free people of color."

My mom's ancestor Coincoin (pronounced "Ko-kwe"), born in 1742, was a slave who was the *placée* (a sort of concubine) of the French merchant Thomas Pierre Metoyer and had ten children by him. In 1778 she was freed, but only after a local scandal. The parish priest publicly accused her of being a concubine because of her relationship with Metoyer. Father Quintanilla threatened to have her sold at auction in New Orleans if they did not end their relationship. Instead, Metoyer freed her.

As a free woman, she remained with Metoyer until 1788, when his growing fortune persuaded him to take a wife who could provide legal heirs. Coincoin was taken care of. She was given sixty-eight acres of land and was able to buy the freedom of eight of her ten children. With that land, she became a tobacco planter and a *medicine*, an unlicensed doctor. She was also a trapper and sold meat and barrels of oil and tobacco at the local market.

On her father's side, my mother is descended from Calise Martinez from Seville, Spain. She even has some relatives from Croatia: Marco Givanovich and Antoine Marinovich, an uncle-nephew team who emigrated in 1835 from what today is Dubrovnik, a city on the Dalmatian coast. Records from the time list Antoine Marinovich as a bachelor, but he had several children, none of whom was legally acknowledged because of the mother's African heritage. You can find black Marinoviches running around Houston and New Orleans to this day.

So what is more important in determining who my mother is? Her genetic makeup or her cultural background?

And beyond that question, does this matter? Should it matter? And what are the implications for the world we live in and will live in?

))▶

No matter how many European genes she carries, my mother's identity and worldview have been shaped by her experiences as an African American woman growing up in the segregated South. She cooks off the African American table, or at least the Creole side of it. She grew up as a "colored" girl. She went to segregated schools. And she is a proud alumni of Xavier University in New

Orleans, a historically black college. She knew the rules of the city of Natchitoches. She also knew that her father, Frank Martinez, along with others risking their lives, was organizing black people to vote.

On her way to school, my mother walked past *Uncle Jack*, a statue of a stooped, elderly black man tipping his hat. The plaque on the statue read, "Erected by the City of Natchitoches in Grateful Recognition of the Arduous and Faithful Service of the Good Darkies of Louisiana. Donor J. L. Bryan. 1927."

When the Jena Six controversy erupted in 2006 — six black teens were charged with the attempted murder of a white student after a schoolyard fight in racially charged Jena, Louisiana — I was a new member of the House Judiciary Committee. Chairman John Conyers Jr., the Michigan Democrat who entered Congress back in 1965, organized a hearing about the Jena Six, and I pulled out some of my fiercest cross-examination skills on some of the witnesses. My mother called me after having watched the televised sessions.

"You know you have your own Jena Six story," she told me.

She went on to explain that when my grandfather Frank went out to organize the black vote, sometimes the Ku Klux Klan would drag logs out into the middle of the road, and Grandpa Frank would have to worry about whether he and his fellow organizers would get shot if they got out of their car to clear the way.

"That was in Jena!" my mother said.

It's impossible to understand my mother without knowing her experience in the segregated South. When she was a little girl, she had to have her tonsils removed. Her father took her to the hospital, and the nurses set her up in a nice room. Now, Grandpa Frank looked more Spanish and European than black, so the nurses assumed he was white and that his daughter was white too. That was until my grandmother showed up along with her mother, Cora Marinovich Balthazar.

"What is y'all?" the nurse asked my great-grandmother, whom everyone knew as "Mama Co" or just "Co."

Mama Co replied, "We jus' plain colored folks, ma'am."

The next thing my mother knew, she was transferred to a huge room filled with beds and sick kids—all black.

My mother adopted her father's willingness to take on the status quo. When she taught us about Rosa Parks and her famous decision to refuse to give up her seat to a white person on a Montgomery, Alabama, bus in 1955, she added pointedly that Ms. Parks was by no means the only person dissatisfied with Jim Crow segregation. She taught us the difference between an individual act of heroism and a freedom movement. She made it clear that Rosa Parks's bold act resonated throughout the city of Montgomery and the South generally because her action took place as part of a movement for justice. Mom described more than a few times how she and her friends would snatch the moveable sign on the New Orleans buses that designated where whites could sit and where blacks could sit. "Yeah, we would just grab it and stick it in one of our big purses." She added, "One time the driver saw one of us take it and said, 'Hey, gal! Gimme back that sign!' We just ran."

My mom also described another time when she was a young married woman, traveling from Detroit back to Natchitoches. The interstate highway was not yet completed, and so my mother and her first cousins Thad and Rita Jones were driving the old surface roads south. My mom was pregnant with her first child, my older brother Leonard, and so she had to use the restroom frequently. Now, stopping at an unfamiliar gas station was potentially perilous for African Americans because of the segregation laws. At one point, south of the Mason-Dixon Line, they stopped for gasoline and for my mom to use the restroom. This pregnant twenty-three-year-old woman walked up to the attendant and asked where she might find a restroom. The man scoffed, "Gal, you know you can't use the one in there! G'wan 'round back and go there." I can just imagine her with her hand on her hip, wagging her finger at him and saying, "You mean, you think I'm not good enough to use your ol' nasty toilet? I wouldn't use it now for love nor money. Let's go, Thad." The way my mom tells it sounds slightly more restrained, but I know she is a little feistier than that.

It's funny how our understanding of racial identity changes as we get older. When I was a kid, I was "black," but I was pretty neutral about it—just as any kid would be. I had no idea that my racial category had any political or social significance. The first neighborhood I remember growing up in was mixed but largely black, but this was before Detroit's white flight. The next neighborhood was decidedly mixed. Our next-door neighbors were white. My buddy Jerry, who lived across the street, was a white kid, and so was David, who lived around the corner.

When fights and scuffles broke out, as they sometimes did, kids picked sides. But not along racial lines. When I was seven years old, the sky was blue, the leaves were green, my family and I were sort of brownish, and Jerry, a mean stickball player, was pinkish. The world would be so much better if we could return to childlike sensibilities regarding issues such as race, but obviously we won't. So we've got to face the problem of racial injustice forthrightly, and this begins with honest discussion and a thick skin.

The social and political ramifications of blackness began to occur to me around the age of eleven, when I started going to junior high school. Well meaning but misguided teachers (ignoring that most children are somewhere in between) introduced the idea of "white" and "black" to kids like me, who hadn't necessarily been raised with these concepts.

"You're smart—for a black student," said one of my white teachers.

"You're one of the best *black* students I have ever taught," said another.

I remember that I didn't feel complimented; I didn't feel praised. I felt like saying, "Thank you . . . I think."

I changed schools between fifth and sixth grades, and that meant a new set of kids and teachers. For the first time, I felt like an outsider. The teachers had low expectations of me. They seemed excessively aware of my color.

In my family, African American personhood was determined by achievement. On both sides of my family, people tended to be hard workers. I couldn't imagine growing up in a household where high expectations weren't placed on me, where achievement wasn't expected. Being black meant living up to that high standard. I was expected to excel. Had I not had such parents and grandparents, I might have fallen victim to those low expectations in my new school.

At home I was taught—not so much directly but by example—that remarks such as "You're smart for a black student" from white people in authority were not compliments, no matter what the speaker intended. My parents valued being the best, not the *black* best. Because of this, I never had the sense that my destiny was beyond my control. I never thought I owed anyone deference, or that I had better mind my place.

As a young adult, I viewed activism through the lens of racial justice, but as I got older, I became more sensitive to any form of exclusion or rejection based on things beyond a person's control or beliefs they hold as a matter of conscience. I immersed myself in the history of the movement and created a new inclusive perspective.

But in this age, when we contemplate a post–civil rights era society but still face dramatic racial disparities in employment, income, test scores, incarceration rates, and health, I ask, What is the continuing significance of race? And, perhaps, how can all Americans see that failure to eliminate racism or the two-tiered ladders of opportunity deprives the country from reaping the full talents of all?

A little history. In America, if you're 1/32nd black, you're black. This was the legal definition in several states to determine who had the right to marry or buy property, or even where a person could eat, sit on public transportation, or attend school. Color or race was a way to assign opportunity and life chances. Is it still? Statistics and life experience suggest that the old determinants of opportunity still have substantial influence.

Ironically, a person can be deemed not black enough. This is a judgment that reaches to the core of blackness. The shared experience. The connection to the culture.

President Obama had to manage this issue of racial "authenticity." Early in his presidential run, the question emerged: Is he really black?

"Well, you know his mother was white . . ."

I was pleased to hear him speak about his father's and grandfather's lives in colonial Kenya. Learning about the experiences of Africans under British rule was actually good for us Americans.

During the 2012 primaries, a Republican candidate for the White House, Herman Cain, questioned President Obama's authenticity: "It is documented that his mother was white and his father was from Africa. If he wants to call himself black, fine. If he wants to call himself African American, fine." Cain, an African American, then went on to say, "A *real* black man is not timid about making the right decisions."

A "real black man"? What does that mean? Not much. In fact, given the political and social nature of race, and its unscientific and transitory properties, a "real black man" means whatever the speaker wants it to mean. Praise. Put-down. Whatever.

))))➤

When I grew up in Detroit in the 1970s, the region of southeast Michigan was so segregated that in 1985, the City of Dearborn—known at one time for its intolerance toward blacks—passed an ordinance that only Dearborn residents could use the city's parks. Violators would face a $500 fine.

A coalition of civil rights and church groups sued, arguing that the ordinance was a political maneuver to keep blacks out of Dearborn. At a public hearing, one elderly white woman testified that while staring out the front window of her home, she saw "those Detroiters" using Dearborn basketball courts. A questioner asked how she knew they were Detroiters from such a distance. She replied, "Why, I was looking right at them!"

The Dearborn parks ban was merely emblematic. As a teen, I read *Detroit: A City of Race and Class Violence* by B. J. Widick, which is among several books detailing Detroit's struggles with racial inclusion. Its point is that race and racial division in Detroit—and in nearly every other city in America—pose barriers to a better quality of life for working-class and middle-class people.

Perhaps Martin Luther King Jr. put it best when he shared

some of his interactions with his white jailers in Birmingham, Alabama, in a February 1968 speech, "The Drum Major Instinct":

The other day, I was saying, I always try to do a little converting when I'm in jail. And when we were in jail in Birmingham the other day, the white wardens and all enjoyed coming around the cell to talk about the race problem. And they were showing us where we were so wrong demonstrating. And they were showing us where segregation was so right. And they were showing us where intermarriage was so wrong. So I would get to preaching, and we would get to talking—calmly, because they wanted to talk about it. And then we got down one day to the point—that was the second or third day—to talk about where they lived, and how much they were earning. And when those brothers told me what they were earning, I said, "Now, you know what? You ought to be marching with us. You're just as poor as Negroes." And I said, "You are put in the position of supporting your oppressor, because through prejudice and blindness, you fail to see that the same forces that oppress Negroes in American society oppress poor white people. And all you are living on is the satisfaction of your skin being white, and the drum major instinct of thinking that you are somebody big because you are white. And you're so poor you can't send your children to school. You ought to be out here marching with every one of us every time we have a march.

I believe that as Americans, we need to seek out what unites us. As King pointed out, issues such as race have been used to keep people distracted while the real culprit gets away scot-free.

I identify myself as a black man, but that describes merely one aspect of me. Maybe it helps communicate something about my experience, my perspective. But I'm also a man of faith, a Muslim.

I'm a parent, a public servant, and a million other things, including a proud American. Identity *does* count. We all are a color, a gender, a religious adherent or not, but our most important quality is how we treat one another.

Beyond being black, my family has ethnic contributions from all over the world, but most of us call ourselves black for political and cultural reasons. We say we are black and proud. What we mean is that people like us who were denied full participation in American society still added to this great country despite the effort to marginalize us. We used to be property. We endured the Jim Crow era. We understand that as a people denied liberty in the land of liberty, we will always be committed to liberty and justice for all—no exceptions.

We're black and proud. Hopefully, not just proud in an egotistical way but in a way that says, "We value ourselves; we value everyone."

But even that notion of blackness has become more and more complex.

Being African American is as much about being American as African. It covers slavery and Jim Crow, but it also includes triumphs despite the odds, like those of Paul Robeson, the actor-singer-activist, and three-time world boxing champion Muhammad Ali. In my town of Minneapolis, saying that someone is African American or black may not tell you much about him. Is he mixed? Is he Somalian? Liberian? Ethiopian? Or is he a "traditional African American"?

Today in Minnesota, we have to talk in terms of traditional African Americans as well as blacks from other countries. For instance, we have a large Somali community, which is thriving in the Twin Cities despite having endured the chaos of war, refugee status, often passing through multiple countries before landing in Minnesota—and, of course, often the loss of loved ones along the way. The Somali population votes, runs for office, opens businesses, and pursues professions. The community is building a world and finding its way in a new environment.

As new Americans, the Somalis have an indirect experience and understanding of Jim Crow, American slavery, and the civil rights movement. In fact, the Somali community is writing a new chapter on the African American experience, and like all new Americans, they are writing a new chapter on what it means to be American, adding to the complexity and richness of the American experience.

Like so many groups of Americans who arrived on these shores for a better life, the Somali community—and the Mexican and Hmong communities as well—understand full well what racial profiling and discrimination are all about. They know exclusion and poverty. They know what it means to watch your traditional culture fray as your young people are lured away by a seductive materialistic culture. This is a problem that many communities face: African Americans coming up north, Latinos coming north, Irish coming west, and Chinese coming across the Pacific. Retaining culture is a common challenge.

I shared the Somali community's pain when its last local bank closed its doors. The people rely on banks to transmit funds to their loved ones in East Africa—in places such as Dadaab, Kenya, site of the world's largest refugee camp, or Mogadishu, Somalia. When I visited Mogadishu on February 19, 2013, it certainly deepened my understanding of what my constituents have faced. Twenty-two years of political chaos, war, famine, and terrorism is an awesome burden for the people of any nation. But by visiting Mogadishu, I also caught some insight into their resilience. I also visited a Nairobi suburb called Eastleigh, which is inhabited by large numbers of Somalis. They have created a thriving business community, clinics, a nice hotel, and more. Historically, Indian-Kenyan business people controlled the commerce in Eastleigh, but Somali refugees, having little choice, have slowly gotten into the game.

I hear these stories of overcoming hardship from Minnesotans of Mexican heritage, too. Many are from rural parts of Mexico, and like so many before them, they came north looking for opportunity. Historically, Saint Paul has been the destination for Mexican Americans in Minnesota. The west side of Saint Paul is home to Minnesota's oldest Mexican American community, and it is still the site of some splendid Mexican restaurants, churches, and Spanish-language schools. It is where the Mexican consulate in Minnesota is located. The new, fast-emerging Mexican American community is on Lake Street in Minneapolis. This community has converted a once-sagging thoroughfare into a vibrant commercial corridor.

But the Mexican American community, like so many new American communities, faces serious challenges. First among these is our broken immigration system. Whether the new American community is Somali, Hmong, Mexican, Ecuadorian, Liberian, or something else, they all are in desperate need of immigration reform. I see it in my congressional office every day. Of all the case categories we help constituents with, immigration tops everything in terms of raw numbers, including Social Security claims, veterans' issues, and housing issues. People come to me describing how they have been separated from their husbands and wives, and children and parents. They talk about how they have lived in the United States for decades, have had their children here, and still live in fear of deportation. Somalis, who have an expansive view of the concept of family, go through great difficulty to bring their "brother" into the United States, only to learn that in America *brother* means the child of your mother or father—not a first cousin who has lived every moment in your household. Many Somalis are called on to supply paperwork that just doesn't exist after twenty-two years of war. America needs an immigration system that works for all, that reunites families, and that allows kids who were brought here at an early age to go to college at a reasonable price.

In Congress, some of my colleagues decry amnesty, and sometimes their arguments are xenophobic. But the twelve million people currently living in the United States without documentation are simply not going to "self-deport"; nor are they going to starve. The only sensible option is to give everyone already here a pathway to citizenship. This is best for native-born Americans too because an undocumented worker is an underpaid and exploited worker. If everyone has a status, and the penalties are high for employers who cheat, then wages will rise because newly documented workers will have legal leverage to demand fair pay and working conditions. The modern immigration debate is in large measure about race, and in order for America to reach its full potential, we need to broaden our understanding of racism beyond Jim Crow. Racial inclusion and justice also entail offering opportunity to new Americans.

))))➤

I hope that we're in the last stages of racism, wiping away its last vestiges in this country. I have watched it erode within my lifetime. The racial constraints I endured growing up—which were usually not spoken but implied—do not apply to my kids and their generation.

I was never told not to date a white girl; I just knew that society thought it wasn't okay. We had read enough history to know that bringing home a white girl would be asking for trouble—not within the Ellison household but within society.

I had a friend in high school named Jaymie who was a very fair-skinned girl, and I used to get teased a lot for going out with a "white" girl. One time my mom asked me, "Keith, do you have a white girlfriend?"

"No, Mom, Jaymie's black," I told her.

I don't think my mother would have had an issue if Jaymie had been white. She was just curious because she'd heard I was going out with a white girl.

My brother Brian had a white friend who was a girl. She had a crush on him and used to come over all the time. When she arrived, we'd go up to his room and tell him, "Brian, the white girl is here looking for you."

We didn't feel any animosity. In fact, everyone liked her. At the time, it was just a little different and a little weird because no one was dating outside of his or her race when I was growing up—at least not in my Detroit neighborhood. We had other races in the area, like Arab Americans, but we just didn't socialize much.

When I was fifteen, I worked in the Chippewa Party Store, which was owned by a Lebanese man who was fair and nice toward me. My job was loading pops (what some call sodas) into the cooler. All day long I would load the hot ones in the back and move the cold ones to the front. The owner's name was Sam, which I'm sure was short for Samir, but he told everyone to call him Sam. (Back then, it was common for Arab Americans to use more American-sounding nicknames. Muhammad would become Mo; Farid would become Fred; and Samir, Sam or Sammy.) I got to know Sam and his family fairly well because they worked at the store too. My mother shopped in the store all of the time, and they always made a huge deal when "Ms. Clida" showed up. Unfortunately, my relationship with Sam never grew beyond work. I never visited his home, and he never visited mine, though I know he liked and respected my family. At the end of the day, he loaded up the car and drove back to Bloomfield Hills, where he lived. The real connection ended because they lived in the suburbs, and we lived in the city.

That no longer holds true for my children's generation. They mix and match and hang out without regard to any separations based on race or ethnicity. When my son Jeremiah introduced us to his Hispanic girlfriend, and when Isaiah introduced us to a half-Hispanic, half-Japanese young lady, I was thinking, *Times have changed*.

My only criterion for my children's future mates is decency. I want them to pick good, honest people no matter what the racial, cultural, or ethnic background. I want this because I believe it's important to be happy. In a world that can be as rough and cruel as this one, if you find someone who you care about and who cares about you, you had better hold on to that person. Period. When I was born, blacks and whites weren't allowed to marry in sixteen states. With my kids, the issue of race is, well, a nonissue. In my generation, dating interracially was still a taboo. A whole lot of drama surrounded a white person bringing home a black, and vice versa. The 1967 film *Guess Who's Coming to Dinner* was considered both controversial and groundbreaking. In the film, a young white woman from an upper-class family shocks her liberal parents (played by Spencer Tracy and Katharine Hepburn) by bringing home her fiancé to meet them: he's a handsome young African American doctor (Sidney Poitier). And his parents, similarly unaware that their daughter-in-law-to-be is white, also react with dismay. Or what about the hoopla that surrounded the interracial love scene between Jim Brown, the football Hall of Famer turned actor, and sultry Raquel Welch in the Western *100 Rifles?* It was 1969, and that just wasn't done.

Today race doesn't even cross a kid's mind—at least not the ones in my family. I have an adult niece who married a white fellow named Tim. Lauren and Tim seem quite happy, and I think Tim gets along with the family better than Lauren does! (She inherited her family's love of arguing and debating.) It looks like my kids probably will not consider race as a factor in choosing a partner. That's a good thing.

This notion, that color and race don't matter, is what attracted me to Islam. Islam teaches that God put us all here so that we could know one another, not hate one another. In his last sermon, the Prophet Muhammad states: "The black is not better than the white, and the white is not better than the black. The Arab is not better than the non-Arab, and the non-Arab is not better than the Arab . . . surely the best among you is the most faithful."

I wonder what the next phase is going to be. I think that America is going to be more accepting of people with different cultures. I can see that the trend is clearly toward tolerance. We're not done with racism. We will see some ugliness. Cases of racially motivated violence will continue to crop up here or there. Racial disparities still plague many aspects of our society. However, this new generation brings hope that the systemic, societal racism that was so prevalent for centuries may be becoming a thing of the past.

Maybe, by the end of the twenty-first century, the color line will be erased. Let's hope.

5

MY DAMASCUS MOMENT

I remember the day my brother Brian bounded into the house with a bold announcement.

"I have some good news!"

"What?" we asked, looking puzzled.

"Jesus loves you!"

Brian was eighteen years old. I was seventeen.

He'd had an epiphany and in that moment knew he would be committing his life to Christ and helping people "find Jesus."

I was like, "Okay. Good for you." And I went back to whatever I was doing.

My dad was less than pleased. That outward display of Jesus loving didn't make a big hit with my father at all.

He had no time for religion. He probably believed in some

concept of God, but organized religion held no sway with him. He had a number of religious people, like his brother, Bob, in his family, but it wasn't for him. He was somewhere between agnostic and neglectful Protestant. "That's a waste of time" was my father's attitude.

So when Brian came home with his grand proclamation, my father said, "You ain't gonna be no jackleg preacher!" (My dad had absolutely no problem telling us what we weren't going to be.) Dad probably associated preaching with the street-hustling con artists from Hastings Street in the Black Bottom, but he never specifically stated why he reacted so negatively to Brian's declaration. I am sure that he'd run into a few preachers who were charismatic types like Father Divine, Reverend Ike, or Daddy Grace.

His idea of success didn't include being an unlettered man of the cloth. My dad had many discussions and some arguments with Brian over his decision to become a clergyman. But in the end, while my dad had strong opinions, he also raised us to follow what we believed to be right.

For Brian, being a man of God was right. Later he would enroll in Virginia Union University's Richmond Theological Seminary— a consolation prize for my father because Brian was getting an advanced degree. (He eventually went to law school as well.) At least his son would be an *educated* preacher. I understood that my dad never wanted any of his children to fail to reach their full potential.

My mother, usually sympathetic and supportive, also had a period of adjustment to Brian's life choice. In her case, it was not merely because she was Catholic but because she was a Mass-attending, candle-lighting, genuflecting, rosary-bead-praying Catholic. What was this Baptist stuff? If Brian had said he wanted to become a priest, that would have been more acceptable to her. But a Baptist preacher? However, she, too, raised us to have our own minds, and while we knew she was a little perplexed by the whole thing, she never made Brian feel like he had made a bad decision. Today my mom leaves her Mass at Gesu Catholic Church in Detroit and then drives over to Brian's church, Church of the New Covenant-Baptist, to catch the end of his service. The two churches are only a few blocks apart in northwest Detroit.

I learned from the way Brian sprang the Baptist surprise on the family that when I had my revelation, I wouldn't make a big deal about it. Whatever I believed was what I believed, and that was going to be that. No grand declarations. Brian wanted to "save" everybody. He wanted to sit you down and teach you the Bible and tell you about all of the wonderful things that Jesus has done for you. And that was cool. But I was on my own journey.

I'm proud of Brian. Today his church is in the Detroit community. Though Brian has several professionals in his congregation, most of the people are working folks. The average income of his congregation is probably less than $25,000 a year. He tends to his people's needs and keeps on preaching the Word. I respect that.

Brian and I don't agree on political and social issues. He supported George W. Bush, and he's a staunch "pro-life" advocate. But his tools are love, persuasion, and acceptance. Brian advises people to see why it's so special to have children—he doesn't vilify them for doing things differently than he would. He and his wife, Sharon, adopted a boy named Christian Nehemiah. He's four years old and the apple of my brother's eye. Brian is also out on the streets helping those victimized by domestic violence and gang violence. He's a true missionary. Brian rolls up his sleeves and gets involved. He is, in my opinion, what a follower of Christ should be.

Growing up, we were never dragged to church. We were gathered up to go with my mom to Mass when we were little, but when we got old enough to make our own decisions, she allowed us to stay home if that's what we chose. I felt that I was sitting in those hard pews for no reason and that the routine had no meaning for me. So I stopped going.

I was also immersed in Catholicism at school, but that actually reinforced my lack of interest. In my sophomore year at the University of Detroit Jesuit High School and Academy, an all-boys Catholic school on Seven Mile Road, I took a Bible course on the book of Mark that I found fascinating, but the religion never spoke to me.

Not the way that Islam did.

))))▶

I discovered Islam as a nineteen-year-old sophomore at Wayne State University. I was carrying on an academic tradition, following in the footsteps of my father, my uncle, and my two older brothers.

I didn't go there for the social life or the athletics. Unlike the University of Michigan and Michigan State University, the other two major schools in Michigan, Wayne State was less of a party-oriented school. It didn't have a big social scene. A lot of students who attended worked jobs or were returning to school after a long layoff. Probably most came to college straight out of high school, like me, but a significant number were working parents. So the campus was more serious and subdued. Some people lived in dorms, but not like the dorms at U-M and MSU, where dorm life was the hub of activity. It was an urban, working-class campus that reflected the aging, industrial city around it.

I didn't live in the dorms but in the apartments surrounding the school. Half of the people who lived in my apartment complex were students; the other half were just people who called the place home. For instance, my roommate, Roger, a friend from high school, didn't go to college when I was attending. I went to class, and he went to work.

When I was a freshman, Leonard was living with his girlfriend, Val, who would become his wife (now ex-wife), and Brian lived at home. I was close enough to go back home for a home-cooked meal from time to time and to do my laundry, but I wanted to be out on my own.

Roger and I shared a tiny one-bedroom apartment. He took the bedroom; I stayed on the pull-out couch in the living room, with Jimi Hendrix posters on the wall. We lived there for three years. During two of those years, I became a practicing Muslim, and he was a nightly beer drinker. We had this whole *The Odd Couple* Felix-and-Oscar thing going on. I'd say I was Felix.

In my sophomore year, I became the sports editor for the daily student newspaper, the *South End*. They paid me for the work, and I made enough money to afford my own place. So I moved out on my own. I loved the job. It honed my writing skills and brought me in touch with everything that was happening on campus.

My conversion to Islam also occurred in my sophomore year. I was majoring in economics. One Friday I was studying for a calculus exam. It was right before noon, and a friend I was with suddenly packed up his books and started to rush out the door.

"Where are you going?" I asked, confused.

"I need to be on time for *Jummah* prayer."

"Jummah prayer? What's that?"

"Why don't you come with me and check it out?"

I was curious about why this Jummah prayer was so important, so I grabbed my books and followed him. We headed over to a room in the student center. I noticed that outside the doorway the floor was littered with shoes. My friend took off his, and I took off mine, and I followed everyone into the open room, which had large sheets spread out on the floor. I sat down on a sheet and listened.

A Muslim preacher talked to us about universal brotherhood, the evils of racism, and the common origins of all of humanity. I liked what I heard. I looked around and recognized other people from my classes. The room was a veritable United Nations: Nigerians, Bosnians, Arabs, South Asians, East Asians, several African Americans, and even Latinos. The preacher spoke of the message of Muhammad being a message of liberation. He recited a portion of the Quran in Arabic, which I did not understand, but then he repeated the passage in English. I have never forgotten these words:

> *It is not righteousness that ye turn your faces towards East or West; but it is righteousness to believe in God and the Last Day, and the Angels, and the Book, and the Messengers; to spend of your substance, out of love for Him, for your kin, for orphans, for the needy, for the wayfarer, for those who ask, and for the liberation of slaves; to be steadfast in prayer, and practice regular charity; to fulfill the contracts which you have made; and to be firm and patient, in suffering and adversity, and throughout all periods of panic. Such are the people of truth, the God-fearing (Quran 2:177).*

I was struck by the call for justice "for orphans, for the needy, for the wayfarer, for those who ask, and for the liberation of slaves." This message fits with nearly everything else I was doing on campus, and I wanted to know more. After the service, my friend gave me a copy of the Quran. He explained that the message wasn't presented in the Quran in the order it was revealed and said not to try to digest it all at once. He suggested that I read a few selected passages and think about them.

In the privacy of my room, I read, and I just thought. I wondered what the spiritual underpinnings of my work were. I was working on campus, and studying in class about fairness. Why was I doing these things? I couldn't answer. I knew only that somehow I needed to. So many of my friends were secular in their thinking. In fact, many of them thought of religion as backward and superstitious. Somehow I felt different. I felt the presence of life in things, and I still do. I also felt that this presence wanted something. Balance. Acceptance. Kindness. What I felt about the world and what I read in the Quran fit for me. "Spend of your substance, out of love for Him." It resonated with me that the abundance we are blessed with wasn't for hoarding but for sharing. I felt like I always knew this. Now here it was written.

As I paged through the Quran, I noticed that nearly every chapter, or *surah*, opened with "In the Name of the Most Generous, the Most Merciful." I felt the need for mercy, as I felt myself make mistake after mistake. I wanted to be a good person, but I knew that I was at times rude, selfish, and insensitive. I was in need of mercy. I was a beginner and didn't know much, but I wanted to know more. I read more, talked with knowledgeable people, and started to pray. At first, I just did it. I didn't feel like it, but I did it. I even told a friend, "I don't feel anything." But I kept at it, and soon I began to miss it when I skipped praying. It started to become my own little refuge in a busy day. I am sure that some of my old associates began to think I was getting weird. I didn't care.

Meanwhile, I kept up my other activities in class and around campus. I had become active with the antiapartheid group on campus, the black student union, and the *South End*, where I was writing about justice and equality. I was new to the cause of racial justice and advocacy, but I was gung-ho to get involved.

At nineteen, while my activism was limited, my reading was

extensive. In high school, I read *The Autobiography of Malcolm X*, *Black Boy*, and *Native Son* by Richard Wright, *Manchild in the Promised Land* by Claude Brown, and Alan Paton's *Cry, the Beloved Country*. After my graduation from high school, my dad gave me a copy of *Black Rage,* by the psychiatrists Grier and Cobbs. On my own, I picked up *Detroit: A City of Race and Class Violence* and also *Detroit: I Do Mind Dying—A Study in Urban Revolution.*

I found Frantz Fanon's *The Wretched of the Earth* fascinating, and I subsequently read everything of his I could get my hands on, such as *A Dying Colonialism* and *Black Skin, White Masks,* both of which were published in the 1950s. I became consumed with understanding racial hierarchy, the economic order, and the structure of society. I read *Rules for Radicals: A Pragmatic Primer for Realistic Radicals,* by Saul Alinsky. Then I read about lawyers who fought for justice, starting with Clarence Darrow and Bill Kunstler, and local legal heroes such as Bill Goodman, George Crockett, and John Conyers. I wanted to be like them.

During my freshman year at Wayne State, in 1981, Coleman Young won his third consecutive term as the first black mayor of Detroit. He'd go on to serve five terms in all. In 1973, the year he was first elected, I was too young to fully appreciate what a victory this represented for the community, but I imagine the elation was similar to the way many African Americans felt when Barack Obama was elected president in 2008.

Young was a legendary trade unionist before I was born. The police had an anticrime program called Stop the Robberies, Enjoy Safe Streets (STRESS), but it seemed to many to be a license for police to target black people. Coleman Young came in and disbanded it. He was a man from the streets who rose up to lead. And folks were plenty proud.

He was one of them.

An oft-told story illustrates how "down" Mayor Young was. He was vacationing in Hawaii when he had to hold a press conference by closed-circuit TV to address a crisis back home. He came on wearing a Hawaiian shirt and said, "Aloha, motherfuckers!" And the audience of Detroit press roared. Detroiters like chutzpah.

))))➡

By my twentieth birthday, I was a full-fledged student activist. But unlike some of my peers, I also had a spiritual yearning. Yes, I was for improving people's material reality, but I also wondered about the answers that faith and values might offer.

The Muslim preacher's words and what I saw at that Jummah prayer gathering moved me. I couldn't tell you the preacher's name, but his message got through.

Something I heard set me on a trajectory that I have been on ever since. What I witnessed that day spoke to me in a way that years of Catholic education never did.

I should mention that today I am a great admirer of Catholic social teaching, such as the Church's position on the death penalty, the rights of workers, our obligations to the poor, and progressive taxation. And, of course, I love my mother, and Catholicism feeds her soul. From my limited vantage point, Catholicism ("the Church") didn't address issues such as apartheid, racial injustice, colonialism, police brutality, and deindustrialization. But, in fact, the Church *was* addressing all those things. I just didn't see it. Many Catholics, both today and in the past, have worked on poverty, hunger, and all of these things. Somehow it escaped me that my own high school had as its motto "Men for others" and that we studied the service-oriented message of the Prayer of Saint Ignatius of Loyola:

Dearest Lord,
teach me to be generous;
teach me to serve You as You deserve;
to give and not to count the cost,
to fight and not to heed the wounds,
to toil and not to seek for rest,
to labor and not to ask for reward,
save that of knowing I am doing Your Will.

While the social justice teachings of my early education didn't stick with me, I was exposed to Catholic and Jesuit social teachings. But all I saw were rules and regulations that didn't have any practical use for me.

I began to lose interest in being a Catholic long before I converted to Islam. In more recent years, my understanding of Catholicism has evolved from reading books such as James Carroll's *Constantine's Sword*, which documented the Catholic Church's transition from the early church—which "held all things in common" and taught universal love—to a state religion that taught anti-Semitism and the Roman emperor Constantine the Great's "in hoc signo vinces" ("by this sign [the Cross] you will conquer"): the edict by which the Church conquered others in the name of God.

I enjoy reading Catholic authors. I have found the works of Richard Rohr, a Franciscan priest and prolific writer, helpful and important to me. I heard him speak at a conference in Washington, DC, in 2005, and picked up his *Adam's Return: The Five Promises of Male Initiation*. He is an awesome speaker, and he, more than anyone I have ever heard, best explains the meaning of original sin. According to Rohr, the newborn baby is not inherently bad but inherits brokenness from Mom and Dad. He has helped me understand the faith I was brought up in much better.

In every era, courageous and committed Catholics have struggled against institutional corruption and indifference to preserve and proclaim the Church's original message. If I'd known then what I know now about Catholicism, I might have looked at it differently. I would have seen that, like other religions, it offers a road, a set of signposts on the path to the divine. But that is not what happened to me. When I walked into that makeshift mosque, a big room with sheets on the floor in the Wayne State student center, the message I heard struck a chord in me.

I was hearing ideas I had never heard before relating to God—God's word and His plan for our lives and the issues of the day.

I wanted to know more.

So I did what I always did when I wanted a deeper understanding of a subject: I started reading and studying. I read everything I could to learn more about Islam.

One day, without an invitation, I walked into the Muslim Center on Rosa Parks Boulevard and West Davison Street. I had been driving back to Wayne State along the John C. Lodge Freeway, one of those famous urban highways like the Dan Ryan Expressway in Chicago or the FDR Drive in New York, lined with billboards. It was a road I had traveled a hundred times before, but this was the first time that I actually noticed one of the billboards. It featured the Muslim Center and directed me to get off at the next exit to find out more. And I did.

As much as I liked what the guys on campus had to say, I wanted my faith anchored to a community of regular people, not students who come and go with each new semester.

At the Muslim Center, I met Imam Abdullah Bey El-Amin and Mitchell Shamsud-Din. These men were the dynamic duo of the center, an old bank that the community had converted into a mosque. They followed the teaching of Warith Deen Muhammad, the son of the Nation of Islam's founder, Elijah Muhammad. They believed in the common origins of all mankind, rejecting the racial exclusion of Elijah Muhammad and his successor, Louis Farrakhan. After attending regularly for about a month, one day, after the noon prayer, I became a part of the community. I recited the *shahada*, the Islamic profession of faith, three times:

"*Ashadu anlaa ilaaha illallah wa ashadu anna Muhammadar rasulullah.*" "There is no god but God, and Muhammad is His messenger."

On that day, on Rosa Parks and Davison, I became a Muslim.

I didn't come into the faith through the Nation of Islam (NOI), as some African Americans have done. Growing up in Detroit, it was hard to ignore the work that the Nation of Islam did on the streets, particularly with young black men coming out of prison. Its members sounded tough, they looked clean and disciplined. But when I took a closer look, I found that it wasn't doing much in the community to change the status quo. I'm not saying that the NOI hasn't helped people get off drugs and stay out of jail. It has helped foster a sense of family, community, and entrepreneurship within the black community. Yet when you look historically at who worked to change society and unjust laws and practices, you won't find the Nation of Islam among them. Its members weren't there during the civil rights movement, getting their heads bashed in or enduring the dogs and fire hoses.

It's interesting to me that Malcolm X is viewed as the tough guy and Martin Luther King Jr. as the soft one. But what is the measure of courage? As much as I admire Malcolm X's courage, one must admit that it takes a lot of guts to know you're going to get your head bashed in and still walk into danger. It takes a lot of courage to have your home firebombed—with your wife and children inside—and still get up the next day to fight the good fight.

It takes a lot of courage to know that your life is on the line, and still be willing to do the things you know are necessary to change a nation.

You don't get tougher than Martin Luther King Jr. in my book.

In the early portion of Malcolm X's public life, he was talking tough, he was saying emotionally satisfying things that many blacks, battered and abused by American racism, may have wanted to say, such as calling the white man the devil. But, in Malcolm X's NOI years, he wasn't confronting the underlying structures that denied black people equality. He was speaking about them boldly and forcefully, but he wasn't changing and confronting them. For Malcolm X, that didn't come until later. According to the historic record, I'm sure he wanted to do more while he was in the Nation, but the organization wasn't set up to take on the establishment. It was designed to avoid racism—not confront it. The NOI preached separation, which was the same message preached by the Ku Klux Klan. The message of "Don't worry about America, worry about yourself" was in the same vein as Booker T. Washington's turn-of-the-twentieth-century philosophy, which was work hard, keep your head down, and don't expect justice. The NOI was able to repackage that message to appeal to the frustrations of young black men and women in the middle of the century. It sold black pride, and members sold bean pies and the *Final Call*, the Nation's official newspaper, on street corners. The NOI posed no threat to the status quo; it posed no threat to the system of racism.

Besides Malcolm X, one of the most noted figures in the Nation of Islam was boxer Muhammad Ali. Few people know that initially the NOI wanted nothing to do with him. It was Malcolm X who reached out and maintained a relationship with the boxer formerly known as Cassius Clay.

Clay had a record of 100–4 as an amateur and was a two-time

national Golden Gloves champion. He won the light heavyweight gold medal in the 1960 Olympic Games in Rome. He returned home to Louisville, Kentucky, thinking he would be treated as a hero, only to find the same racism he'd left behind. As Ali wrote in his autobiography, after being refused service at a local restaurant because he was black, he threw his gold medal into the Ohio River. He started searching for a cause and found the NOI and Malcolm X. But the Nation of Islam wasn't sold on him. NOI leaders thought that Clay was going to get beaten by the heavyweight champ, Sonny Liston, in their upcoming February 1964 title bout. They thought he talked too much, and they didn't want to be associated with a loudmouth loser. Malcolm took a different position, saying, "I don't care whether you win or lose, I'm with you."

When the twenty-two-year-old Clay won and, as he proclaimed, "shocked the world," the Nation of Islam opportunistically embraced the newly crowned champ. But it was Malcolm, not the Nation, who had the vision, the heart, and the plan. And both Muhammad Ali and Malcolm X eventually found out that each had to cut his own path. Of course, each man cut his own path in his own time. Each was on his timeline, but each man reached the conclusion that human beings were more than a skin color, that America could change for the better, and that the principles upholding America were worth the fight. The NOI, to this day, has never figured this out.

))))➤

When I became a Muslim in 1982, I was fascinated by the life of Malcolm X. Actually, I was influenced by El-Hajj Malik El-Shabazz, the name he took after leaving the NOI and embracing Islam.

I had read *The Autobiography of Malcolm X* five years before, and I liked that Islam had the power to transform him. He seemed more focused on justice, not less, as he gravitated toward Islam. Only after leaving the Nation of Islam in 1964 did Malcolm find his true purpose and voice.

In July 1964, Malcolm X spoke at the second meeting of the Organization of African Unity (OAU) and asked its member governments to bring the issue of racial injustice in the United States to the United Nations Commission on Human Rights. He spoke on the same subject before the Kenyan parliament, moving that nation to pass a resolution in support of the human rights struggle for African Americans. In other words, it was after *leaving* the Nation of Islam that Malcolm X became an activist.

Malcolm X criticized Martin Luther King Jr.'s "nonviolent" approach. He said there is a difference between the "black" revolution and the Negro revolution, led by MKL, which was based on nonviolence and love for one's enemy. Malcolm X said that there was no such thing as a nonviolent revolution and chided the nonviolent approach as an inadequate response to the violence many blacks were facing in the country. "We're nonviolent with people who are nonviolent with us. We are not nonviolent with anyone who is violent with us," he said.

After being critical of MLK's nonviolent approach, Malcolm X reached out to work with him in the struggle for justice and equality. He even went to Selma, Alabama, at the invitation of the Student Nonviolent Coordinating Committee (SNCC), a civil-rights organization that led the drive for voter registration and the sit-in movement. In a tough, fiery speech at the famous Brown Chapel AME Church on February 4, 1965—less than three weeks before he was murdered—he once again criticized the use of nonviolence in the face of violence. He felt that violent racists shouldn't get a free pass and should at least be concerned that their actions might return an equal reaction. Following Malcolm X's speech to a group who were ostensibly followers of MLK, who was jailed at the time, Coretta Scott King was scheduled to speak in her husband's place. It is said that Andrew Young, one of the organizers, whispered to Mrs. King to lighten up her speech to counterbalance Malcolm X's.

Within the Nation of Islam, however, Malcolm was never a real threat to the racial hierarchy. He was merely a man venting anger with fiery rhetoric.

Outside of the NOI, Malcolm X was an organizer and mobilizer around a workable plan to achieve justice and to change the status quo. This is apparently what made him most dangerous. Interestingly, Malcolm X's passion for justice never waned, but his public mood and demeanor appeared more relaxed after he abandoned the NOI philosophy. Malcolm seemed, even with daily threats against his life, at peace. This is not surprising to me. Islam has brought me, a passionate man, inner peace. What I found in Islam is that you can be happy and still practice your religion. You don't have to be angry or seek an enemy in order to serve God. Islam, like Christianity, Judaism, Hinduism, and Buddhism, is not constructed on opposing anything or anyone. You can love everybody and still develop your spiritual self. In the NOI, if you're not angry in opposition to some group of people (whites, Jews, so-called "sellout" blacks), you don't have a religion.

In Islam, your religion is what *you* make of it. How you decide to worship your God and what you decide to do within the confines of that religion is your choice. For me, the core of Islam was about things that I held in high esteem: mercy, justice, generosity. I could point to real people who embodied those characteristics. I admired Muhammad Ali. Here was a guy who in 1967 refused to be drafted into the army—losing his boxing title as a result—based on his belief that the Vietnam War was immoral. I remember thinking, *What would make someone do that?*

I was fascinated by Malcolm X's pilgrimage to Mecca, or hajj. He discovered the universal brotherhood of mankind, that we are all "created from a single pair," as stated in the Quran. I'd always known that at the center of my being. When reading about Malcolm's experience at Mecca, I came to see Islam as a religion that accepted all humanity without regard to tribe, race, or ethnicity. There are Muslims who are racist, but the basic tenets of the religion teach that all people are the same under God.

I like the story of Bilal ibn Rabah, a slave who was freed because of his devotion. His owner discovered that he was learning about God from Mecca's leading troublemaker, Muhammad, who had taught Bilal not to submit to or worship anyone but God. To try to force Bilal to deny his faith and return to worshipping the owner's deity of wood and stone, the slaver put boulders on his chest as he lay on the hot sand under the sun. Near death, Bilal never gave in. All he said was *"Ahad, Ahad,"* which means "One God, One God." Bilal was a black man, an African from Ethiopia, and he was given the honor of being the first prayer caller, or *Mueddin*. This was a sign to any and all among the companions of Muhammad that race, tribe, lineage, and nationality were not important but that faith and consciousness of God are.

After Muhammad left Mecca under threat for preaching one God, he went to the Arabian city of Medina, which had a substantial Jewish population. There Muhammad issued a charter granting everyone constitutional rights based on citizenship. At that time, tribe was the ideal of community. Your security was within a tribe, and your tribe was what kept order. A person without a tribe was extremely vulnerable. But Muhammad said, "There are no tribes." It was as if someone said, "There is no race."

What Muhammad did was radical at the time. He called for equal treatment and freedom of faith under the law, with Jews and Muslims living together in peace. This was a society based on a constitution rather than on cultural, racial, or ethnic identity. He left Mecca in pursuit of freedom. Freedom of faith, freedom of worship. Sound familiar?

When Muhammad attained power, he didn't just impose his will. He set up a constitution for the rights of all. This message kept me coming back. I wanted to learn more. My reading taught me that Islam reveres Jesus, referring to him as Messiah in the Quran.

I was not raised in a household where we talked about Jesus as our personal Lord and Savior. My brother Brian came to speak in those terms, but no one else in my family did. My mother clearly holds this belief, but in her tradition, they didn't phrase it that way. When I decided to study and then follow the teachings of the Quran and ways of Muhammad, I made sure that my conversion would not be more disruptive than necessary. In fact, my conversion to Islam came up by accident at Thanksgiving dinner. My mother was serving ham, and I refused to eat it.

"Have some of this honey-baked ham; you're going to love this," she said.

"No. I can't eat none of that," I told her, and scooped some mashed potatoes onto my plate.

"Why can't you eat my ham?"

After a pregnant pause, I finally said, "I'm a Muslim," and busied myself with the turkey.

It's funny. Looking back on this moment, it probably didn't last as long as I remember it. But I can recall her eyes widening, blinking; she looked bewildered. Then, as she lowered her chin slightly, she raised an eyebrow suspiciously, furrowed her brow, and looked sideways at me.

"You ain't no Muslim," she said incredulously.

"I am."

"What? Really?"

"Yep."

"So you can't eat my ham?"

"Umm, no."

"Well, what about the greens? You can eat the greens, can't you?"

"No, I can't," I told her. "It has pork in it."

"Well, you can just pick out the pork."

"No, I can't just pick out the pork," I told her.

My mom seemed more upset that I wasn't eating her food than by my declaration that I was a Muslim. I admit that I did miss her ham and greens. But that was a minor sacrifice for me. Mom eventually seemed okay about it. Mostly she was curious and asked questions: "Do you believe in Jesus? Can you still go to church with us?" One of my brothers asked, "Can a man really have more than one wife? How many you gonna get?" He laughed. Everyone seemed okay with my decision because I wasn't imposing it on anyone else. My family is amazingly tolerant and accepting—and willful and strong headed, too.

You can't push beliefs on anyone, and I didn't want to push Islam. I was still finding my way, and it was more important that I understood for myself what my relationship with God would be. I wanted to find my purpose within and beyond my spiritual life. What would this new journey bring for me? What was I supposed to do on earth? What was my purpose?

I returned recently to Detroit to talk about how the 2009 American Recovery and Reinvestment Act can be shared among unions and the community, and how we in Minnesota were able to make it work through cooperation. I talked about how we were able to negotiate among the neighborhoods, environmental groups, and labor so that the stimulus money could be shared and put to good use.

It was different in Detroit. Folks I met in the city weren't interested in sharing anything with the groups in the neighboring suburbs, and vice versa. Groups in the suburbs did not want to work with folks in Detroit and definitely weren't interested in splitting the pot with them. These divisions were an impediment to cooperation and growth.

I see many religions in the same way: polarizing people in the world in a way that's counterproductive to change and growth.

Through Islam, I saw a different vision. That vision called me to do more than simply be a part of a group, write for a paper, and lend a voice here or there. It taught me that everybody matters.

After I accepted Islam, I continued to pursue my education. I graduated from Wayne State with a bachelor's degree in economics, and did some graduate work in economics. I remained active on campus, writing for the *South End* and doing other things, but I had changed. My faith was woven into all of it, even though I never wanted to pursue a career as a religious leader or teacher. My role was to be active on the issues of the day, which led me to consider law school. For some time, I thought I might become an economist. Following this pursuit, I became a graduate teaching assistant and took graduate courses for a year until I realized that it wasn't something I could do as a career. All I knew about economics as a profession was academia; I didn't have any exposure to the practice of economics, and I didn't want to be a college professor. So I applied to law school, and the next thing I knew, I was moving to Minnesota.

6

ANY JACKASS CAN
KICK DOWN A BARN

October 16, 1995

I boarded the DC Metro at about five in the morning. The trains were already full, and I realized that this rally was going to be big—really big. I was in Washington already attending the annual meeting of the National Conference of Black Lawyers (NCBL), so I had missed taking the bus from Minnesota to the big event: the Million Man March.

I had spent months organizing the event, and I was disappointed not to be riding down with the guys from our group, MARCH (Men Are Responsible to Cultivate Hope). It still meets once a week in Minnesota, and I try to stop by occasionally. I also helped to organize attorneys who would serve as a legal observer committee to monitor and report any unlawful or improper behavior at the march.

I could only imagine the emotions on that bus, because I was feeling them myself on the train. Exhilaration swelled within my chest as I rode the Metro escalator up to the Washington Mall. On the steps I saw black men, boys, teenagers, and old fellows, all moving forward with a single purpose. As I walked onto the long, grassy expanse of the Mall, I saw families taking down tents in which they had spent the night. The milling crowd had a benevolent aura, and it occurred to me that legal observers might not be needed. In the cool early morning air, I could tell that there would be no fights, no arguments, and no disruptions generated by the participants. Everyone was exchanging handshakes, hugs, and "Brother this" and "Brother that." I am sure these men did not know each other as they exchanged hugs and greetings, but they had something in common: a shared experience of wanting change in their communities. The gigantic number of men gathered on the Mall was nothing short of amazing.

The men on the Mall came for various reasons, but common threads propelled us. This was 1995, thirty-two years after the March on Washington. Our parents represented the generation that had defeated Jim Crow, but they hadn't defeated racism— particularly institutional racism, which seemed to predetermine racially disparate outcomes without any individual to blame. My generation was expectant and hopeful. We overcame, right?

So why were so many of us incarcerated, in failing schools, brutalized by the police, and being murdered by other black men in our own neighborhoods? Why were so many of us who went to school and played by the rules still the "only brother working here" or the "only brother in this class" or "on this campus." Why did Rodney King get his brains beaten in by the Los Angeles Police Department in 1991, and no officer on the scene moved to stop it? And why did the Simi Valley jury give his torturers the thumbs-up a year later? All these questions swirled in the minds of American black men in the late 1980s and early 1990s. Many songs we sang, like "My Country, 'Tis of Thee" and "We Shall Overcome," rang hollow. This is why Malcolm X caught a revival around this time, X caps became popular, and message or movement rap caught on. The Million Man March was a chance to do something; to express the popular sentiment among so many black men that "Hey, we ain't overcome *yet,* guys!" To make our communities better. To stand in solidarity with people who knew exactly what Chuck D of the rap group Public Enemy meant when he cried out, "Fight the Power!" What power? Who's Chuck D? You know, brother: the Power.

From listening to the news, I got the impression that some folks throughout the country were scared of the huge gathering on the National Mall. They didn't want all these black men gathering at the Capitol talking about change. They wanted the status quo. But the status quo meant record rates of incarceration and a massive drug war aimed, it seemed, at black communities. The status quo meant a black unemployment rate double the national average, and a declining national commitment to full inclusion and parity. These were the issues propelling people to join the Million Man March. Louis Farrakhan originally called for the march. It was not Farrakhan's charisma but the lived reality of black men that fueled the march. So when the national dialogue kept focusing on Farrakhan, I resented it. In fact, I concluded that the reason for harping on Farrakhan was to avoid a larger conversation about how the circumstances of the black community were stagnating, not improving. If the powers that be could identify the march with Farrakhan alone, they could minimize the importance of the event itself, and thereby dismiss the demands of the march's participants.

I resented the spotlight on Farrakhan because I saw it as a way to avoid the issue, which was the unmet promise of the civil rights movement. With all of the movement's earthshaking achievements, it seems almost ungrateful to speak of it as having made unmet promises. But embodied in a song like "We Shall Overcome" is the idea that we would deliver more than the end of government-sanctioned exclusion: namely, real inclusion.

What I didn't know at the time was that the black community was not alone. It seemed that way from where I was standing. But the wages of nearly all working-class and middle-class Americans had been stagnant since 1980. I saw that nearly every concern I had for the black community was shared broadly throughout American society. As stagnant salaries, offshoring, an imbalanced tax system, and declining union membership took hold, many Americans were feeling the pinch.

The only speaker who didn't meet the moment was Farrakhan himself. The moment called for a sharply focused plan, some inspirational words that could motivate the men gathered on the Mall to action. Thirty-two years before, Dr. King spoke of "the fierce urgency of now." He spoke of universal acceptance. He articulated a vision to hold and inspire generations. Farrakhan, despite his flaws, was usually a powerful speaker, but this time he fell flat. Not only was his speech a dud, but his follow-up after the march was zero. Instead of touring the nation and organizing, he left the country! Millions of African Americans were ready to organize voters, tutor kids, take control of their communities, and stop the violence—and he left. His exodus, I think, revealed how starved the black community was for national leadership to address its challenges. Farrakhan's weakness as a movement leader became apparent, as he showed that he had no answers and could not move people forward to take on real problems. He could only wax eloquent while scapegoating other groups.

In spite of him, the Million Man March was miraculous. I was excited about the possibility of what organized people could do. That day, I wasn't thinking about who'd called it; I was in awe at what an amazing scene it was.

We stood at the place where so many hopeful Americans had stood in 1963, listening to Dr. Martin Luther King Jr. deliver his "I Have a Dream" speech. They, like me, were holding on to a promise. Of course, I also stood where, two hundred years before, black people had been bought and sold. The Mall was the site of some of Washington's most notorious slave markets: just below Capitol Hill, very near the site of the Smithsonian Institution's National Museum of African Art. President James Madison's staff fretted that foreign dignitaries might observe "such a revolting sight" as the "gangs of Negroes, some in chains, on their way to a Southern market." As I walked the crowd as a legal observer that day, I was amazed. I could not have known that fourteen years after the Million Man March, Barack Obama would be sworn in as the first African American president of the United States. I also had no inkling that I would be standing nearby as the first Muslim member of the US Congress, watching President Obama being sworn in.

As I looked out upon the sea of black men gathered that day to make a change, something changed inside me. Another conversion, of sorts. I was witnessing firsthand that a concerted effort around an important cause could succeed. It was billed as the Million Man March, and it certainly seemed that a million of us had arrived, pledging to come together to be better fathers, better husbands, and better citizens in our communities.

We were joining together for the march to make a difference in our communities. I was already doing that, albeit on a small scale. I imagined that we could build a movement throughout the country and thereby achieve positive change—much like the civil rights movement. The march may have been called to draw attention to past grievances, but it awakened in me a sense of possibility. A sense of what could be. We were going to take our future into our own hands and improve our condition. That was an ideal that I supported and wanted to work toward. The broader meaning of the march superseded the reservations I had about its convener.

God says in the Quran, "O mankind! We have created you from a male and a female, and made you into nations and tribes, that you may know one another (not that you may despise each other) *(Surah* 49:13)." In his final sermon, Muhammad spoke these words: "All mankind is from Adam and Eve."

The Nation of Islam proclaims that Elijah Muhammad, who lived from 1897 to 1975, is the messenger of Fard Muhammad, who they say is Allah in person. Muslims contend that Muhammad, who lived fourteen hundred years ago, is the last prophet of God. That is why Islam and the Nation of Islam are not the same religion. The NOI has a sprinkling of Islamic esthetics, but it is profoundly different in its beliefs. The media attacked Farrakhan and often extended its criticisms to the Million Man March. At the time, I resented attacks on the march, and I was reminded that our country had a long legacy of negativity toward black leaders who dared to speak their minds.

For example, in 1829 David Walker, a free black man during the antebellum period leading up to the Civil War, published a pamphlet titled *An Appeal to the Coloured Citizens of the World,* which detailed the horrific aspects of black life in pre–Civil War America and called for unity and self-help within the black community in the fight against oppression and injustice. Walker's work was branded as seditious, and legislation was introduced to ban it. His life was threatened, and he died a year later under suspicious circumstances. Many believed that he was poisoned.

When you move ahead to the twentieth century, Jamaican-born Marcus Garvey, who rallied millions of African Americans around notions of pride and dignity, was discredited, arrested, and deported. In that same era, W. E. B. Du Bois, America's foremost African American scholar, a cofounder of the National Association for the Advancement of Colored People (NAACP), and the first African American to earn a doctorate from Harvard University, had his passport confiscated. Then the US government refused to renew it while he was traveling in Africa, so that Du Bois became a citizen of Ghana, where he eventually died in exile.

Paul Robeson, Phi Beta Kappa, all-American athlete, world-renowned singer and actor, had his passport withdrawn as well, and then in 1956 he was dragged in front of the House Un-American Activities Committee. Within the next generation, Malcolm X and Martin Luther King were both spied on by the government, and were harassed and persecuted. America's leading law enforcement officer, Federal Bureau of Investigation Director J. Edgar Hoover, called King "the most notorious liar in America." The persecution of American leaders seems to hold no regard to race, religion, or sexual orientation, as no community has escaped targeting throughout American history. These black leaders were leading the community toward greater freedom and equality within the United States. I concluded that Farrakhan was leading the black community in a different direction, especially young black people in search of answers. The appeal of the NOI was strongest during the late 1950s and 1960s and again in the late 1980s and early 1990s.

We had eliminated Jim Crow and legal segregation, but we hadn't ended racism. Police brutality was a frequent occurrence in black neighborhoods throughout the country. In the 1980s and 1990s, a crack epidemic had led to a horrific crime rate in the inner cities. Black communities suffered from high unemployment, and the justice system was delivering blacks straight to prison. The climate was perfect for a movement like the Million Man March.

))))➤

In Minneapolis, I was doing my part to shed light on the issues affecting our community. I was one of the hosts of a public affairs radio program on KMOJ-FM called *Black Power Perspectives*. Three years after I graduated from law school, I had been offered this slot replacing Ron Edwards, the original host.

Edwards was an iconic figure in Minneapolis, known throughout the black community for his show *Black Focus*. He was entertaining, and the bulk of his topics addressed race, racism, and black history. He would call out folks and make up names for them. For example, he called the *Star Tribune*, the major daily in Minneapolis, the *Star Tribune Johannesburg Times*.

When Ron left the show, a friend of mine on the radio station board asked me if I wanted to take Ron's Thursday slot for one night. Malcolm X's birthday was coming up, and he wanted me to do a show on Malcolm X because I'd studied his life so much.

I called another friend of mine, Resmaa Menakem. He follows Kemetic spirituality, which is a set of ideas and practices based on ancient Kemet, or ancient Egypt. Resmaa was and remains a knowledgeable fellow, and I asked him to cohost the show with me. Well, rather than doing a one-night stint, we ended up staying on for eight years. Resmaa would sign off each show with the Kemetic word "*Hotep*," to which I would add the traditional Muslim greeting "As-salaam alaikum." (Both phrases translate roughly to "peace be unto you.")

KMOJ-FM was originally chartered to meet the needs of public housing residents, and because so many of them were African American, the shows catered to that format. So the station featured hip-hop, gospel, jazz, blues, and live talk-radio shows focusing on issues of concern to the black community. We broadened the topics to also cover welfare reform, domestic violence, and gangs—issues that were having a direct impact on our community.

I remember a show we did on welfare reform, because we had a lot of callers saying that people on welfare were lazy and that the system needed to be reformed. Some of the callers had been on welfare themselves yet still perpetuated stereotypes about recipients. But that was the beauty of the show: you never knew what to expect. One night we even debated whether or not parents should spank their kids. (I was against it, for the record.)

The radio program was a great platform to give residents a voice and also to find out what was really happening on the streets. The show helped forge my place within the community.

Whenever a police shooting occurred, certain people in the community would speak out against the brutality. I became a part of that group, which included Spike Moss and Rev. Randy Staten, well-known activists in Minnesota. We would speak out whenever an incident of racial injustice occurred—from police brutality, to unfairness in government contracting, to the low graduation rate among black kids.

My activism in Minnesota dated back to my law school days, 1987 to 1990. I joined the Black Law Students Association (BLSA) and became its president. We were involved in a case known as the Embassy Suites Five. Several of our friends were having a party at the Embassy Suites Hotel in Minneapolis in 1989, and someone complained about the noise. When the police showed up, the situation turned hostile, and partygoers were beaten and charged with disorderly conduct. The case had racial overtones that struck a raw nerve in the black community.

So did the disparity in sentencing for drug-related crimes. Once I became an attorney, I represented people who were getting serious time for crack cocaine, while white people were merely receiving probation for possessing the same amount of powder cocaine. We also were facing the explosion of gang violence connected to the drugs. We engaged in gang intervention. The BLSA believed that if gangs could understand that they were pulling down the community, they would stop. I have since come to the conclusion that we were naïve. Back then, though, everyone was calling for gang truces.

We held several gang summits. I represented quite a few defendants who were gang members. While I don't believe that the truce strategy was the most effective approach, I do believe that many people who get caught up in the gang culture aren't necessarily criminals. For many, it's a phase they will outgrow. All they want is a connection to something larger. We have to provide constructive alternatives.

))》➡

Around this time, I too was trying to figure out what I wanted. I was a grown man, thirty-three years old, with kids, practicing the respectable profession of law. But I kept wondering, *What is my future?* This didn't seem to be enough. I was handling cases, and I felt like I was making a difference for my clients. But the forces that brought them to me seemed systemic. Most of my clients were low-income people of color, and they found themselves having a lot of contact with the criminal justice system. It seemed to me that if they had jobs, they wouldn't be in need of my services. If they had better education and training, they could get jobs that paid a livable wage. It began to seem to me that the criminal justice system was society's solution for structural problems in the economy. I wanted to get more to the root of the problem.

I wanted to do more to contribute positively to my children's future and to my community. I had never considered running for office. I thought that most politicians were participants in an ineffective system. But being involved in the Million Man March changed my perspective. I realized that all those guys, united around a common agenda, could drive the change to help make things better. The Million Man March showed me that passion for change wasn't dead among large numbers of Americans. African American men needed to do better by their families, but to do that, we needed public policy that promoted higher wages, public investment that would result in meaningful work, and education and training. We needed better politics. But being good fathers and husbands was something in our power to control. We couldn't control the system, but we could control ourselves. And if we could control and organize ourselves, we *might* control the system.

After graduating from the University of Minnesota Law School, I landed a job with one of the top firms in Minneapolis: Lindquist & Vennum. It was a large firm, and I was the only black lawyer. I really enjoyed the people I worked with. In fact, it was one of the best work experiences I've ever had.

It was a family firm, and when I started working there, several of the children of the original founders were senior partners. So they were committed to a family environment. I had a great relationship with everyone while I worked there and still do.

My respect for them grew during my first year with the firm, when I was assigned a death penalty case. A man in Louisiana named Albert Burrell was facing execution for his alleged participation in a double murder, and Lindquist & Vennum thought that his treatment in court had been so egregious that it wanted to get involved. We rented a van, and the partners sent me and a team of lawyers to defend Mr. Burrell.

The details of the case had me scratching my head. I couldn't believe that they would even put the man in jail, let alone on death row, based on such specious "evidence." The main witness in the case was a man known in Louisiana State Penitentiary at Angola as Lyin' Wayne Brantely. He was a trusty in the prison: someone who trades information for personal favors. Lyin' Wayne claimed that Albert Burrell had confessed to him.

Burrell's first attorney—who later ended up disbarred on a drug conviction—failed to deliver a closing argument on his client's behalf, claiming he was sick. But this lawyer also failed to request a continuance so that he could deliver some kind of defense for his client.

When Lindquist & Vennum decided to get involved, the Union Parish district attorney told us, "Lookie here, we'll let him off death row and back into the general population if you drop this appeal now. But if you guys want to fight, you will lose, and he will die."

That was all we needed to hear. We would fight, and we would win. Mr. Burrell regained his freedom in 2001. And I loved the firm for taking a stand. Arguing this kind of case was what I'd imagined for myself when I decided to pursue a law career.

Unfortunately, cases like this were few and far between. Like most law firms, we had to take cases that earned money in order to be able to take cases like Albert Burrell's. Eventually I lost interest in representing corporations fighting other corporations over a king's ransom. It was standard commercial litigation, but my heart wasn't in it. So I left the firm and took a job as the executive director of the Minnesota Legal Rights Center (LRC).

I went from the forty-second floor of the IDS Center—the tallest high-rise building in Minneapolis, all glass and steel—to a run-down second-story walk-up above the Chef Cafe, a greasy spoon in a low-income neighborhood. I did experience culture shock, I must admit. But I had no regrets. At Lindquist, I had a beautiful office with a new computer. At the Legal Rights Center, we had to be a little scrappier.

The Legal Rights Center was a nonprofit founded in 1970 on the heels of *Gideon v. Wainwright.* This landmark 1963 Supreme Court decision ruled that under the Fourteenth Amendment, every person is entitled to an attorney and, further, that the government is required to provide counsel if he or she can't afford it.

Following the ruling, the courts didn't have any idea how to implement the law, and a number of mistakes and bad results ensued during the early days because judges would appoint any old lawyer to cases. You could be a tax lawyer and find yourself on a death penalty case. That's a serious difference, because criminal law is a specialty that you need to know inside out.

I had always wanted to do this kind of work, but I realized that I had a lot to learn. Despite being the executive director, I was the youngest person on the staff. I had no idea how I got the job, and a lot of people there didn't think I deserved it.

Once I came to know them better, I understood the decision. Certain people may be brilliant, but they are not good leaders. Legal Rights needed someone who could provide leadership, and I could do that. And I honored the legacy and was committed to seeing the center live up to its original mission and help it evolve to address community needs.

The Legal Rights Center has a unique and interesting history. Doug Hall, Gwen and Syl Davis, Peter Dorsey of the law firm Dorsey & Whitney, and leaders of the Way—a North Minneapolis organization devoted to serving African American youth—all united to establish a law firm they called "Of and for the People."

Also among its founders were Clyde and Peggy Bellecourt, two leaders of the American Indian Movement (AIM), which was the equivalent of the Black Panthers for Native Americans. The history we learn about Native Americans usually includes the Indian Wars of the nineteenth century. But many people may not know what happened in the twentieth century to native people, who were still being oppressed and whose rights were violated regularly.

In Minnesota and the Dakotas, children of native people were taken from their homes and placed in boarding schools where they were literally stripped of every cultural practice. For example, among certain tribes, you cut your hair only when someone died, but when these kids went to the boarding schools, their hair was cut, and they were forbidden from speaking their language, eating their food, or practicing their religion. They became "Americanized"—or, more appropriately, "anglicized"—which is a form of genocide called ethnocide. Instead of killing the people, you harm them from the inside out by eliminating connections to their culture.

It was systematic. It was justified by the claim that the kids' new culture was "superior." It's like the popular 1980s television sitcoms *Webster* and *Diff'rent Strokes*, which look innocuous and almost positive until you see what's really happening.

Pernicious, ugly racism against Native Americans exists even to this day. Can you imagine a sports team called the Saint Louis Niggers? Or what about the Brooklyn Wops or the San Francisco Wetbacks? But we have the Washington Redskins football team, and the Cleveland Indians and Atlanta Braves teams. While there is a movement to change the names, it hasn't been successful yet. Just imagine how other groups in America would react to these persistent stereotypes, yet we readily accept or ignore the pain of Native Americans. And that's just one example of what they continue to endure.

Minnesota has the largest urban Native American population in the nation. Some of the founders of the American Indian Movement lived in Minneapolis, including Clyde Bellecourt, and brothers Russell and Bill Means. In 1973 Bellecourt and other AIM leaders led approximately two hundred members of the Lakota tribe in seizing the town of Wounded Knee, South Dakota site of the 1890 Wounded Knee Massacre, in which the US Cavalry slaughtered more than three hundred Native American men, women, and children. Bellecourt and his fellow activists were protesting the government's failure to uphold treaties with the Indian people, among other grievances. A tense two-and-a-half-month standoff between the protesters and federal law enforcement ensued. Bellecourt and AIM also fought to have a Federal Indian Commission address the needs and concerns of Native Americans.

Leaders from that community joined with leaders of the black community to form the Legal Rights Center. They were seeking a higher quality of justice for all people. How could you have equal justice under the law when there was such a disparity in representation between poor and displaced minorities and the majority?

I was the third director of the Legal Rights Center. The first was Doug Hall, a civil rights lawyer who had won several very high-profile cases on behalf of the rights of Native Americans. The second was Billy McGee, my mentor, who died of cancer at the age of forty-seven. I joined the LRC just as the court system was changing rapidly. When the center was founded, no public defender's office existed, and there was a significant need for qualified, experienced lawyers to take these cases. But as public defenders became standard, organizations like ours were becoming obsolete. I needed to have a plan to reinvent the center.

As I mentioned before, I was engaged in gang intervention in poor communities. At the time, some in law enforcement were rounding up gang members and assigning them a special category within the criminal justice system. Some members of the community argued that gangs were an appropriate target because an organized group of criminals was more dangerous than a single individual. While many gang members were certainly dangerous, involved in drug dealing and other crimes, many others were just lost kids. This latter group often had mitigating circumstances that had to be considered as well—miseducation, low income, poor job prospects, tough backgrounds, and racial exclusion. I believed they needed some compassion and help.

Street-corner drug dealing had its share of victims, and it was a conspicuous nuisance in the neighborhood. Neighbors could see their activities, and from time to time their turf battles would have deadly consequences for innocent bystanders. I represented a grandmother named Mary whose adult daughter was gunned down on the street when she went out to buy Mary's grandchildren ice cream from the Good Humor truck. The police could not ignore street-corner drug dealing, by any means. But at the same time, it's also true that a lot of small-timers and hangers-on got hurt in America's scramble to stamp out gangs and drugs. Instead of rehabilitation and job training, they were getting long jail sentences. I thought we needed an approach that might save some kids who wanted a future. I knew that so many young people who drew the attention of law enforcement could perhaps turn themselves into something if given a chance. I also knew that many of these guys fit a profile, dressed a certain way, or got caught because the police tended to enforce the drug laws, especially with regard to crack, with extra vigor. They weren't up in hotel suites; they were on the streets. They were poor and mostly black and brown. They had no advocates, no family support, and no community connection. The police weren't going after other kinds of organized criminals with the same fervor. So I became an activist on this issue.

The demographic makeup of Minneapolis, as in many post-industrial cities with a shrinking manufacturing base, was changing rapidly. New populations were looking for work and finding none. Youths couldn't find jobs, and they were coming together to form gangs. There were the Crips and Bloods, Native American gangs like the Club and the Native Mob, Hispanic gangs, and even gangs plaguing the Hmong community from Southeast Asia.

We believed that we could get better justice for people if we understood our clients. We organized local community workers who would conduct interviews and screen cases so we knew the stories of the kids we were working with. Our black community worker was Sonny Anderson, the older brother of local musician-songwriter-producer Andre Simon Anderson, better known as André Cymone. (His childhood friend and fellow musician Prince lived in the Andersons' basement for a time while growing up.) We had a Hispanic community worker, an Asian community worker, and a Native American community worker, Walter Yellowhammer.

As the executive director of Legal Rights, I took our findings to the state legislature, and I told legislators that their approach to rounding up gang members and creating a special category under the law was wrong. I testified before committees of the Minnesota State Legislature quite frequently, arguing against unequal justice and a lack of police accountability.

I told them the issue wasn't gangs as much as it was crime.

You can't target the gangs widely or say that just because a kid is in a gang, he or she must automatically be involved in criminal activity. The legislature wanted to declare gang members guilty by association. Its approach targeted the gangs and dealt with them as harshly as possible. But at the center, we were seeing kids who were parentless, directionless, and in survival mode. Many gravitated to the gangs for a sense of belonging; anything to help them get by. Crushing them wasn't going to solve the root problem.

I stood before a legislative committee and asked, "What about the gang members who aren't committing any crimes? And what about criminals who don't call themselves a gang but act together to commit crimes? How do we throw a bunch of resources and cops at gangs and still not solve the problem?" I believed that law enforcement's job should be fighting crime, not targeting groups of people. "You should be color blind when applying the law," I said.

I loved that I could just walk into a legislative committee and state my case. You can't do that in Congress, where there is an elaborate process in order to testify before a committee. But at the state level, you can be heard. It is citizen friendly. It doesn't mean that the legislature will actually act on what you recommend, but at least you get to speak.

What struck me at the time was the absence of ethnic or gender diversity among the members of the committee who attended the hearing. They were all white men. And I wondered if they could truly relate to the kids I was talking about. I went home that night frustrated. I shared my feelings with my wife, Kim, and she said, "I think those people do an important job, and it's a really hard job they do in the legislature. But if you think you can do it better, maybe *you* should run for office."

Hmmm. I had never thought about being part of the system. I'd always seen myself as an activist, someone who agitated and pushed for change from outside.

I will admit that my psychology from the age of sixteen to about thirty was "Fight the Power!" I loved Public Enemy, and I was in line with the spirit of that time. I saw society as structured to keep the powerful holding down the powerless, and not much in history presented me with evidence to the contrary. In fact, in 1992, following the acquittal of the Los Angeles Police Department officers *caught on film* brutally beating Rodney King, I was convinced that the system was corrupt. I considered that America might not have the capacity to be fair to people of color. Our only recourse would be to chip away at the corruption from the outside. To protest. Going to the Million Man March was about pushing change from the outside.

If you think you can do it better, maybe you *should run for office.*

That stayed in my head. And it reminded me of a phrase I'd heard my father say: "Any jackass can kick down a barn, but it takes a carpenter to build one." He used it to refer to protest-oriented leaders. My dad admired Martin Luther King Jr., but I can't say that he had positive feelings about other leaders on the national scene.

My mother expressed the same sentiments, but in a gentler way. "You can curse the darkness, or you can light a candle. It's much better to light a candle."

If you can see, you have no excuse for walking around blind.

))))➤

I decided to run for the state legislature. I thought I *could* do a better job. I understood the root causes of gangs, and I didn't think it was okay to lock people up without addressing these problems. People were not disposable to me.

I started to see a change in my faith, too. I began to be more conscious. When I got home from the Million Man March, I started bringing my kids to the mosque with me more often. I wanted to help them become part of a faith community. Before, I had sometimes seen my faith as a refuge from society or like a cocoon. I used religion to make me feel better, safer, and to consider essential truths. But the march provoked me to reflect deeply. What kind of society should we build, and shouldn't we take responsibility for it? Can't we do more than complain about it? I felt more earnest, and more serious. This went for my spiritual life as well. I studied a little more and prayed more regularly. Why? I don't know. I just felt I needed to. It calmed and soothed me like before, but it also connected and strengthened me. From the outside, I am sure I looked more confirmed in my faith as a journey; a way to connect to a divine spirit, to a higher power.

Gradually, I felt myself mellowing, taking small things less seriously and life more seriously. I also started emphasizing calmness, peace, and love, but I also felt urgency. I felt more purposeful, and looking back now, I know that the march helped me to evolve. I moved from cynicism to optimism. As people get older, usually it's the reverse, but I became more hopeful.

I was doing well personally. I owned my own home and was making decent money. My four children were healthy, and I began to think about a better world for them. I wanted to help build something, not just criticize what was wrong.

When I was younger, my activism was protest oriented. I wanted to protest police brutality, inadequate housing, inequality, injustice. I was more energized by protesting than by actually starting to construct a better world. But this was 1998. My oldest son was ten years old. I wanted something more for him and his siblings. It didn't seem adequate to build my life around what I didn't like; I needed to do something more proactive. It wasn't a conscious decision. It just happened.

I left the Legal Rights Center and started my own law firm devoted to public service. A friend had founded a school, and I helped him to eliminate the drug houses in the surrounding neighborhood. I joined a group called Sincere and Loyal African American Men (SALAAM, meaning "peace" in Arabic). We were in the community every week, wearing our green T-shirts, tackling the issues facing our neighborhoods. I was taking positive action to address my concerns rather than just talking about them.

While on the streets, I was approached by a local drug dealer I'd once represented. He asked me, "How can you represent me and now stand here protesting my business?"

"I never thought what you did was right," I told him. "I believed you had a right to representation. But make no mistake about it: you're having a negative impact on our community, and you have to go!"

If I was going to complain about injustice, didn't I have an obligation to try to fix it? Complaining without offering a solution is whining.

It was time. I threw my hat in the ring for an open seat in the Minnesota State House. Gregory Gray, a friend of mine, was also running. I thought he was a good person, but I also thought I had a better handle on the important issues. Gregory had the support of most of the Democratic Party leadership, so he was the odds-on favorite to win. I had my work cut out for me. I would have to build from the outside and hope that we could gather enough support to challenge him for the Democratic-Farmer-Labor Party (DFL) endorsement.

When we arrived at the delegate convention, I felt good. I thought we had a chance to win. On the first ballot, we made a good showing, forcing another round. On the second ballot, Greg ran away with it. We lost. I was more upset than I'd expected. I had run hoping to serve my community, but I realized after losing that I had also wanted to win.

I went home and sat with my two oldest kids, Isaiah and Jeremiah, ages ten and nine. They had been involved in the campaign with me and were very supportive.

"Well, sons, we lost," I told them.

"Did they cheat us, Dad?!" Isaiah wanted to know. I looked in his eyes, and he was serious. He figured something had to be fishy for us to lose.

"No, son," I said. "They beat us fair and square."

"But why?" Jeremiah wanted to know.

"Because they had more votes; more people chose them."

"Are we going to get them next time?" Jeremiah asked.

"Yes, son. Next time we're going to win."

And I meant it. I spent the next few years building coalitions, forging political relationships, and becoming active in party politics. For the first time, I was working for change within the political structure. I was inspired by Minnesota senator Paul Wellstone, Minneapolis City Council president Jackie Cherryhomes, and others, to believe firmly that it was possible to be in politics and still have integrity; to stand for something beyond self-interest.

Four years later, Greg decided to run for state auditor, and I ran for his seat in the state legislature. This time I won handily. My kids were elated, and we went to dinner to celebrate.

Looking back, I needed those four years not just to gain credibility as a viable candidate, but also to cement myself in my home as a father. During those four years of working in the community, I spent a lot of time with my kids. I coached them in track and field and attended most of their sporting events and extracurricular activities. I was there for them, and it was an important time for us. Once I stepped into politics, our lives changed forever.

7

SEPTEMBER 12

I was sitting around my house waiting for a furniture delivery. Our couch, a fixture of our household for eight years, was on its way out. It was so ratty that we used a throw blanket to camouflage the wear and tear caused by four kids.

I had received a nice check for a case I had been working on, and splurged on a leather couch. The delivery company gave me the usual four-hour window, between eight and noon. As it turned out, September 11, 2001, was a rare day off for me between court appearances.

The movers arrived early, just before eight. I helped them maneuver the sofa through the tricky doorways to the living room. The television was on in the background. We had just set the couch in place when I noticed breaking news on the television. The movers and I plopped onto the new couch in disbelief. We all offered opinions about what might have happened. Maybe the pilot of the plane that had crashed into the North Tower of New York's World Trade Center was incapacitated in some way. Maybe he was sick, or had a seizure or a stroke.

Then the second one hit the South Tower.

I instantly knew *that* wasn't an accident. We sat there stunned. All I could think about were those poor people on the planes and in those buildings. I could see people jumping from the windows—from ninety to one hundred stories up—and I knew I was watching pure terror.

I had friends and family in New York City. I immediately tried to call my cousin Carol. I couldn't reach her. All the circuits were busy. Then I got in touch with my family. I immediately wanted to connect with my family. To be with those I loved.

The attacks happened on a Tuesday. Two nights later, my weekly radio show was focused on the tragedy of the terrorist attacks. Our audience was mostly black, and we had all kinds of listeners—some who were really out there. But I had never imagined the kinds of comments a few callers made on the heels of this national tragedy.

We opened the program by paying homage to those who'd lost their lives that day, honoring all of the first responders and citizens who helped out and praising the resilience and unity of our nation as the world rallied to support us. We posed a few questions about what must be done next and how, as Americans, we should handle this crisis.

Most of the callers expressed sympathy for the victims, along with outrage for what the terrorists had done. Several spoke of loved ones in New York City. But I also fielded calls from some bitter, deluded people.

One man called to say that he thought the attacks had been carried out by Mossad, the Israeli spy agency.

Good-bye!

Then someone else started talking more nonsense.

"See, man, America thinks no one can get to them. But see, someone got them!"

"Someone got who?" I asked, trying to make sense out of his inane comment.

"America!"

"Sir, aren't you an *American*? They got *us*. Innocent people died. Innocent *Americans* died."

"Yeah, but America has been doing this stuff all over the world. America had it coming."

Good-bye.

Outraged, I think I called him a fool or worse before hanging up on him. The station manager reminded me to stay cool. And my cohost, Resmaa, took over most of the broadcast because I was definitely not in the frame of mind to entertain the opinion of anyone trying to justify what had happened, and how innocent lives lost somehow constituted "payback."

The people who attacked our nation that day didn't care if they were killing black, brown, beige, or white, Christian, Jew, Muslim, or atheist. They wanted to harm America and kill Americans.

I had intended to have dialogue on the broadcast, not demagoguery. I thought the nation needed to grieve. I thought we needed to contemplate what brought forth the terrorist act and explore it. People wanted to know why these men hated us, and I thought it would be okay to ask that question.

The 9/11 attacks stunned America. How did this scale of terrorist attack with such devastating losses occur on US soil? Understandably, there were many different reactions. During the days and weeks following the attacks, we stood united as a nation. Honor and bury the dead. Care for the injured. Comfort the grieving families. Help the communities that were attacked—New York City and the Pentagon—recover and move forward. Initially, the normal divisions took a backseat. We had right on our side, and we had the world's sympathy. President Bush and his administration had an infinite number of opportunities to engage the world.

The other impulse, which was widely supported, was to go after Al Qaeda and capture the evil mastermind of the terrorism, Osama bin Laden. Eventually it was under President Obama's command that the US military found and killed bin Laden, crippling Al Qaeda in the process.

There were differences of opinion regarding our role in Afghanistan, but there was national and international agreement about the need to bring Al Qaeda to justice.

The post-9/11 consensus fell apart when the Bush administration decided to invade Iraq despite no evidence that its leader, Saddam Hussein, was connected to terrorism. Some foreign policy actors around the president had broad motives, using 9/11 as an excuse to pursue a grandiose notion of remaking an Arab society by force. It was opportunistic, and a bad decision on all fronts.

In those days, weeks, and months following the 9/11 attacks, very few people were willing to publicly question the administration, and most people supported the attack on Al Qaeda in Afghanistan. There were widely different views of how to help Afghanistan root out the Taliban, an extremist political movement, and establish a democratic country.

At this time, I came to admire Representative Barbara Lee, a member of Congress from the Ninth District of California. Shortly after 9/11, she voted to deny President Bush authorization to use military force—a principled stand for which she was savaged. She stood up on September 14 and delivered a ninety-second speech that left me knowing what true courage truly is.

It was a highly emotional time. President Bush was popular and had the nation behind him. Congresswoman Lee stood on the floor of the US House of Representatives, her voice cracking, and said, "This unspeakable act against the United States has forced me to rely on my moral compass, my conscience, and my God for direction."

When she finished, I thought that I'd love to be her ally. I was not even considering running for Congress at this point. I remember seeing this person get up and stand alone. She warned the nation to be "careful not to embark on an open ended war with neither an exit strategy nor a focused target." House Joint Resolution 64, the Authorization for Use of Military Force, had a single opposing vote: Rep. Lee's.

Watching her speak on the House floor, I could tell that she was afraid and vulnerable emotionally. But it didn't stop her from a brave act. If the country had listened to her, maybe we wouldn't have gone to war in Iraq. More than 4,486 US servicemen and -women, and more than 125,000 Iraqi civilians, would be alive, and we wouldn't have spent more than $1 trillion and counting.

It's not that Congresswoman Lee *knew* the next step in that moment. But she was moved to speak out for her beliefs. In America, we pride ourselves on being smart. We develop our minds, but our hearts need cultivating. What Barbara Lee showed was heart.

She was no wiser than her colleagues. Most of them knew that giving President Bush carte blanche to engage in war was a bad idea, but they also knew it was politically risky to oppose him. People told Representative Lee that it would be politically expedient for her to vote for the war. She would not.

"As we act, let us not become the evil we deplore," she said. Everything she warned against came to fruition. She was prescient. "We are not dealing with a conventional war. We cannot respond in a conventional manner. I do not want to see this spiral out of control."

As she predicted, the war in Iraq did spiral out of control, and the country chose a different direction in 2008 with the election of President Barack Obama, who pledged to end the Iraq war.

Later in 2001, Congresswoman Lee came to Minnesota to receive an award. I was excited to meet her and remember thinking that this brave woman should have people standing with her. Subconsciously, that moment pushed me toward my decision to run for Congress.

I knew that our country had declared unnecessary wars before. In 1846 the United States went to war with Mexico when it refused to give up what is now California and the US Southwest. President James K. Polk provoked a border skirmish and used it as an excuse to seek a declaration of war. The opposition, the Whig Party, feared that the acquisition of new territory would lead to the expansion of slavery. The invasion of Mexico was costly, and many Americans lost their lives. Sound familiar? Just as with the decision to go to Iraq, government leaders were afraid to speak out against it. But one junior congressman from Illinois stood on the House floor and spoke against the war. Just one.

Abraham Lincoln.

More than a century later, President Lyndon Johnson used a skirmish between a US destroyer and Vietnamese torpedo boats in the Gulf of Tonkin to seek congressional authorization to use military force in Southeast Asia. Only two people in Congress voted against that joint resolution: Senators Wayne Morse of

Oregon and Ernest Gruening of Alaska. They were widely criticized at the time, and President Johnson used the blank check he'd been given to plunge the nation deeper into the Vietnam War.

I was inspired by the courage of Barbara Lee and remembered the prescience of Senators Morse and Gruening. I was propelled by the legacy of Abraham Lincoln. Little did I know that one day I would stand where Lincoln stood and Representative Lee would be my colleague. After 9/11, everything changed. But I knew that our future as a nation was in our hands.

))))➡

In 2002 I decided to run again for the Minnesota House of Representatives, to represent House District 58B in North Minneapolis. The country was still reeling from 9/11 and sorting out the aftermath. We were engaged in Afghanistan and marching toward war in Iraq. My campaign platform, inspired by Representative Barbara Lee, included opposition to the invasion of Iraq. I thought it was the wrong war for the wrong reasons. My community supported this position, as well as work I had been doing against social injustice and inequality. I now had the support of several DFL leaders, including Senator Paul Wellstone.

I had grown to respect and admire Senator Wellstone over the years, and he had a huge influence on my political career. Originally from Virginia, he went to the University of North Carolina at Chapel Hill. Wellstone, like me, found his place in Minnesota when he went to teach at Carleton College. Before I met him and watched him work, I thought that a lot of politicians were in government mostly for themselves. Sure, they would do things for "the people," but only as it furthered their individual pursuits.

One afternoon, during Paul Wellstone's first term, around 1993, I was at a community festival in the Glenwood-Lyndale housing projects, near where I lived in North Minneapolis. Wellstone attended, and when I saw him, I viewed him skeptically. I figured he would shake a few hands, squirt out some hand sanitizer, hop in his black SUV, and go on to the next event.

Those thoughts were born out of ignorance.

Not only did Wellstone not skip out, he stayed for most of the afternoon. I approached him with all of my cynicism.

"What are you going to do about police brutality and the tensions between the police and the black community?" I asked him.

I expected him to dodge the question and find a way to get out of there. Instead, he looked me straight in the eye and said, "Keith, I want you to tell me about your experiences. I want to know what's really going on."

He stood there and listened as I told him about how the people in our community distrusted the police and how crime went unchecked because people were fearful of what the police might do. We needed to address these issues. He nodded his head as I spoke and never disconnected from what I was saying.

Wellstone stood about five foot five, making him one of the few men shorter than I am. That day, he grew immeasurably in stature for me. Here was a United States senator in the projects, listening to the concerns of the people, and it wasn't a stunt. He spent time. He stayed. After we finished talking, he sat at a picnic table and chatted with more people.

The next time I saw Senator Wellstone, he was marching over the issue of police brutality. I just smiled. He was dedicated and a truly amazing human being. He single-handedly changed the way I thought about politicians and showed me that it was possible to be in office and retain your humanity. I had imagined that the ugliness of politics would swallow me up. I had assumed that a good person couldn't be in politics. Paul Wellstone proved me wrong.

A couple of weeks before the election, Senator Wellstone came to one of our campaign events at the Minneapolis Urban League.

Paul stepped up and addressed the crowd.

"I want you to support Keith Ellison," he began, "not because he's a lawyer. But because he's a *justice* lawyer!" And the crowd cheered.

I'm almost embarrassed to share this, but I got all choked up. What an honor to have this revered figure say something nice about me. I felt like Paul stood for what I was trying to do.

A month before, Wellstone had given an impassioned speech on the Senate floor against our "go-it-alone" approach to Iraq, warning that it would be a critical mistake. Just like Barbara Lee's bold prediction, his warning proved to be correct. At the time of his speech, the senator was engaged in a close race for his seat. Some pundits suggested that his opposition to the war could cost him, but, true to his principles, Paul decided that he would rather risk losing than remain quiet on an issue of such tremendous importance.

It is often said that leaders should be more thermostats than thermometers, setting the temperature instead of taking it. Paul Wellstone was a thermostat. The polls showed that opposing the president was not prudent. But after the speech, Wellstone's numbers went up. He stood his ground on that issue, and Minnesotans appreciate people who stand up for their convictions. Paul was popular even among conservatives, among whom I heard quite a few say, "I don't necessarily agree with his politics, but I like him. He stands up for what he believes."

I didn't agree with Paul Wellstone on all the issues. For instance, I didn't agree with his position on gay marriage, and he voted in favor of the federal Antiterrorism and Effective Death Penalty Act of 1996 because it contained some worthy provisions to help domestic abuse victims. (Minnesota hasn't had the death penalty since 1911.) But he always stood up and explained why he'd voted the way he had. He answered to the people and did so with honesty and conviction, and people appreciated that.

Paul Wellstone was my model; my exemplar of an effective politician. During parades when elected officials rode on floats waving to the crowd, Paul jogged on the sidelines, shaking hands and greeting people. Whenever I have the opportunity to ride in a parade, I do the same thing. I get out on the street and shake hands.

On October 25, 2002, eleven days before the election, we heard a report of a plane crash a couple of miles from the airport in Eveleth, a town in Minnesota's Iron Range region. Then came the report that Paul Wellstone, his wife, Sheila, his daughter, Marcia, three staff members, and two pilots had all perished. I felt stunned beyond belief. Things like that don't really happen, do they?

Paul's death was heartbreaking. We lost a giant that day. His death strengthened my resolve to serve, if the people elected me, in the spirit of Paul Wellstone—with integrity, with honesty, and with sincerity.

I won the election and served in the Minnesota State House of Representatives on the Governmental Operations and Veterans Affairs Policy Committee, the Judiciary Policy and Finance Committee, and the Local Government and Metropolitan Affairs Committee. In 2004 I won reelection with 84 percent of the vote, and in the following years, I worked on a wide range of issues, including slumlords, lead poisoning, and the prevalence of asthma in our neighborhoods.

I was committed to the job.

8

MINNESOTA NICE

On the University of Minnesota campus, which straddles the Mississippi River, there is a well-traveled pedestrian bridge. I crossed it often from one side of campus to the other while attending law school. Some of the most outrageously racist graffiti I had ever seen was written on its walls.

"Minnesota *is* for white people," and "Nigger go home!" were some of the tamer comments. The slogans had been there for a while, and several African American students said they were afraid to cross the bridge at night.

I thought the city and the university knew about the problem but had done nothing, so I decided to do something. I was a second-year law student and president of the Black Law Students Association. Jordan Kushner, a student who hung out with us, organized members of the predominantly white Progressive Student Organization to join us. We bought spray paint from the local hardware store and painted over the racist comments. Our group was mixed racially. We all took offense at this graffiti.

Afterward, we alerted the local news and the police department. The story got traction. I had realized that we could get into trouble—perhaps even get thrown out of school—but I didn't care. I knew that we could have petitioned the university to do something, but how long would that have taken? The racist slogans had been there long enough. They had to go.

One of our crew was arrested for defacing school property. We went to bail him out and explained what we did and why, and the police let him go. That amazed me. Instead of the campus authorities coming down on us, they supported what we'd done. The next day, they had the bridge painted professionally. After that, whenever some miscreant decided to tag the walls with hate-filled graffiti, the university continued to paint over it.

Some local television shows invited me to talk about what we'd done. There were news articles written about it, too. I was pleased that we were able to make a positive difference. It felt good to be in a community where you can organize if you see something wrong. Some people cared. I don't expect perfection, but I was encouraged that people would listen and respond when we tried to solve a problem. Minnesota was that kind of place. It became my kind of place.

Minnesota was becoming my home. I had put down roots. All my children were born there. And it was in Minnesota that I felt I could make a difference.

Even before getting involved in politics, I must have known in my soul that I needed to break free and cut my own path. And I ended up in Minnesota.

After graduating from Wayne State in 1987, my plan was to attend grad school and earn a PhD in economics. I didn't know what being an economist meant in terms of making a living. After taking some graduate economics classes at Wayne State, I decided instead to attend law school. One thing I knew for sure: I wanted to leave Detroit. I applied to the University of Wisconsin, University of Notre Dame, George Washington University, and the University of Minnesota.

When the financial packages arrived, I narrowed my choices to Minnesota and Notre Dame, because they offered the most. I decided on Minnesota. I had never set foot in the state before going to law school there, and I didn't know anyone there. But I packed up what little stuff I had and moved to the Land of 10,000 Lakes.

I had heard how cold it was—even colder than Detroit in the winter. How true that turned out to be: I haven't experienced anyplace in America quite as cold as Minnesota. It's funny when people say "Minnesota Nice," the reference being that the people are genuinely nice. But there is another saying, "Minnesota Ice." Nice on the outside, chilly on the inside. I've never experienced the chilliness. Just the opposite. Before moving to Minnesota, I'd heard about the state's open-minded progressiveness. And I found that to be true.

I had been involved in student activism, particularly around apartheid, at Wayne State. When I got to the University of Minnesota, I fell right back into it. In my first year, I was elected president of the Black Law Students Association. At Minnesota, we could complain about the lack of diversity among the professors and actually have fruitful conversations with members of the administration. They listened to us and seemed open to change. (We never had to challenge the administration at Wayne State University about diversity among the student body and professors because it *was* diverse.)

If you wanted to get something done in Detroit, you needed to be ready for a battle. There were entrenched interests trying to preserve the little power they had. For Detroit to ever succeed again, it needed radical thinking, which is something the city didn't have then.

I noticed immediately that the culture was different in Minnesota.

One evening I was driving through North Minneapolis. Two SUVs were blocking the street, music blaring. The drivers were carrying on a conversation in the middle of the street, blocking traffic in both directions.

In Detroit, you might lean on your horn or yell out your window for them to move, but it was at your peril. A horn blast might be met by some profanity. If you yelled for them to move, you might be cursed out; you might also get threatened, and getting shot was not out of the realm of possibility. You just never knew.

I wanted to ask these guys to move and not take too long doing it. Who were they to block the street while people were trying to go places? So I leaned on my horn, expecting one of them to curse at me, which I knew could possibly lead to a confrontation. One of the guys waved to acknowledge me, and they both drove off without incident.

Wow, they moved, I thought.

There is a reason why Detroit has always seemed on edge. Detroit, like many other cities, had suffered deep job losses due to offshoring and the increased automation of American manufacturing, leaving millions without work or in low-paying jobs. Economic hardship causes social stress and undermines family life and community stability. Over time, people fell into survival mode, and that carried over into tension on the streets.

To juxtapose Detroit with Minnesota would be irresponsible without putting this issue in perspective. At the time, Minnesota was working with a robust and diverse economy; its unemployment rate stood at just 3 percent. Detroit's rate was more than twice that. Frankly, I didn't see a solution to Detroit's ills, whereas I did see room to have a voice and make a difference in Minnesota. The state was not a perfect model, especially in terms of race and ethnicity: the disparities between blacks and whites regarding incarceration, unemployment, and academic achievement are among the highest in the nation. However, the culture of openness and space for political leadership meant that people would listen, and things could change.

The contrast with Detroit was showing me that there were alternatives; that there were places in the country where people could work together and get things done.

I retained thoughts of returning to Detroit after I graduated from law school. How could I walk away from the city of my birth and its deep history? Detroit was a stop on the Underground Railroad. And it was there that Dr. King first tested out his "I Have a Dream" speech at the Great March on Detroit, on June 23, 1963, where Dr. King, arm in arm with Rev. C. L. Franklin and followed by a crowd of 125,000, strode down Woodward Avenue on that Walk to Freedom. And the largest chapter of the National Association for the Advancement of Colored People could be found there.

My family and many other good people lived there. But in 1987 I felt that Detroit was in the midst of a free fall that would take more than my desire for change to stop it.

In Minnesota, I could breathe. I *could* make a difference. I could have allies from different backgrounds. It was not so desperate. It wasn't so dog-eat-dog, intense, and on edge.

Minnesota has black history of its own. The great African American playwright August Wilson moved to Saint Paul in 1978. He wrote scripts for the Science Museum of Minnesota and received a fellowship at the Playwrights' Center in Minneapolis. In 1987 the mayor of Saint Paul declared May 27 August Wilson Day because he was the only playwright from Minnesota to have won a Pulitzer Prize (for *Fences* in 1985). A Saint Paul clothing store helped launch the career of photographer Gordon Parks by featuring the fashion photography that eventually led to his being discovered. Parks was a multitalented genius, a photographer and a playwright who chronicled African American culture for a quarter of a century. His photograph *American Gothic* depicts the black person as a laborer, salt of the earth, hardworking. It speaks to the dignity of African American people and our contribution to America. It also speaks to our pain and our inability to rise. The reality is, the backdrop is the flag. It's helped us. It's honored. But you have this black woman in a servile role. And there's something in her face that says, I deserve respect and dignity, and if you ever let me loose, there's nothing that I can't do. It's a compelling, gripping picture.

In the 1840s, Frederick Douglass passed through Minnesota as part of the American Anti-Slavery Society's Hundred Conventions project, a six-month tour throughout the East and the Midwest pushing for the abolition of slavery.

Detroit felt set in its ways. The world was changing, but it was refusing to budge, to grow, to do things differently to get ahead. I didn't see much movement happening in Detroit. And no fresh ideas coming from newcomers because very few people were moving into Detroit at the time. Minnesota had its own history of leaders who went against the grain, who stood up for what they believed. In addition to Paul Wellstone, there was former vice president Hubert Humphrey, who returned to the US Senate not long after he narrowly lost the 1968 presidential election to Richard Nixon.

In 1977, a year before his death from cancer, Humphrey said in a speech, "The moral test of government is how that government treats those who are in the dawn of life: the children; those who are in the twilight of life: the elderly; and those who are in the shadows of life: the sick, the needy, and the handicapped." Those weren't just words for Humphrey, it was his personal credo, and I quote it quite often. In fact, I have written twenty different speeches containing that quote. Humphrey helped Minnesota carve out a new way of seeing itself.

The state also gave us Walter Mondale, who followed Humphrey into the US Senate, serving from 1964 until 1976. He became the forty-second vice president, under Jimmy Carter, and ran for president against Ronald Reagan in 1984. He got trounced by Reagan, losing every state except one: Minnesota. Mondale said candidly that he would raise taxes if elected. Reagan pledged that he wouldn't, but ended up doing it anyway. People in Minnesota didn't necessarily vote for Mondale just because he was a son of Minnesota. They appreciate honesty. They'd rather you tell them what you're going to do and explain why it's in their best interests, and they will roll with you, as they did with Mondale.

Minnesota also produced Eugene Joseph McCarthy. He was a member of the Democratic-Farmer-Labor Party, a representative from the Fourth Congressional District, and he served in the Senate. In 1964 he was considered for vice president under incumbent LBJ, who ended up picking Humphrey instead.

McCarthy cosponsored (with Ted Kennedy) the Immigration and Nationality Act of 1965, which removed quotas and prejudice from our immigration policy. Prior to this act, Asians and Africans were excluded, as Western Europeans were preferred for US citizenship. It was an unpopular act, as Americans were nervous about allowing "others" into the country.

McCarthy never shied away from being unpopular. He opposed the Vietnam War long before it was popular to do so and in 1968 ran against the incumbent president of his own party in order to try to bring it to an end.

I stand on the shoulders of these great leaders of Minnesota who stood up for what they believed and who didn't back down, no matter how unpopular their position. But I also owe Detroit and its rich history. I am a product of both, and grateful to both.

After I won a seat in the Minnesota State House, I served in the minority for both of my terms. I introduced legislation to protect kids from lead exposure, to increase the rights of parents in the schools, and to allow felons on probation to vote.

I introduced and passed a bill revoking a person's driver's license if he or she deliberately drives off without paying for gasoline. The idea came from daily life, the source of many legislative ideas. I'll explain:

The House was in legislative session, but we weren't meeting because we didn't "gavel in" on Fridays. I frequently worked as a contract public defender in the suburban courts in Hennepin County on such days. One Friday I took a case in which an eighteen-year-old kid was charged with gassing up his car and then leaving without paying. He was a smart aleck with a wide grin. When I asked him what had happened, he said, "Hey, dude, I just forgot. You know what I mean? It's just some stupid gas. I mean, damn."

I said, "So, you took the gas?"

To which he replied, "Whose side are you on, man? It's just a little gas."

I looked at him, stood up from my desk, and said, "Anything else you want me to know?"

"Naw. Just get me the best deal you can."

"Let me see what I can do."

I talked with some more clients, and when I had five cases ready to negotiate, I picked up my files and went to the prosecutor's desk to talk about plea bargaining to avoid trial. It's a normal part of the process. The courts couldn't operate unless most cases were resolved this way. When we got to my little gas thief, the prosecutor said, "I will dismiss this one in a year if the kid pays for the gas."

That was it. I went back and told my gas thief, and he said, "Man, couldn't you get it dismissed now?"

I said no and directed him to the place to pay restitution. I had a duty as a lawyer to represent this guy zealously. But as a legislator, I had a duty to protect everyone from him. I was clear on my various roles, and performed both. So I introduced the bill. Now, if you pump gas in Minnesota, you will probably see the stickers on pumps all over the state, warning gas thieves about the risk to their driving privileges.

I was an active state legislator and spoke frequently on the House floor. I called community meetings to discuss key issues. A friend named Cheryl Morgan Spencer, an organizer for the Minneapolis Urban League, was my usual collaborator at community meetings. Cheryl bubbles with enthusiasm; she is thoroughly convinced that ordinary people can transform society.

I popped into Cheryl's office at the Urban League one day and asked if she had noticed the prevalence of asthma cases in North

Minneapolis. Nearly every house seemed to have a child on an inhaler or nebulizer. Neither of us knew exactly why, but we knew there was a connection to the local environment. We decided to organize a community meeting. One of the speakers we invited was an experienced environmental organizer who was working to reduce dangerous emissions, which lead to health hazards such as asthma.

Our speaker focused her words on the Xcel Energy Riverside coal-fired power plant, which was emitting mercury, lead, cadmium, and barium. She explained that coal plants release fine particulate matter, which creates a light haze in the atmosphere. Eventually the particles settle and are inhaled by people. They seep into the deep structures of the lungs and cause respiratory illnesses.

The Minnesota Public Utilities Commission was in the midst of deciding whether to allow the Riverside plant to be converted to natural gas, which, though still a fossil fuel, is far less polluting than coal. It wasn't a simple decision because to do so meant raising the rate on people who could least afford the price increase.

Based on this community meeting, I, along with several others, proposed that we start a community organization dedicated to environmental justice. We started Environmental Justice Advocates of Minnesota (EJAM). I'm very proud of the work EJAM did and continues to do. One of the first things we did was to convene a public meeting. More than two hundred residents showed up to testify about how this plant was affecting their lives.

One man, a grandfather, brought a bucket of fish he had caught the day before.

"Part of the way I grew up was fishing with my grandpa. We caught it, cleaned it, and ate it. I can't do that with my grandkids," he said, holding up one of the fish. "These fish are contaminated, full of mercury. And it is disrupting the generational traditions of my family and many others."

There were people from the Hmong community, a group from Thailand and Laos that fought on the US side in the Vietnam War and was forced into exile after it ended. Minnesota has a large Hmong community. They talked about how they fished not for sport but for sustenance and how the lake's pollution was having a serious negative impact on their lives.

There was a teacher who talked of having to hand out inhalers to her students who had breathing problems that she tied to the particulate matter coming from the plant. There were dozens of stories like these. And each story was important because it made the case for converting to natural, cleaner energy, which the plant did.

We were making a difference.

9

The Politics of Generosity and Inclusion

My phone rang around eleven in the morning. It was my friend Ken Martin.

"Are you ready?" he asked.

"Ready? Ready for what?"

"Ready to be a congressman, representing the Fifth District of the great state of Minnesota!"

It was March 17, 2006. A Friday. That was the day my life was to change forever.

I did not know that Congressman Martin Sabo, who had represented Minneapolis and surrounding communities in Congress for twenty-eight years, had announced his retirement. Ken's call was a surprise. Representative Sabo, a member of the Democratic-Farmer-Labor Party, was a quiet man who represented the district effectively during his long service. He knew budget and appropriations issues inside out and did well for the Fifth District. Before going to Washington in 1979, he'd been Speaker of the Minnesota House of Representatives. His seat was now open, but I had never imagined filling it.

I was active in my community. America was at a crossroads with the Iraq War. There was a growing movement for us to withdraw. I spoke at rallies, went on marches, and was vocal about the need to end the war in Iraq. I was a state legislator and involved in local government. But Washington? That wasn't on my radar. Not until Ken Martin asked me if I was ready.

"The story about Sabo is going to break tomorrow," he said. "So you don't have much time to decide. Are you in or out?"

I had about five minutes to make a decision. An antiwar rally was scheduled for the next day. I thought to myself, *This is my chance to speak up about the Iraq War.* This was my chance to speak up against torture, which our country had been using. This was my chance to speak up about the decline of the American working class and the increase in income inequality. It was my chance to speak up about the hold of corporate and economic interests of the rich and powerful on policy. This was a chance to point out how they used their economic advantages to hire lobbyists who delivered loopholes, which then bought them more lobbyists to find more loopholes!

This was my chance to jump in and say something. To do something.

My biggest competition for the DFL nomination was Mike Erlandson, Representative Sabo's chief of staff, the former chair of the DFL Party, and Congressman Sabo's first choice. Whoever won the DFL nomination would be in an excellent position to win the general election. The DFL was the party of Walter Mondale, Hubert Humphrey, Eugene McCarthy, and Paul Wellstone. The real race—the tough, competitive race—would be the primary.

My race for office was unconventional in many ways. I didn't think much about fund-raising or whether I would have enough money to run. Had I done that, I probably would not have run. I didn't think about whether I could get enough votes to actually win or where those votes might come from.

Ken asked me a simple question: Are you ready? I had a short time to think about it before reaching the conclusion that yes, I was ready. I was ready to step up and step out. I was already active in the trenches, especially on the antiwar front. But now I had a chance to apply my values in Congress and make a difference beyond my district. Money and popularity did not determine if I would run. My decision was based on whether I could actually do something or represent a vision that was different from those of others in the race.

I didn't hear anyone talking about how to get out of the war. I knew that the war needed to be raised in the campaign debate. I didn't hear anyone speaking up for poor people. No one running was speaking for disenfranchised youth in our community. No one was talking about immigration—at least, not in the way it impacted my community.

I asked myself, *Are any of the candidates going to speak effectively on these issues?* It wasn't clear to me that they were; therefore I needed to jump in. I called a friend of mine, Peter Wagenius, who is a political guru in the Twin Cities, and told him I was thinking about running.

"What should I do?" I asked him.

"There's a *Star Tribune* reporter named Rochelle Olson, and she's starting to do stuff on the election and Sabo's retirement. If you're seriously thinking about doing this, you'd better call her up and let her know. And do it now."

It was around five o'clock, and he told me her deadline was soon. So I called her. I figured that if I decided to change my mind, I could drop out at any time. What did I have to lose?

The first question Rochelle Olson asked me was why I was running. To me, this was the most important question. I had spent a lot of time asking myself this question, so I was prepared.

"It seems to me that another vision of this country needs to be asserted," I said.

Our country was in a wrongheaded war in Iraq. Wages for working- and middle-class families had been stagnant for decades. Families throughout the country were losing their homes to foreclosure due to the predatory practices of mortgage lenders and large financial institutions. I ran for Congress to address these issues. I ran to offer a vision that I eventually called the politics of generosity and inclusion.

There were several visions that I did not agree with. Some argued, "America is broke; we need more budget cuts." Others suggested, "If we give tax breaks to the wealthy and large corporations, they'll create jobs, and the money will trickle down." That approach doesn't work. It's never worked.

My vision was about helping people in need and strengthening the weakest links in our chain. And my vision had four components.

The first was peace.

"Get out of Iraq and get out now!" That was my stance. I wanted to take a stand against the Iraq War and talk about how we should look at war differently. War should be a last resort, for the defense of our country against an attack—not to be used for economic interests or to rearrange the global map. I was concerned about military spending, and believed that diplomacy and development had been relegated to an inferior position in the management of global affairs.

The second component of my vision was prosperity for working people. The third was environmental sustainability, and the fourth, civil and human rights. When I say civil and human rights, what I mean is human solidarity. Every human being in the world should be embraced and accepted. Everyone should have the opportunity for liberty and justice.

I developed my purpose for running from many sources, including the Islamic perspective on social justice. However, my vision of the politics of generosity and inclusion developed after speaking with a rabbi from Northern California and reading the New Testament. Rabbi Michael Lerner, author of several books, including *The Left Hand of God: Taking Back Our Country from the Religious Right*, and I discussed the issue of scarcity and generosity and how these ideas could inform a political vision. The idea that America was broke was not about a financial balance sheet, it was a political culture geared toward scarcity. Instead of trying to figure out how to get people what they need, the prevailing thought of the "ownership" culture was that you are on your own.

When I graduated from college, I owed $12,000 in student loans. I had a job and had received some financial help from my parents. It was a time when tuition was low enough and salaries were high enough that a young person could work her way through college and be able to get a good job.

Working your way through college today is next to impossible. And the enormous debt that many of our young people carry after college makes it all but impossible for them to excel. I grew up in a society where we believed that educating the next generation was a social good. Today's national policies don't support this. We practice the politics of scarcity. Instead of sharing so that everyone has enough, we say there's not enough for everyone, so only a few can have more than everyone else.

My mother cooked dinner every night. Some nights our friends would come over. When my mom made a pot of gumbo, there might not be enough for three or four extra mouths. Do you know what she used to do? Add water and stretch the gumbo. Put out more bread, and we all ate until we were full.

In our society, we're not stretching the gumbo. Some people will eat, some will not. That's the politics of scarcity. And that's what I was running against.

One day I visited Saint Joan of Arc, a Catholic church in Minneapolis. A guest speaker talked about the passage in the New Testament where Jesus fed the masses with two fish and five loaves of bread. I went home that night and studied the scripture myself.

Jesus was talking to the multitudes, which means a whole lot of people, and it was time for dinner. He asked his people, "What do we have?" Jesus was always inviting people to banquets and having meals.

They replied, "We have a couple of fish and some barley loaves." Clearly, there wasn't enough for the multitudes. At this point, Jesus looked to heaven and blessed the food. Then he started handing it out. And after everyone ate, there wasn't just enough, there was more than enough. They had to gather the leavings.

Many look to this story as an example of Jesus's supernatural ability to perform a miracle by transforming two fish and a few loaves into many. But what if Jesus actually prayed for the transformation of people's hearts? What if he prayed for generosity? What if people actually went back and got more food to share? Did people already have food with them and share that with others around them? The meaning of this story to me is that what the disciples saw as scarcity, Jesus saw as abundance. What they thought was not enough, Jesus saw as another invitation. Jesus added water and stretched the gumbo.

When my mother cooked and fed our friends, each of us went to bed feeling more full than if our friends had been turned away. My mother must have known that some of our friends were going home to a bare kitchen or an empty house, and so it was important to provide enough for everyone.

The politics of generosity were fostered in me at an early age in my home. And that was the vision I was bringing to my campaign.

One of the things that helped me be successful was that I didn't have doubts about why I was running: we needed to get out of Iraq right away. And we needed to institute a more humane vision for the American people — one with generosity and inclusion at its core.

))))➤

Minnesota has a party endorsement system. It's a caucus state, and the caucus delegates decide who will receive the DFL endorsement before the September primary. It was six weeks until May 6, the date of the endorsing convention. I had a lot of work to do to get my name in the race. The *Star Tribune* article by Rochelle Olson helped. And I also met a lot of people for coffee, knocked on doors, called folks, and sent out mailings letting everyone know my vision for the American working class and middle class.

When I declared my candidacy, so did about fourteen other people. Many individuals saw opportunity in Representative Sabo's retirement. Officeholders, former officeholders, and people from various walks of life entered the race. Only two people of color—Jorge Saavedra, an attorney born in Chile, and I—declared their candidacy.

With the race so crowded, there was a mad scramble to build momentum ahead of the endorsing convention. The nomination requires 60 percent of the vote. It seemed unlikely that any one of us would get 60 percent. If there was to be a nominee, it could take several ballots and last until the wee hours of the morning.

The day of the convention, I arrived at the St. Louis Park High School auditorium bright and early. I wore a dark business suit with a red tie, and I noticed that some of the political veterans were wearing casual clothes: jeans, sweats, and tennis shoes.

All the candidates were called to the auditorium, where the nomination process was taking place. Mike Erlandson, the assumed front-runner, seemed focused on the primary in September and not engaged in the endorsement process. Each of us was asked to give opening remarks, and we were asked, "Will you abide by the endorsement?"

Mike Erlandson gave his speech, and I think it was well received. But then some people in the audience asked whether he would abide by the convention's endorsement. He said simply, "I'll see you in September," and left the stage. He indicated that he was going to run in the primary. That didn't help him, because the delegates came there to endorse someone. If the candidate wasn't going to abide by the endorsement, then some delegates didn't feel obliged to consider that candidate. I was abiding. I was either getting the endorsement or running for the state legislature again, leaving the US Congress to others.

I expected to be there all day and throughout the night. My campaign brought food and found a spot in the auditorium to set up camp. I was nervous. The first round was under way. The folks counting ballots sat on the stage. When the first ballot came back,

I had twice as many votes as the next highest candidate. But I was not close to the 60 percent needed to be the nominee.

So then it went to a second ballot, after which I was still leading the pack, and a few people dropped out. Under the rules, if you failed to get a certain percentage of the vote, you had to drop out. When you dropped out, you could give a speech.

Jorge Saavedra, who didn't make it past the second ballot, went to the stage.

"Everybody, it's been a great race," he began. "I enjoyed being here. My Chilean American roots mean so much to me, and the fact that you guys, of diverse backgrounds, have supported me means a lot. I've been an advocate for immigration reform. And I believe there's one person who's going to carry on my values here, and I want all you guys to vote for Keith Ellison!"

I was stunned. I had no idea he was going to do that. I sat there for a moment and didn't move. I felt incredibly humbled, and my emotions started welling up to the surface. A few others also asked their supporters to vote for me, and it started to look as if I might actually win.

I hugged Jorge and thanked him.

There were only three of us left on the third ballot. My opponents were Gail Dorfman, a Hennepin County commissioner, and Jack Nelson-Pallmeyer, a professor of justice and peace studies at St. Thomas University. We shared similar views regarding the antiwar platform. Jack was and remains a voice for peace around the world. He has written and spoken widely on peace, and I call on him regularly for advice.

Before the ballot, they brought Gail, Jack, and me to the stage for a mini debate. I knew something about all of the questions and had solid answers. They asked me about Israel and Palestine. I said, "America needs this conflict to be resolved. There has been too much loss of life by innocents on both sides. We need to use our power as a nation to help facilitate a two-state solution."

Then they asked us a question about the Constitution. I'm a lawyer, and I knew the answer.

I felt like the character Jamal Malik in the film *Slumdog Millionaire*, who said something like "I don't know everything, but I knew what they asked me." It was purely an accident that I happened to have answers to the questions that were asked.

Before the results were in, I pulled Jack aside in the parking lot. He had trailed both Gail and me on the second ballot. I asked him if he would throw his support behind me.

"We're both antiwar, and I will definitely carry that platform," I told him.

"I think you'd make a good congressman," Jack said to me. "But I think I would too. I'm not dropping out."

"Come on, Jack. Think about it . . ."

As I was trying to convince him to concede, my staff ran out to me.

"Gail's about to drop! Get in here!"

When I walked in, the counters were still calculating the ballots. Gail was at the podium with her family and staff standing behind her.

"This has been an amazing campaign," she said. "I'm so gratified by all of the support, but I am bowing out."

I don't even remember what she said next. I knew that with Gail pulling out, I would have the 60 percent needed to win.

It was three o'clock in the afternoon, and I was heading to the primary as the DFL-endorsed candidate for the congressional seat. Historically, the DFL endorsement ensured that the endorsee would be elected to Congress. But not in this election. The primary race would prove to be hard fought and highly competitive. I was thrilled, shocked, excited. My knees were shaking as I walked to the podium after they made it official. I was barely able to keep from bawling.

After my acceptance speech, I walked outside, and reality hit me. There were about twenty microphones taped to the podium, and I saw just about every reporter in the state of Minnesota. I had never stood before such a gaggle of press. They were all waiting for me to say something.

I didn't know what to say. So I clicked into automatic pilot.

"I want to thank everybody. I want to thank my supporters. I want to thank . . ." and I must have thanked everyone from my mother to my high school English teacher. "We still have a long way to go."

It was only May. The general election was in November, and I still had to get by Mike Erlandson in the September primary. I didn't know how much I would have to endure to get to Washington. And nothing prepared me for how my life would change so dramatically. Once I heard the first question from the press, I knew that it was going to be a long and interesting ride.

"Aren't you a Muslim?" the reporter asked.

I paused. That question came out of left field for me. I expected to be asked something about Iraq or what I would do for the middle class or about immigration. But "Aren't you a Muslim?" I didn't think *that* was an issue. I was a Muslim when I won my seat in the Minnesota State Legislature. Nobody seemed to care then. It never even came up.

"If you win, will you be the first Muslim in Congress?" The reporter obviously knew the answer. I, however, did not.

"I don't know," I responded.

It never occurred to me that I would be making history if I won this seat. That wasn't on my radar, nor was it part of my platform. But it seemed to become an issue for many others, especially my opponents. And there were other things besides being a Muslim— things I had never imagined being issues.

Before they decide to run for office, some people think about all of the bad things they ever did. I didn't review everything that I had ever done or said. I thought that important issues in the country needed to be addressed, and I was willing to fight for them.

Actually, I didn't have time to think about my blemishes. I threw my hat in the ring around March 17. The delegate convention was on May 6. The primaries were on September 12. It was a long summer, and I went through the wringer.

I didn't expect the degree of scrutiny I was receiving, because during my service in the state legislature, no one seemed to care about my personal life. In fact, my faith didn't come up at all until I decided to run for Congress. Then came the stories about unpaid tax bills (they had been paid by the time I ran, but I did have some delinquencies in my past) and parking tickets.

When I won the DFL endorsement, it was like stepping through the looking glass. It was unlike anything I had ever experienced. It was a whole new deal.

In the state legislature, you can have personal shortcomings, and no one comments on them unless they are really bad. But when you run for Congress, reporters examine your background. I wasn't just the first Muslim to run for Congress, I was the first African American ever nominated to represent Minnesota. In fact, I was the first brown person. So we broke historic ground when we won.

We attracted a bright spotlight.

After my nomination, I was invited to a local television station to talk about gun violence. The first question was about unpaid parking tickets.

"Are you kidding me?" I asked, wondering if I heard the question correctly. "You're asking me about *parking tickets*?" That was the wrong response.

I didn't realize that unpaid parking tickets were a big deal to a lot of people. Many folks would never dream of not paying their tickets immediately. Not paying your tickets is not being a good citizen. I was a scofflaw to them, and how could a scofflaw represent them?

I accumulated parking tickets when running from case to case at the Hennepin County Courthouse, working to represent people. I got a few at the courthouse that I didn't pay right away and picked up a few others at the federal courthouse nearby. Because I was so busy, they fell through the cracks. I never thought I was above paying my tickets. But it was a big deal and, in hindsight, I didn't handle the questions well.

I was dropping in the polls and losing support quickly, which shocked me. Several weeks before the primary, I was invited on KSTP-TV, the local ABC network affiliate. I was sitting in the greenroom with Governor Wendell Anderson, who would be discussing the political landscape. I was there to talk about my candidacy.

Governor Anderson had been the thirty-third governor of Minnesota, serving from 1971 to 1976, before resigning to take Walter Mondale's senate seat when Senator Mondale became vice president. He was a striking man, about six feet tall with thick, wavy silver hair. We were chatting about the race, and Wendell offered me extremely helpful advice. He put his hand on my shoulder and said, "Keith, you need to apologize. You need to go out there and look them straight in the eye and say, 'I'm sorry.' If you don't, this story is only going to get worse. I know you were probably out there doing God's work, but people see it only as a sense of entitlement. You simply have to apologize. People are forgiving."

I said, "You're right. I was careless. I owe people an apology."

When we got on the set, before the first question, I looked straight into the TV camera and said, "I'm really sorry. There's no excuse. I could tell you what happened and how it happened, but the bottom line is, I was wrong for not paying those tickets on time. Those rules are there for a reason, and I didn't do what I was supposed to do. And I'm truly sorry."

I was already embarrassed and ashamed, and I'd just wanted the problem to go away. I was beginning to feel I was letting people down. I felt I had to do well because anyone coming behind me would be judged by my failure. I'm grateful for Wendell Anderson for seeing me drowning and throwing me a lifeline.

This issue had been dragging me down for three weeks steady. One blogger wrote, "Ellison, dead man walking. He's going to lose!" Conservative columnist Katherine Kersten of the *Star Tribune* attacked me regularly. It got to the point where I didn't want to get out of bed.

Betty Folliard, a former state legislator and longtime activist, called me and said sternly, "You have to get up and get out there. We're going to hit coffee shops. You have to talk to people and shake hands. I don't want to hear about your pity party. I know you don't want to hear it, but you have to hear from the people. You have to listen to what they say. You want their vote, you have to talk to them."

June was the roughest month. By mid-July, the narrative about the race started to shift. People stopped talking about parking tickets and an old tax lien all of the time, and started asking me about what policies I stood for. Like Governor Anderson, Diane Feldman, a pollster from Washington, DC, gave me some campaign-saving advice. She knew Minnesota well because she had worked hard for Senator Wellstone and done a lot of research in Minnesota. We asked her to find out where we stood. She met us at Pizza Luce on Franklin Avenue in Minneapolis to give us her findings.

"I have good news and bad news," she began. "The bad news is you're going to lose this election if you don't do something. The good news is that you *can* do something. If you can expand the electorate by ten thousand voters—people who have never voted in a primary election—you will win."

Now, getting folks who don't vote in primaries to come out is no small feat. It takes a huge effort and a compelling message. But this was our only path to victory, so we decided to increase the electorate. We organized neighborhoods and constituents who'd rarely voted in primary elections. We focused our efforts on grassroots organizing rather than on television. The Minnesota progressive community brought its talents, creativity, and energy to build our awesome field program—our "ground game," as we referred to it. People stepped forward to help. People like Dr. Josie Johnson, Dan McGrath (executive director of the community organization group Take Action Minnesota), Larry Weiss, Pam Costain, John Stiles, and Shayna Berkowitz. They all came to the table to map out our strategy for attracting ten thousand new voters and winning the primary.

I think Carla Kjellberg and Dick Kaspari, two progressive friends and leaders from the National Lawyers Guild, took extra shifts. Vic Rosenthal, Frank Hornstein, and others were organizing in the Jewish community. Donna Cassutt, vice chair of the DFL Party, went beyond what anyone could expect. Folks in the Muslim community such as Asad Zaman, Ziad Amre, and Makram El-Amin jumped in with both feet. Javier Morillo of the Service

Employees International Union (SEIU), Bill McCarthy of the Central Labor Council, and Eliot Seide of the American Federation of State, County, and Municipal Employees (AFSCME) brought labor friends to the table. Diane was telling us to do something that had not been done at this level in the Fifth District. It was going to be difficult to find ten thousand people who had never voted in a primary election and then convince them to vote for us. And we had only a few weeks to do it. The good news was that we had the right team to get the job done.

10

All Colors, All Cultures, All Faiths

September 12, 2006

As I sat in the business office of the Blue Nile Ethiopian restaurant, I could hear folks shouting and chanting and cheering one floor below. I could barely breathe.

This was our primary election headquarters. All colors, all cultures, all faiths—that was our campaign mantra. The house was jam-packed; standing room only. Lil' David was pumping up the crowd. David Gilbert-Pederson, a five-foot-three dynamo, was a Minnesota phenomenon—a sixteen-year-old activist heavily involved in social justice causes and politics.

R. T. Rybak, mayor of Minneapolis, and Sharon Sayles Belton, his predecessor—onetime political rivals—were taking turns firing up the people, too. The feeling was electric, connected, and powerful.

My campaign manager, Dave Colling, poked his head into the office.

"It's time for you to get down there," he said. "They're calling for you."

My fate was about to be decided: either I would be going back to private life, practicing law, working on issues that I care about, building the progressive movement, or I would be going on to the general election as the DFL primary winner in one of the most Democratic congressional districts in the country.

As I reconciled myself to both of these alternative futures, I wasn't neutral. I burned for the chance to articulate an inclusive vision for my country in this fearful and angry post-9/11 world.

))))➤

Two hours earlier, I was walking through the Somali Mall, making that final push before the polls closed at eight o'clock. The mall is a festive and lively place in an old warehouse, divided into stalls for each vendor, not unlike the souks of Mogadishu. It's also like the Mercado Central, a Latin American mall a little farther south on East Lake Street. We had been campaigning practically nonstop since the night before. I was beyond tired. Too tired to be tired. But then I heard a sound that made me forget my fatigue and the stress of the election. I heard the *adhan*, the Muslim call to prayer. Though I had heard it thousands of times, I felt like I was hearing it for the first time—that melodic call, which ends with the phrase *"Laa ilaaha illallah"* ("No god but God"). I took comfort in it.

As I headed toward the exit, I passed vendors selling hair products, clothes, phone cards, and money-wiring services. Amid all the stalls, there is a mosque ready to accommodate the prayers enjoined on Muslims five times a day. I headed there. Not only was it exactly what my soul needed, it also marked eight o'clock. The polls were closing. It was all over but the counting. I could do nothing more but pray.

We had worn out our feet, hands, and throats campaigning all day. In the mosque, I let it all go as I stood there for evening prayers with my hands crossed over my midsection, right over left, reciting Al-Fatiha, the first chapter in the Quran. My mind drifted back over the whirlwind of the last several months. I had faced humiliation and shame, but I also experienced joy, renewal, and indescribable elation.

I'd thrown all of myself into it, and it had taken a toll.

As I bent over in the prayer position of *ruku*, I thought about how I'd missed taking my oldest son to Drake University. He was leaving home for the first time. Kim and her parents, Harvey and Elizabeth, ended up doing a job that should have been mine.

"That's all right, Dad," Isaiah said.

I guess the poor kid knew how I felt about not being there, and he was trying to comfort me.

As I knelt down in prostration, in the prayer position of *sujud*, I thought of all we'd gone through as a family. I was relieved that it was almost over.

"Glory to God, the most high," I said in Arabic as I completed the *raka'at*, the prayer positions.

Afterward, I shook a few hands and said *"Mahadsanid"* ("Thank you" in Somali) to many in the mall, some new Americans, young and old, male and female. I was met with the greeting "As-salaam alaikum." People were reaching out their hands, letting me know that their very first vote in America had been for me. Some were sporting red-and-white "I voted" stickers on their shirts and jackets. No matter what the polls would say, I knew I had already scored a major victory. We had helped these new citizens, many of them refugees seeking a safe haven from a war-torn nation, feel democracy in action. They had a sense of power and control over their own lives. It was delicious.

When I was done, I walked out of the mall, feeling renewed but also reflecting on how my faith had become a big issue. I didn't quite understand this. I had spent four years in the Minnesota legislature, and no one seemed to care about anyone else's religion. Now it seemed to be all anyone wanted to talk about.

Before heading to the Blue Nile, where we would receive the election results, I stopped by our campaign office. My younger brother Tony was in the parking lot along with Batala, an old friend, swapping primary-day stories and smoking cigarettes. I gently chided them about the hazards of tobacco, while Tony smiled from ear to ear. He had taken leave from his law practice and family to help me campaign, as had my older brother Brian. I was emotionally raw and kind of in a daze at this point, but Tony picked up my spirits, boldly proclaiming victory. He was certain that we had won the primary. He gave me a high five that was caught on camera and appeared in the *Star Tribune* the next day.

I went downstairs to my office to work on my speech and refine our message. While I wasn't certain I had won, Carla Kjellberg, my lawyer and adopted big sister, reminded me that I had to be ready anyway. She, like Tony and everyone else, was sure. I couldn't wrap my brain around it yet.

I knew we had done the work. We knocked on thirty-seven thousand doors—some more than once—in the final days before the primary. We placed ninety thousand calls before the polls closed. The folks in the mall were sure. Brian was sure. Carla was sure. I couldn't explain why I still wasn't sure.

Carla is the practical idealist, the hopeful but realistic progressive liberal, sentimental about Paul and Sheila Wellstone, Jack and Bobby Kennedy, and, of course, Martin Luther King Jr. She's a committed member of Saint Joan of Arc Catholic Church—the premier progressive Catholic congregation in Minneapolis. There the message is love, generosity, and peace. She was a tireless worker, and in my campaign earned the nickname "Chairperson of CCK": Concerned Citizens for Keith.

Her candidates usually lose—an exception being Paul Wellstone and, tonight, maybe me. *Maybe*. The interesting thing about Carla was that she was not on my staff; she was there because she believed in our vision. She was there more than the hired staff, around every day, plotting strategy and helping to refine our message. She is tough and takes crap from no one—including me.

Carla started lecturing me as soon as I entered the office. "We've got to practice, Keith. Remember our message of inclusion: 'all colors, all cultures, all faiths!' "

"Yeah, Carla. I remember—I'll remember."

"We're not going to have time to practice later," she said. "You're going to be mobbed. Get your head together now."

"Okay. I got it."

We headed over to the Blue Nile, located in the heart of the Seward neighborhood: a mix of recent immigrants, vegetarians, intellectuals, and working people—my kind of place. It's home to organic food co-ops, ethnic restaurants, and thriving immigrant life.

Dave, the campaign manager, greeted me at the door and pulled us upstairs. The Blue Nile's owner was already up there, and he was all smiles and hugs, like he had a feeling that something cool was going to happen this night and he was going to be a part of it. He was very attentive. Gesturing to his staff, he said, "Hey, bring the congressman something to drink."

Congressman? Did he say what I thought he said? I wasn't ready to be called that.

Dave had been running the show all summer, and on primary night he was as calm as if he hadn't a care in the world. During the campaign, a band of supporters—that would be Carla and the CCK—thought he was *too* laid back. Not me. I needed somebody calm because I was frantic throughout most of the summer. Dave had kept me sane, confident, and ready for the next challenge.

Handing me the phone, with his hand cupped over the receiver, Dave mouthed, "It's Mike. He's going to concede."

He's conceding?

For me, it just wasn't real.

I took the phone.

"Hey, Mike . . . Oh yeah, thanks . . . Sure. Uh-huh . . . Uh-huh . . . Yeah. Thank you. Best of luck to you. Thanks again."

"What did he say?" Dave asked.

"Well, he congratulated me. He said somebody had to win and others were not going to. He said best of luck and feel free to call."

Mike Erlandson was more than a worthy opponent. He was not only the odds-on favorite but also a nice guy, an experienced campaigner, and a native son of the district. I'd had no reason to think I could prevail over him, but here I was accepting his call congratulating me on a primary win.

"But all of the returns aren't in," I started to say.

"Oh yeah, it's certain. You won." Typical Dave.

Whatever happened that night was fine. God had been good to me. I was surprisingly centered, and I would accept the outcome no matter what it was.

My kids were there, too. Isaiah, my firstborn, was standing proud. Jeremiah, sixteen, had worked for the campaign right up until football practice started in mid-August. Now he was working the crowd. He's gregarious, like his uncle Tony, and loves people. Amirah, ten, was doing the same. And my sweet, quiet son Elijah, the one who enlisted in the US Army after high school, was silently soaking it all up.

By this time, even cool Dave was getting a little jazzed.

"It's Ember," he said, smiling and handing me the phone again.

"Let me congratulate you," Ember said. "Great field operation."

Ember Reichgott Junge was another tough opponent. She had the endorsement of Emily's List, a great organization dedicated to electing more women to public office, as well as twice the amount of money that we had and way more experience. She'd been a state senator for sixteen years, representing a suburban area in the Fifth District, and had ushered charter schools into Minnesota, which was both a help and a hindrance to her campaign.

It didn't help her with the teachers' union, but, of course, there are a lot of people who crave education reform. Ember was formidable also because she had visibility. She was a television commentator, delivering the liberal side of the point-counterpoint segment of a KSTP Sunday morning show called *At Issue*. In addition, she was a poised presenter, having honed her skills with the popular clean-cut singing ensemble Up with People in the 1970s. But on this day, she was calling to concede.

As I hung up the phone, I could hear the chants from downstairs: "Keith! Keith! Keith!"

"Time to go," said Dave. "Time to go down to address the people."

I hesitated.

"Hey, man, we haven't heard from Paul yet."

I wanted to hear from Paul Ostrow, my final opponent. Paul was a council member from the city's northeast side. We had worked together for the city of Minneapolis. I really liked his mother, who was a dedicated peace activist. I liked Paul, too, and had found him to be a very decent man. But things had gotten ugly during the campaign. He even had to fire a staffer who was caught trying to smear me. I never held it against Paul, because I knew that politicians can't always totally control their staff members. I wouldn't have held it against him anyway. He's a dedicated public servant.

In these campaigns, there is an enormous pressure to win. You can get swept up in it if you're not careful. People tell you to "go negative," that you have to do it to win, and sometimes you feel pressured to agree.

Paul had reason to believe he could win. He was from Minneapolis, which took up 60-plus percent of the district, and he was on the ground as a city councilman dealing with day-to-day problems. And, unlike me, no embarrassing past personal missteps had surfaced about him during the campaign.

As I was waiting for his call (and I later found out that he *had* called to concede, but we'd missed it), I remember someone touching me on my shoulder.

"They are calling for you."

))▶

I moved through a sea of people as I headed to the stage. I'd never seen such a gathering in my life. It was completely integrated by race, age, class, religion, and gender. There was a millionaire standing next to a homeless person. I saw a Somali woman wipe away the tear of a working-class white organizer. As Mayor Rybak, one of the speakers that night, said, "I have been in lots of rooms like this on many election nights, but I have never been in one that actually looks like my city."

"Do you have your statement ready?" Carla yelled over the crowd. "You know what we worked on. There's 'only' about a thousand people stuffed in here, and you can't be shooting from the hip like you usually do."

The music was blaring, and the people were jubilant. I heard Carla's question, but I was still kind of drifting along, staring into the crowd. It was all very surreal. Then the weight of winning finally hit me.

I noticed the women in the headscarves known as *hijabs* and the men wearing kufi hats. I hadn't jumped into this election to represent the world's 1.3 billion Muslims—I ran to represent all the people—but I was so happy to have the community's support. My religious faith had been made an issue in the campaign, and my Republican opponent would only intensify the issue. It was ironic because the only Muslim I'd ever tried to represent before was me. I was neither an imam nor an Islamic scholar. I had never led a religious service in my life. I never delivered the Friday sermon (the *Jummah khutbah*) or even conducted congregational prayer. I was motivated to run for office by a burning desire to assert arguments in favor of the common good and for peace. Obviously, voices for our shared prosperity were being drowned out by the voices of greed and fear. Peace needed an amplifier, and needed it where it would make a difference: in the United States Congress.

As I arrived at the stage, time seemed to slow down. I climbed up onto the stage and looked out over the room. I spotted Sam and Sylvia Kaplan, a husband-wife team, stalwarts of the progressive DFL. Sam, with Sylvia beside him, went on after the historic Obama victory of 2008 to represent the United States as ambassador to Morocco. Their help, at a critical stage, sustained us. After the barrage of news stories about my failure to pay taxes and tickets on time, Sam and Sylvia held a fund-raiser at their house. It was the turning point in the campaign. After that amazing event, things began to look up.

I saw Karen Northcott, an old friend with whom I'd spent many years practicing law. Karen is a private investigator—tough and smart. Despite the human suffering and pain she has seen in her work, she is optimistic and yearns for justice. When I first heard her Texas accent, I honestly didn't know what to expect, but she was in my corner 100 percent.

Shayna Berkowitz, Liz Brookins, Todd Jones, Michael Guest, Kathleen Murphy, and Rev. Ian Bethel were all there. The multitude. All colors, all cultures, all faiths. Old friends, new friends.

I began:

> *Do you believe this?!*
>
> *We made history. We came together.*
>
> *When the great Martin Sabo—the great Martin Sabo—decided to take his retirement as he so richly deserved to do, we said our goal was to increase voter turnout. And you know what? We did. We said we wanted to reach into the community, to empower communities that have not had a voice in electoral politics. And we did. We said we wanted to affirmatively and deliberately reach out into the diverse communities to improve all God's children, each one of us. And we did. In this campaign, we had people who say* shalom. *We had people who say* as-salaam alaikum. *We had people who say all the words of greetings in peace, because peace must be the guiding principle of our nation. All colors, all cultures, all faiths came together. We brought them together.*
>
> *And, let's be honest: we faced some tough days. But we weren't derailed. And we proved, we proved, we proved, that you can win an election by being positive and staying positive. We know that negative campaigning has its effect, we know it can work. But it does not lift us up, it does not lift up the debate. We know*

it can be effective, but it does not build bridges, it builds walls.
And so we're about being positive. We're about bringing people
together. We're about love!

The audience chanted, "Love! Love! Love! . . ."

Let me tell you, we got a call a little while ago—a classy thing
for Mike Erlandson to give us a call—and he congratulated us
on the campaign we ran, and I congratulated him back on your
behalf. And we got a call from Ember, who ran a classy campaign,
and, on your behalf, I congratulated her right back. And I asked
them, I asked them, I asked them, I said, "Look, we've got a state-
wide election to win in only a few weeks, and as we exploded the
electorate, and as we boosted up the turnout, we're going to need
all that plus more to win in November." But let the word go out,
the Fifth Congressional District is here to turn it out.

Let me tell you, from day one, from March 17, to this moment,
we said we were running a peace agenda, and we mean that. We
are running on universal single payer, and we mean that. We say a
caring nation provides for all, our seniors matter, our kids matter,
all our people matter. We care. No more do we tolerate an owner-
ship society in which you are on your own. You are not on your
own. We are with you. We do this thing together, y'all. We do this
thing together, y'all. We accept you as you are, you are why we are
here, you are our own, we love you and will show it through our
caring, through our public policy, through our outreach, through
our fellowship, through everything that we do.

And you know what? I'm going to let you have a great party.
I'm going to say this: thanking people is a risky business, because
everybody helped do this. Everybody helped do this. Everybody
helped do this.

I went on to thank my family and to talk about all the people who had made this moment possible. No day could ever match it.

After the speech, I hung around. I talked with folks and thanked them. Thank God, I ran into Reverend Ian Bethel. My old friend instinctively knew that I was tired and spent, but I still wanted to thank people. He pushed me out.

After a round of back slaps, congrats, hugs, and love, we jumped into our Honda Accord and went home. I had to get up at four in the morning to do a round of press calls. We were in demand.

I would do well to savor the moment because, little did I know, I would go back into battle in short order.

))))➤

The next day, Jim Linefelter, our communications director, scooped me up around four in the morning. We did several media interviews. We talked with everybody. But we didn't get to bask in the glow for long. My Republican opponent, Allan Fine, in a stark departure from his earlier behavior, had turned up the heat.

I had known Allan Fine as a gentleman. He was a business teacher at the Carlson School of Business at the University of Minnesota. I'd heard that he was an expert pianist.

During the primary campaign, a south-side school invited all the candidates — Republican, Democratic, Green, and Independent — to debate educational policy issues. One black parent asked about the so-called achievement gap: the racial disparity between black students and white students in standardized testing results.

Allan responded by saying that he didn't know much about the achievement gap, but, he said, "What about the happiness gap?" He went on to describe how we need to get out there and tackle that happiness gap and make folks happier. My kids thought it was funny. Me too. The last thing I associated Allan Fine with was meanness, but the day after the primary results, he came at me with both barrels blazing.

"Keith Muhammad, Keith X, Keith Hakim" is how he started his press conference. He didn't link these words to anything. He appeared to be raising suspicion about my faith. His approach seemed connected to an overall Republican strategy, because the onslaught was similar to attacks posted on conservative blogs such as *Power Line* and *Minnesota Democrats Exposed*. Katherine Kersten, the *Star Tribune* opinion writer, tried to tarnish me in the same way. She also tied me to the overall DFL ticket, including Minnesota Attorney General Mike Hatch, who was running for governor, and Amy Klobuchar, who was running for US Senate. Kersten ran me into the ground and then launched into a diatribe about how the DFL (which she hated) used to be the "Party of Humphrey," but now it had descended and become the—dramatic pause, please— "Party of Ellison."

It wasn't funny when I read it. But it was not a surprise. In a September 13 *Star Tribune* story, Patricia Lopez reported on a Republican National Committee (RNC) strategy to find "damaging material about challengers" and how to "define your opponent immediately and unrelentingly." Lopez quoted University of Minnesota professor Larry Jacobs saying, "Given that Keith Ellison is a left-of-center black Muslim . . . you can see national Republicans putting some real resources into this race as a way of characterizing other Democrats running."

Allan Fine said he wasn't taking orders from the RNC or the Minnesota Republicans, but it sure sounded like they were singing from the same hymnal.

The day after the primary, the *Star Tribune* wrote, "State Rep. Keith Ellison overcame setbacks and questions about his past to win the DFL nomination to succeed U.S. Rep. Martin Sabo, placing him on the verge of becoming the first Muslim elected to Congress."

Someone said that my election was like a Japanese American being elected to the US Congress five years after Pearl Harbor, while the memory was still vivid.

I don't remember *Muslims* attacking this country on 9/11. I remember hateful terrorists, who were part of an extremist group that happened to be Muslim, attacking this country on 9/11. Not only was I being attacked for my religion, but so were millions of law-abiding, devout, God-loving people.

My candidacy went from being one of inclusion, peace, and solutions to the problems of my district and the nation, to being a defense of one of the core tenets of our Constitution: the freedom of religion.

We made a decision that we would not respond negatively to the attacks. As they became more vicious, I received more support from the voters. Minnesotans do not appreciate negative attacks. That is still true today. When I get attacked, I receive more support.

We worked just as hard in the general election. We had an impressive get-out-the-vote program, and I received 56 percent of the vote. The good people of Minnesota judged me by my platform and my track record. I believe my vision for the district and the nation reflected the views of most people in the Fifth quite well.

))))➤

January 4, 2007

My right hand was over my heart and my left hand was on Thomas Jefferson's Quran. Standing with me were my wife, whose mother had immigrated from the Dominican Republic; my mom, a Catholic from Louisiana who can trace her roots to a French aristocrat, an African medicine woman, and Croatian immigrants; my dad, a lifelong Republican and overall contrarian, who could not be more proud; and my older brother Brian, a Baptist minister. Other family huddled all around.

There was so much history, controversy, and pride over this moment: the first Muslim being elected to the US Congress. There was pride from my family and my district. Indeed, there was pride throughout the entire Muslim world; I received calls and even saw headlines from throughout the Muslim world. On the other hand, there was anger and bitterness from some quarters too. On one level, I understood all of these reactions.

On that day, I also recognized that my faith—the practice of my faith in Allah—is fundamentally American. The irony is that this nation was founded by people escaping religious persecution, seeking freedom to worship God in their own ways, however they chose to worship, *if* they chose to worship. But there was a sentiment in America running counter to that notion of freedom. Every day, Americans—*citizens*—were being labeled as terrorists, and became targets for violence and other unthinkable acts, simply because of their faith.

I hadn't originally planned to swear on the Quran. In fact, I hadn't even thought about it.

A couple of days before the election, as a favor to the host, I agreed to go on a local Somali public access cable TV show. It was late, and I didn't expect there to be many viewers outside of a few Somali insomniacs. The interviewer asked me the usual questions about my campaign and my plans to serve the district. Then he asked, "So, if you win the election, will you swear in on the Quran?"

We had been totally focused on getting through the primaries, and then the election and the tasks to be completed once in office, and the swearing-in wasn't on my mind.

"I don't know," I answered honestly. "I never thought about it."

He asked again, "If you win—you can imagine yourself winning, right?"

"Yes," I said.

"Well, imagine yourself standing up there getting ready to be sworn into the United States Congress. What book is your hand placed on?"

"I don't know."

"Is it a Quran?"

"Yeah, I guess it would be a Quran."

We moved on to other topics, and I didn't think much of it until it exploded into a national issue a few days later. Having won the election, what I had said in that interview would become a reality. This sent a lot of people into a frenzy.

Dennis Prager led the charge. He was a syndicated conservative radio talk-show host who wrote an editorial on the website Townhall.com entitled "America, Not Keith Ellison, Decides What Book a Congressman Takes His Oath On." According to Prager, I was undermining American civilization. He said that I was a bigger threat than Osama bin Laden. My mother, who regularly listened to Prager's show, was so outraged by what he was saying that she called in to give him a piece of her mind.

It became clear that not only Somali insomniacs had watched the interview. People were flooding *the US Capitol* with letters and phone calls expressing their displeasure at my intention to be sworn in on the Quran. Letters of support came in too. (I later found out that members of Congress do not take their oath of office on *any* book when they are sworn in officially on the House floor. The whole swearing-on-a-Bible thing is ceremonial, not official.)

One of my colleagues-to-be in the House, Virgil Goode, a six-term Republican (and former Democrat), got involved in the controversy. The congressman, who was working on an anti-immigration bill at the time, raised fears of a "Muslim invasion" and declared that he wanted to keep "terrorist states" from entering our country. He wrote in a letter that was distributed to news organizations such as CNN: "When I raise my hand to take the oath on Swearing-In Day, I will have the Bible in my other hand. I do not subscribe to using the Quran in any way. The Muslim Representative from Minnesota was elected by the voters of that district, and if American citizens don't wake up and adopt the Virgil Goode position on immigration, there will likely be many more Muslims elected to office and demanding the use of the Quran."

But I wasn't a terrorist. I wasn't invading America. I was born here. I *am* an American. And this is *America*!

We received a letter a few days before the swearing-in that suggested we contact the Library of Congress and request Thomas Jefferson's Quran. The letter even gave us the reference number for it. I know a good idea when I hear one, so we contacted the Library of Congress. They confirmed Jefferson's Quran and said that they would be proud to let me use it.

After the swearing-in, two of my fellow Democrats, Dennis Kucinich of Ohio and Jim Moran of Virginia, grabbed Virgil Goode and introduced us. I greeted him, and we shook hands. I suggested we get together for a cup of coffee. It's easy to throw mud and promote hatred from afar. But sitting across from a person and talking has the potential to ease fear and suspicion. Too bad we never actually got that cup of coffee together. I was willing.

I knew there were a few members who were hostile to the idea of serving with a Muslim. But folks like Congressmen Kucinich and Moran helped squash that sentiment. And Speaker Nancy Pelosi definitely set the tone. She didn't do so only for my benefit. I am sure she made certain that I was welcomed because she believes in inclusion. Perhaps she did it for the caucus. But that's good leadership. She didn't want us to be divided, especially not over the issue of whether I would be swearing in on a Quran. She grabbed me by the hand and told everybody that I was on the team. I really appreciated that.

The next day was the big ceremonial swearing-in that everyone had been waiting for. (The real one was a collective swearing-in on the House floor. No Bibles. No Qurans. No drama.) House rules allowed for children under twelve to join their member parents on the House floor for the real swearing-in, and I had my son Elijah and daughter Amirah along with me. Elijah, now nineteen, serves as a combat medic in the army.

But then came the ceremonial swearing-in. The swearing-in that drew all the attention but did not have the force of law.

I went first. There was a horde of reporters and photographers present.

Speaker Pelosi leaned in and whispered to me, "You draw quite a crowd."

"You're the first woman Speaker," I said. "I think they're here for you." We shared a laugh.

11

HILLS AND VALLEYS

All newly elected members attend an orientation in DC before joining the House of Representatives. New members arrive and they say, "Here's your binder with the administrative information you need to have." You fill out employee forms, and it's just like starting a new job. There are two days of meetings about House ethics rules and floor procedures, hiring staff—everything you need to know to get a new office started. Then all new members go through a lottery for office space. The House administrative staff provides a long list of available office suites, and we toured them. They tell you to decide on your first, second, and third choices in advance, because they don't give you much time when your lottery number comes up.

Members can choose from one of three buildings: the Cannon

House Office Building, the Rayburn House Office Building, or the Longworth House Office Building. My first choice was room 1130 in Longworth, the building nearest to the Capitol. I also chose Longworth because some great colleagues were there, such as Representative Mike Honda, a Japanese American who spent time in an internment camp during World War II. Mike, a Democrat from California, is one of the most beautiful human beings I know.

I'd learned on my tour that being close to the Capitol is essential. When Congress is open, a bell rings, letting you know it's in session. When votes are called, members have fifteen minutes to get to the floor—no matter where you are or what you're doing. If you are in the middle of lunch or a meeting, you have to be close enough to get to the floor on time.

The lottery results came in. Maryland Democrat John Sarbanes got the number one pick. *Please don't pick my office*, was all I was thinking. Room 1130 was one of the larger suites in the Longworth Building. He didn't. I was number two. Relief.

I couldn't wait to set up my office. I have the best staff in the world. I chose Kari Moe as my chief of staff. She has a PhD in public policy, making her Dr. Moe. But we playfully call her Dr. No because, while I am known as a pushover, she stops me and says no. You need somebody in your camp who puts the brakes on things and makes sure that you're making the best decisions. Dr. Moe was Senator Paul Wellstone's chief of staff during the 1990s. In the 1980s, she served as a deputy mayor for Mayor Harold Washington, the first black mayor of Chicago, who had also been a member of Congress. So I was in good hands.

Members are given the option to change offices with every new Congress, since new offices become available as members retire or leave for other reasons. Many of the heavy hitters have their offices in the Rayburn Building, the newest of the three House office buildings. That's where I am today, along with Democrats John Conyers of Detroit, Charlie Rangel of New York, and Maxine Waters of California. Most of the committee chairs, too, are in Rayburn, such as Connecticut's John Larson, chair of the Democratic caucus. Several members like the Cannon Building, which dates back to 1908, because it is more traditional, but I prefer Longworth or Rayburn.

Being in Washington was surreal for me. When you are in your district, you're the only member of Congress. There's a singularity to that experience. But in DC, there are four hundred thirty-four other members of the House and one hundred senators. You're part of a team. In DC, you bring what your constituents asked you to represent. Your work in the Congress is where you try to maintain the trust that your constituents placed in you. This is where you justify your election. Why else are you here? But it is crucial to remember—and I always tell my staff this—that the good folks of the Fifth Congressional District are the bosses. We work for them. I go back to Minneapolis almost every weekend and feel renewed. And I get a lot of my ideas from talking to people at home.

New members, including me, are eager in the first year. I wanted to tell people about my district. I was fresh off the campaign trail, which demands a particular kind of discipline. I spent months debating, defending my record, advancing my vision, and responding to citizens. This process had honed me. I came to DC fired up and ready to go, ready to fix Washington.

You hear a lot of anti-Washington rhetoric on the campaign trail. All candidates campaign against Washington a little bit, which is part smart and part cynical, considering Congress's approval rating. It's also odd, because why would folks criticize a job they are fighting to have? But when you actually get there, you discover that there are many hardworking, decent people—which you might not know by listening to the commentary about DC. Most politicians are sincere. Sometimes they are sincerely *wrong*, but, nonetheless, they are regular people who are there to advocate for their constituents and to serve the nation.

During my first week as a congressman, President Bush invited all freshmen to the White House. However, there was an AFL-CIO (American Federation of Labor and Congress of Industrial Organizations) event at the same time. I wasn't trying to be impolite to President Bush, but I thought the most important thing for me was to connect with the working people whose values I shared. When the story came out that I had attended the AFL-CIO event instead of going to the White House, some people found that strange. But I didn't snub the president; I merely spent time with workers and leaders, many from Minnesota, who believed that the economy needed to reflect the needs of working men and women.

My first day at the office was a big deal. My dad, who'd suffered a stroke years ago and didn't travel well, made sure he was there. All my brothers were there. Even my childhood babysitters, Cicely and Genie (who are my father's first cousins), came. Genie passed away in 2013, and I will always remember her. My cousins from Louisiana who lived in New York, Tina and Cole, came down with her sister. And there were several people who traveled all the way from Minnesota to celebrate this day. We hosted a reception in my new office, and it was standing room only, with an overflow crowd in the hallway.

I felt weight and responsibility. I had been entrusted with something very precious and couldn't even contemplate anything but success. I felt the power of that moment.

My Baptist minister brother, Brian, and my Catholic mother had been interviewed by the press and were telling me what they'd said. I thought it was all hilarious. I wasn't used to the attention, quite frankly.

We prioritized the Minnesota press on swearing-in day and into the first year—and continue to do so now. But we also sat for some national and international interviews because I wanted to talk about my election and the promise of America.

There were also some trade-offs in the early days between hunkering down to do the work and telling our story to a wider audience. In retrospect, we passed up an invitation that I wish we had taken. In the early weeks, Jon Stewart invited me on *The Daily Show*, but after internal discussion, we declined the request and told him that we were focused on the Minnesota press. We may have erred on the side of caution, not wanting to do much national media before we got to work on legislation. However, for many people, *The Daily Show* is more important than CNN. That's where they get their news. In hindsight, I wish I had taken the opportunity. But this story shows the shifting nature of how people consume information. When I was growing up, it was Walter Cronkite and the major networks, and now it is Jon Stewart and Stephen Colbert, among others. And cable news, Facebook, and Twitter.

My main priority, however, wasn't Washington. It was setting up my office in Minnesota and getting to work for the people. There was a lot of pressure and attention, and I wanted to make the right moves out of the gate. I wanted to convince folks in my district that I would do everything I could to deliver on the promises of our campaign. They voted for me not because they thought I was great but because they believed that I *could* be. And I wanted to live up to their faith in me.

Balancing the two worlds between my district and DC was more difficult than I anticipated. I was sent to Congress by the people of the Fifth District to represent them in Washington, and that was at the forefront of everything. Some folks in Congress make an early mistake and start to think that being a member of Congress is about *them*. They become attracted to the spotlight and the status of serving in Congress. The power and the access can tempt folks to get disconnected from the folks back home.

You learn quickly about lobbyists when you arrive in Congress. And it is important to distinguish between the top corporate lobbyists and all of the other advocates you meet. There are a lot of regular "lobbyists" for every issue you can think of, from research on Alzheimer's disease to support for public transit. But the corporate lobbyists appear to have the most power. A lot of the old-fashioned perks such as gifts, meals, and golf outings have been outlawed, but lobbyists still have more access to members of Congress than just about anyone else. They are paid by corporate interests to hang out around the Capitol and knock on doors. The average citizen generally can't afford to do that.

Some members of Congress have access to valuable economic and market information. When I arrived in Congress, insider trading wasn't explicitly illegal for members, although I believe it's always been a conflict of interest for a member to consider his or her private financial interests when making a legislative decision. When this practice came to light in the media, I was proud to support Congressman Tim Walz, a Democrat representing Minnesota's First Congressional District, as he championed the 2012 passage of the Stop Trading on Congressional Knowledge (STOCK) Act, which finally banned this practice.

My first few days in Congress, I was absorbing everything. The history. The tradition. I was in awe as I walked the halls to my office and to the House floor. Imagine Abraham Lincoln walking across that same floor in 1847 as a freshman representative from

Illinois, a member of the Whig Party. During his only term in Congress, Lincoln authored a bill to abolish slavery in the nation's capital. The bill didn't win much support, but he never abandoned the idea that slavery as an institution must one day cease. That freshman representative would become president and shepherd the Thirteenth Amendment to ratification through Congress in 1865.

This was the same House floor where Charles Sumner, a freshman Republican senator from Massachusetts, was nearly beaten to death by a fellow congressman in 1856. A few days before the beating, Sumner delivered a three-hour speech that included an attack on the Fugitive Slave Act of 1850 and the entire institution of slavery. The Harvard-trained lawyer, who was also a powerful orator, stood before his fellow congressmen on that sunny day and said:

> *The wickedness which I now begin to expose is immeasurably aggravated by the motive which prompted it. Not in any common lust for power did this uncommon tragedy have its origin. It is the rape of a virgin Territory, compelling it to the hateful embrace of Slavery; and it may be clearly traced to a depraved desire for a new Slave State, hideous offspring of such a crime, in the hope of adding to the power of Slavery in the National Government. Yes, Sir, when the whole world, alike Christian and Turk, is rising up to condemn this wrong, making it a hissing to the nations, here in our Republic, force—ay, Sir, force— is openly employed in compelling Kansas to this pollution, and all for the sake of political power.*

Sumner, whose father once said of slavery that it would "do us no good" unless the slaves were treated equally by society, was denouncing the Kansas-Nebraska Act, which the senator believed would spread slavery into these territories. He also chastised Democratic senators Stephen Douglas of Illinois and Andrew Butler of South Carolina, who coauthored the act. Of Butler, Sumner said:

"[He has] a mistress who, though ugly to others, is always lovely to him; though polluted in the sight of the world, is chaste in his sight—I mean, the harlot, Slavery." And he likened slaveholders to pimps.

Sumner's words set off more than a negative backlash from the slaveholding and slave-promoting members of Congress; it provoked a physical assault by Butler's nephew Preston Brooks, a Democratic representative from South Carolina. Brooks beat Sumner unconscious on the floor of the Old Senate Chamber two days after the speech. He didn't stop beating Sumner until his thick gutta-percha cane had broken in two. Nearly three years passed before Sumner recovered from that attack and was able to return to Congress. His speech, and the subsequent beating, have been cited as a major catalyst for what would become the Civil War.

I imagined standing in the very spot where George Henry White stood as he delivered his final speech before leaving Congress. White, the last of the Reconstruction-era blacks elected to Congress in 1896, was a representative from North Carolina's Second District who served two terms and introduced the first bill in Congress condemning lynching. The climate in the country had become so hostile and violent toward blacks—particularly those with political aspirations who fought for social justice—that White, fearing for his life, chose not to run for a third term.

In his final speech he said, "This is perhaps the Negroes' temporary farewell to the American Congress. But let me say, like the Phoenix he will rise up some day and come again. These parting words are on behalf of an outraged, heartbroken, bruised and bleeding, but God-fearing people; faithful, industrious, loyal, rising people—full of potential force."

There was not another black person in Congress until 1929, when Oscar De Priest was elected from Chicago. He was followed by New York's Adam Clayton Powell Jr. in 1945. Powell, my father's favorite politician, is one of my heroes because he didn't just go to Congress, he arrived with a vision, a plan, and a purpose. Of course, he ran into trouble in the latter part of his service (he was stripped of his committee chairmanship by the House Democratic Caucus in 1967, and despite being reelected in 1969, was denied his seniority), but for a while, he was awesome. As I stood there, I reminded myself that I was sent to Washington to make a difference for my constituents and to fight for the rights of all American citizens.

Powell served not only his district in Harlem for thirteen terms but black America as a whole, and as a result, all of America. He put equality on the front burner. He served his larger constituency among the black and poor populations of our nation. When President Lyndon Johnson passed the Civil Rights Act of 1964, Project Head Start, Medicare, Medicaid, and the other elements of his Great Society, he achieved goals that Powell had pursued for decades.

Powell's presence chipped away at a congressional culture that was content with the status quo and mired in prejudice. He used to take black constituents to eat in the whites-only House of Representatives dining room in the Capitol building, daring his colleagues to say a word. He also challenged congressmen who used the word *nigger* on the House floor. And he continually attached to bills his "Powell Amendments," which denied funding to any organization practicing racial discrimination.

I had a private chuckle when I learned that my office in the Rayburn Building is located directly above Adam Clayton Powell's old office. My dad would love that. My father admired the congressman's intelligence, but he was more enamored by his nerve and unabashed style. My father would become animated when talking about Powell's exploits:

"Adam Clayton Powell rode up in the baddest Cadillac, and those other folks were so jealous!"

Adam Clayton Powell was not perfect. He liked his scotch and women too. But for a long time, he was serious and on the job. Powell made a difference.

))))⟶

Standing among all of that history, with the legacy and the promise, was overwhelming, especially in the early days. I was in awe. I had visited Washington about three times in my life—mostly just passing through as a state legislator. I'd stay in my hotel and not do much else. I had never *seen* Washington, DC, up close. In fact, I had never even been to the Capitol building until I went there as a congressman.

The first thing that struck me is that Capitol Hill is literally on a hill. You get a serious calf workout walking up there. At dusk, you can see the light at the top of the Capitol dome, with its blue background. Capitol Hill was designed to inspire awe, and it does.

It felt special and rare. I didn't think I deserved to be there.

That December, during the orientation meetings, I found my way to Statuary Hall, where a dinner was being held for the freshmen who would be sworn in the following month. The lights were dimmed. The atmosphere was mystical. Statuary Hall served as the House Chamber before 1907, and it has the ghosts of Congresses past. There is a spot where you can whisper and hear clearly what is said on the other side of the room. Rumor has it that when John Quincy Adams was in Congress, he positioned his desk there so that he could covertly eavesdrop on conversations.

As we were finding our seats for the dinner, Speaker Nancy

Pelosi came over and introduced herself to me. *Wow.* The first woman Speaker of the House in the history of our nation.

I was a freshman congressman attracting a lot of attention. The first Muslim. The swearing-in on the Quran. Dennis Prager likening me to Osama bin Laden. Fellow congressmen setting off all kinds of fear across the country. And throughout the world, I was receiving attention: people in countries such as Egypt and Indonesia celebrated my election as a win for them, while people in other places wanted to know more about this Muslim congressman.

I didn't know how I was going to be perceived by Speaker Pelosi. Maybe she would consider me a distraction. And she certainly could have treated me like that. But instead, she embraced me.

"We want you to give the opening prayer," Speaker Pelosi said, grabbing my hand. She is a small woman—she can't weigh more than 115 pounds—but what I felt in her grip was strength and resolve. She pulled me close to her and whispered, "And you can swear in on whatever you like."

Men often do things with testosterone, macho, and ego. Women often have a more diverse approach, as Speaker Pelosi demonstrated. She has a very sure and gracious style, in addition to being determined and tough. I have always had a lot of admiration for women of achievement because I know they've had to go through a lot to get to that place. That night, I became a true Nancy Pelosi fan.

When it was time, I got up and prayed from my heart over the meal, and when I was done, Speaker Pelosi said, "See, colleagues, a new member of our democratic body—and his prayer was just like any one of us would give."

12

A Plan and a Purpose

During that first run for Congress, I spent a lot of time in the community, knocking on doors and introducing myself to people. I didn't just want to do a bunch of posters and flyers. I wanted them to know who I was and what I stood for, in person.

One Saturday I was in southwest Minneapolis, in a modest working-class neighborhood. I knocked on one door, and a guy answered. I noticed a ladder up against the house, and there appeared to be another guy on the roof.

"May I help you?" the man said, standing in the doorway.

"Hi, I'm Keith Ellison," I said. "And I'm running for Congress."

"I've heard of you," said the man, who was distracted by the man on the roof. He called out, "You need to get down from that roof! You know what happened last time. You fell, and we had to call the ambulance!"

"Well, if I don't fix this, who's going to fix it? We don't have enough money to get it fixed!" shouted the guy on the roof.

"Okay, okay," the other one said reluctantly. "Just be careful."

The man at the door told me a story about how the hospital bill had been $1,800. They didn't have the money, so they paid with their credit card. When they couldn't pay the bill, the interest rates were raised on their other credit cards.

I thought that was incredibly unfair. And I told him that working people's prosperity was the top priority in my campaign for Congress.

"I sure hope you win and do what you say," said the man.

I decided to do some homework about his problem. How prevalent was this family's situation? In fact, two-thirds of all family bankruptcies were caused by medical debt. Regular families facing bankruptcy weren't simply spending too much—they were trying to pay medical bills and had to use credit cards. Household income for the majority of Americans declined during the George W. Bush years, while the cost of living—especially fuel, education, food, and so on—went up. I learned more about how the credit card industry was taking advantage of consumers. And the folks who have the least resources or have a family emergency pay the highest rates for credit. Working families in America were anxious and overstretched with health care bills and trying to help their kids get an education. I went to Congress to fight for these folks.

I wanted to sit on a congressional committee where I could have a direct impact on the financial opportunity and security of working-class and middle-class people. A few committees address these issues: Ways and Means, Appropriations, Energy and Commerce, and Financial Services. I joined the House Financial Services Committee.

The very first bill I introduced was a ban on universal default. Remember the man with the medical debt? This situation was happening all over. If a person was late or stopped paying on one credit card, the companies who owned your other cards could change your status even if you'd never been late paying them. My logic was, if a person is paying a credit card on time and has a positive history, companies should not be able to change the fees or interest rate on that person's card just because he's having problems with a different credit card. This bill would prevent credit card companies from penalizing customers for adverse activity on a card issued by another firm.

My bill passed and was incorporated into the 2009 Credit Card Accountability, Responsibility and Disclosure (CARD) Act, also known as the Credit Card Bill of Rights—a great piece of legislation shepherded by Congresswoman Carolyn Maloney of New York. Now a credit card company can take adverse action against you only if you miss paying *that* company. If you find that you're getting higher costs on your cards for no reason, you should contact your congressperson, because it's now illegal for credit card companies to do that.

After I had been in Congress for a while, a reporter asked me who in Congress I wouldn't mind being stranded on an island with. Remembering Carolyn's generosity and the role she allowed me to play on the CARD Act, I said, "Carolyn Maloney." Next thing I knew, a volleyball with a red face painted on it arrived at my office. Carolyn had seen the piece and sent me a version of Wilson, the volleyball that Tom Hanks befriended in the movie *Cast Away*. Clever.

When I was running for Congress and still in the state legislature in 2006, the financial system hadn't collapsed yet, but the signs were there. We had a campaign within the state legislature called "Don't Borrow Trouble." We were trying to alert folks and discourage them from taking out subprime mortgages. Irresponsible lenders were pushing loans that seemed like a good deal, but in the fine print the interest rates would be raised beyond what a family could afford. These practices and high-risk activities of Wall Street financial firms resulted in the foreclosure crisis, the collapse of the housing market, and ultimately the Great Recession.

When I was campaigning in 2006, I didn't fully understand how dangerous the housing mortgage scams were to the economy. High-risk mortgage refinancing and home equity lines of credit were pushed throughout the country. A shady practice known as the yield-spread premium made it possible. Mortgage companies and banks would steer someone from a prime loan to a higher-interest subprime loan even if he or she qualified for the prime loan. Why? There was profit in pushing people into subprime loans. They also saddled these people with prepayment penalties.

Why were some lenders pushing through loans that people couldn't afford? The mortgage lenders and banks profited. They weren't keeping these loans on their books but, rather, selling them to third parties. That's called securitization. As long as the banks and lenders could sell the loans on the secondary market, they didn't care. The loans were like hot potatoes. As long as they could sell them, they would issue them. Whether a person could pay it back didn't matter to the banks because they weren't going to hold them for very long. When this financial house of cards collapsed, the banks got bailed out, and the American people paid the price.

Now, I voted for the bailout because a massive failure on Wall

Street would have had a devastating impact on Main Street, meaning working- and middle-class families. Unemployment would have spiked even higher than it did. A vicious cycle would have ensued, and we wouldn't have experienced "merely" a recession but a depression. Also, the terms of the Troubled Asset Relief Program (TARP), known as the bailout, allowed the US Treasury to purchase the troubled assets—that is, the bad mortgages. In 2008, Bush administration officials told many of us in Congress that they would simply buy the mortgages and then modify the terms to allow people to stay in their homes at a monthly payment they could afford. Of course, that is *not* what Treasury Secretary Henry Paulson did. Instead of the Treasury acquiring the illiquid, hard-to-value mortgage-backed securities as promised, he merely infused capital into banks via preferred stock in order to clean up their balance sheets. As a member of Congress who was called upon to vote yes on TARP to save the economy, and then further induced to vote yes based on the idea that the Treasury would help home owners, I felt betrayed. But as of June 2013, the TARP money has nearly been repaid, with taxpayers reimbursed $414 billion of the $457 billion committed to TARP.

These mortgage scams had a more negative impact on African American and Latino home owners, but they hurt everyone. Many banks, including Wells Fargo, which settled a $175 million lawsuit for pricing discrimination, took advantage of two communities that historically have placed a high premium on home ownership. Now many families are losing their homes and are in serious financial trouble because of it.

The financial crisis has been one of the Obama administration's top challenges since 2009. While it moved effectively to manage the financial and economic crisis, it has not done enough to hold accountable the financial companies responsible for the crisis. As of this writing, not one major banker has been successfully prosecuted for predatory lending or mortgage fraud. Families throughout America were financially ruined, and those responsible have not been held accountable. The foreclosure crisis hurt the African American and Latino middle class very hard, since most of these families hold their wealth in their houses. The US Justice Department should continue to hold accountable those responsible for such financial damage. The federal government should make it easier for home owners who are "under water"— the situation where the mortgage is higher than the value of the home—following the collapse of housing prices to refinance their mortgages and have their principal reduced. This is a better strategy because it helps people keep their homes, avoid foreclosure, and get back on track to paying their mortgages.

What happened to tenants if their landlords couldn't afford their mortgages because of subprime loans? They lost their apartments, with no recourse. In 2007 I invited Massachusetts representative Barney Frank, the chair of the House Financial Services Committee, to hold a field hearing in Minneapolis on the housing foreclosure crisis. Some folks in the audience pointed out that tenants were being hurt by the crisis too. After the hearing, I wrote and introduced a bill called the Protecting Tenants at Foreclosure Act (PTFA) of 2009, which gives a tenant ninety days to find a place to live if the landlord's property is lost due to foreclosure. I'm proud to have received the 2010 Edward W. Brooke III Housing Leadership Award from the National Low Income Housing Coalition (NLIHC) in recognition of this law.

I'm also proud of the Preserving American Homeownership Act, which I introduced with Gary Peters, a moderate Democrat from Michigan, and John Campbell, a Republican from California. This act includes a principal-reduction program that allows homes to be revalued at a more accurate price. It will cut fore-closure rates and strengthen the housing market. When the value of the home increases, the owner would share in that profit with the government.

This is a win-win proposition that resulted from a moderate Democrat, a progressive Democrat, and a Republican working together to help home owners. When members of Congress talk informally about the things happening in our individual districts, we find that we share many common issues. The Preserving American Homeownership Act—which remains a viable means for millions of Americans to realize their dream of home ownership, but has been held up from passage by a Republican majority—made a lot of sense, and we decided to work together. This is the way that Congress should function all the time, but politics sometimes trumps common sense.

We still need to do more to help home owners and support affordable rental housing. There has been a lot of discussion about reforming Fannie Mae and Freddie Mac, organizations created by Congress to maintain stability and affordability in the housing market. The Congress has not made progress on improving regulation of Fannie and Freddie. Why? Some Republicans on the House Financial Services Committee want to eliminate Fannie and Freddie altogether. These agencies have not been perfect, but they have supported the expansion of middle-class home ownership throughout America for decades. This would not have occurred if mortgages were managed entirely in the private market.

The GOP caucus itself is split. Many Republicans are reasonable and willing to work with those across the aisle for the good of the American people, but what makes the news is the acrimony. We can do better.

13

WHAT HAPPENED TO THE PARTY OF LINCOLN?

I grew up in a household with a lifelong Republican. My dad's philosophy was "Leave me alone; I can do it myself." He was an Eisenhower Republican. Ronald Reagan might not have been conservative enough for today's Republican crowd. While my dad had strong opinions on just about everything, he also didn't believe in imposing those views on others (except for his kids, of course). He believed that people should live and let live. My dad wasn't into movements and marches. He just wanted to be able to do whatever he wanted to do—especially make money. And for him, the Republican Party had some answers, but he also tended to focus more on candidate than party. He hasn't voted for a Republican since Reagan's first term, and he was quite proud to vote for Obama.

While my dad was all about self-reliance, he also understood that there was nothing wrong with an earned helping hand. He proudly benefitted from the GI Bill following World War II and was a product of public schools. But he believed those were rights, not handouts, and that stripping Social Security and other government safety nets would do more harm to society than good. He voted for Ronald Reagan in 1980 but not in 1984, because he believed that Reagan went too far in cutting and dismantling middle-class programs. He could never have gotten behind the current crop of Republican leaders and their Tea Party ideology.

Former senator and Republican presidential candidate Bob Dole noted recently how far his party has fallen into the grip of obstructionist ideology when he commented that the GOP headquarters should hang a "Closed for Repairs" sign on its door until the party can advance a positive plan for governing—besides "Government is the problem."

The GOP was founded in the 1850s to oppose the spread of slavery and promote commerce and industry. Many believe that the Civil War was about ending slavery, but it was really about preserving a unified nation. On this, Lincoln was perfectly clear when he said, "If I could save the Union without freeing any slave, I would do it; and if I could save it by freeing all the slaves, I would do it; and if I could do it by freeing some and leaving others alone, I would also do that."

Freeing slaves was initially a military strategy, not a moral imperative. Lincoln hoped that doing so would cripple the South and cost it European support. His Emancipation Proclamation of 1863 freed only the slaves in the Confederacy, leaving slaves in bondage in several Northern states. Near the end of the war, Lincoln saw a political opportunity to end slavery once and for all, and he seized the moral moment. The Thirteenth Amendment finally ended slavery everywhere in the nation in 1865.

For a few years after the Civil War, Reconstruction policies conceived by Lincoln and implemented after his death allowed freed slaves and poor whites to make economic and political progress in the former Confederate states, under the protection of federal troops. In 1870 several African Americans were elected to Congress.

But in the late 1870s and 1880s, the Republican Party suffered from compassion fatigue. It grew tired of trying to keep Reconstruction going and of fighting the Confederate remnants that still maintained an iron grip on Congress. So the Republicans stopped fighting.

The Compromise of 1877, in which Congress settled the contentious 1876 presidential race between the Republican Rutherford B. Hayes and the Democrat Samuel Tilden, awarded Hayes the presidency provided that he pull federal troops from Southern states. The original compromise was supposed to honor the rights of freed slaves, but that simply didn't happen.

Perhaps Hayes presided over the end of Reconstruction due to circumstances beyond his control, or maybe he was a weak negotiator whose heart was never in it, but civil rights took a step back under his presidency—a dubious distinction.

He was known as a strong advocate for education and social reform. But very little of that got accomplished during his time in the White House because of that compromise. He returned the South to the control of white supremacists and brutal racism. The Supreme Court, to which Hayes appointed two justices, one of whom was a Southern Republican sympathetic to the Southern cause, began striking down many of the gains won by blacks during Lincoln's presidency and Reconstruction—especially voting rights.

By 1887, there were no blacks left in Congress. The Republican

Party abandoned its justice-and-rights platform and went back to what it was all about from the beginning: Northern industrialism.

With the Tilden-Hayes Compromise came Jim Crow laws (state and local mandates that enforced segregation), Black Codes (laws passed by several Southern states to all but circumvent the Thirteenth Amendment by forcing Negroes into economic servitude), and a reign of terror for many blacks throughout the South with the spread of the Ku Klux Klan to enforce those laws and the brutal customs that went with them.

Following the war, the only blacks to serve in Congress belonged to the Republican Party. Blacks remained sympathetic to the party well into the 1950s. Just to put this into perspective, Martin Luther King Jr.'s father was a Republican. In fact, my father and his father, Zollie Crawford Ellison, probably derived their Republican affinities from this earlier era.

Franklin Delano Roosevelt, the thirty-third president of the United States, brought blacks to the Democratic Party in the 1930s and 1940s, particularly by desegregating federal employment. However, many felt that FDR's other New Deal programs didn't help them much. Those programs were designed to assist mostly white working-class and middle-class Americans during the Great Depression. Black folks—particularly those migrating to the cities in search of work—often met with poverty, despair, and racism.

That was my father's reality for most of his life, growing up in the Black Bottom of Detroit during Jim Crow. It wasn't until Presidents John F. Kennedy and Lyndon B. Johnson that the Democratic Party established a stronghold among black voters. Before them, most blacks still felt an allegiance to the Republican Party, especially in the South. My father wasn't an anomaly.

The turning point came when President Kennedy called Martin Luther King's wife, Coretta Scott King, while Rev. King was in jail. Black people had been so thoroughly ignored up to that point, the simple gesture established a bond.

While many blacks hung images of John F. Kennedy on their walls in the years following his assassination—right next to the photo of Dr. Martin Luther King Jr. JFK's civil rights legacy was more a matter of promise than product. But the promise was great and helped to signal a new direction for the country. I still draw inspiration from his June 11, 1963, speech on civil rights in which he identified the cause of civil rights as a "moral issue." Perhaps his life was cut too short to deliver, and therefore, other people, before him and after him, were left to advance justice and equality in our laws and culture.

))))➤

There must be something in the water in Minnesota, because historically, despite its seemingly homogeneous population, the state has produced some of our more radical political thinkers, and its people have put their prejudices aside to vote for them.

Among them was Hubert H. Humphrey, born over a drugstore in a tiny South Dakota town with no black residents. Yet he had a deep sense of fairness. He saw the changing tide in America and what that tide should bear.

Humphrey served as a popular mayor of Minneapolis from 1945 to 1948, and his reelection in 1947 was by the largest margin in the city's history. At that time, Minneapolis was known as the anti-Semitic capital of the country. The few people of color living there faced the same kind of discrimination seen throughout America. But Humphrey decided to make fighting discrimination part of his platform.

In 1948 he stepped to the forefront on the issue of civil rights, jumping right into the rift within his party over whether civil rights should be a states-rights issue or a national platform. In a powerful speech he delivered at the Democratic National Convention, Humphrey laid down the gauntlet and challenged his fellow Americans to do what was right.

"To those who say, my friends, that we are rushing this issue of civil rights, I say to them we are one hundred seventy-two years late!"

Humphrey and a few others, such as Senator Paul Douglas of Illinois and California congressman John Shelley, both Democrats, proposed adding to the party platform a minority plank calling for an end to school segregation and job discrimination, and for federal laws against lynching. Several delegations—all of Mississippi's and half of Alabama's—walked out of the convention. They were not happy campers.

Think about how radical this speech was in 1948. Humphrey was speaking at the convention of the party of the Ku Klux Klan. The party of Jim Crow. The party of a short-lived faction called the States' Rights Democratic Party—the Dixiecrats—which formed after this speech. The Dixiecrats put forth South Carolina governor Strom Thurmond, a virulent segregationist, as their presidential candidate to challenge incumbent Harry S. Truman and the progressive movement within the party.

The fractured Democratic Party presented Republicans with a golden opportunity to make inroads with Southern voters, but they weren't able to capitalize on it initially. The Republican Party, too, was conflicted, changing from within, while throughout the 1960s, the Democrats built a growing legacy of publicly fighting for civil rights, the working class, and women. A series of events eventually helped the Republican Party find its identity and seize control of the political landscape.

While blacks shifted in droves to the Democratic Party on the heels of Kennedy's election, some, like my dad, held out. I think he knew that political parties are vehicles for agendas. You have to drive with whichever party gets you to the destination. In the early 1960s, it still wasn't clear which party was going to carry the civil rights mantle. The Democratic Party had taken more affirmative steps toward civil rights, but even the Democrats had lingering issues.

At the 1964 Democratic Convention, the party's commitment to civil rights was put to the test when forty-seven-year-old Fannie Lou Hamer joined a racially integrated group that attended the convention and demanded to be seated as the official delegation of Mississippi. The Mississippi Freedom Democratic Party (MFDP), established in opposition to that state's all-white convention delegation, shook things up. Mrs. Hamer stood up and shocked the world. She brought the civil rights struggle in Mississippi to the attention of the entire nation during a televised session at the convention. She said, "I question America. Is this America, the land of the free and the home of the brave, where we have to sleep with our telephones off the hook because our lives be threatened daily because we want to live as decent human beings—in America?"

Fannie Lou Hamer brought the spirit of the movement to the forefront, and her frustration was fueled by a series of tragic events that redefined America in the 1960s.

On the other side, there was Barry Goldwater, the Republican candidate for president against President Johnson, claiming that civil rights laws were unconstitutional because the government shouldn't tell someone what to do with his property or business.

Property-rights fundamentalists propelled the party. On the other side sat a halting and reluctant Democratic Party, whose members believed that a full embrace of the civil rights agenda would cost them the South in the election. The Democratic ticket of Johnson-Humphrey steamrolled Goldwater on Election Day. When President Johnson signed the Voting Rights Act of 1965, he conceded that the Democrats had undoubtedly lost the South for a generation. The Republican Party was there with open arms waiting for those Southern Democrats. But the seeds of what would become the modern Republican Party were starting to break through the ground. To this day, racial resentment and free-market fundamentalism remain pillars of the Republican identity.

In 1964 the GOP was actually on the ropes. A growing distaste for harsh Southern tactics had been brewing for several years and spread across the nation. In August 1955 a fourteen-year-old black teenager named Emmett Till was brutally murdered in Mississippi for allegedly flirting with a young white woman. That December, Rosa Parks refused to give up her seat on a city bus to a white man, setting the stage for the yearlong Montgomery bus boycott.

Nineteen sixty-three was a crucial turning point in our nation's history. In June, civil rights activist Medgar Evers was gunned down in front of his home in Jackson, Mississippi, and President Kennedy identified civil rights as a moral issue. The famous March on Washington occurred in August, when King delivered his "I Have a Dream" speech. In September came the bombing of the 16th Street Baptist Church in Birmingham, Alabama, killing four little girls. And in November, President Kennedy was assassinated.

The following June, three civil rights workers, Andrew Goodman, Michael Schwerner, and James Earl Chaney—two of them white; one black—were murdered in Mississippi. In February 1965 Malcolm X was assassinated.

In April 1968, Dr. Martin Luther King Jr. was assassinated at the Lorraine Motel in Memphis, and in June presidential hopeful Bobby Kennedy was assassinated at the Ambassador Hotel in Los Angeles. Those murders were the final sparks; the powder keg exploded. There were riots from DC to Chicago; from Kansas City, Missouri, to Berkeley, California. The unrest came in waves, and there was a sense that things were out of control.

At the same time, in 1968, a growing anti–Vietnam War movement shook the nation's campuses. There was a budding women's rights movement, led by Shirley Chisholm, Bella Abzug, Betty Friedan, Fannie Lou Hamer, and Gloria Steinem, that was making itself heard. In 1969 Steinem wrote a piece for *New York* magazine entitled "After Black Power, Women's Liberation." In San Francisco, Harvey Milk was leading a movement to fight discrimination against gays and lesbians.

While the voter rolls for blacks were sparse in the South (in the early 1960s, only 1 percent of blacks voted in Alabama, and about 3 percent in Mississippi and South Carolina), the black vote in large industrial cities counted. There was John Conyers in Detroit, Charlie Rangel and Shirley Chisholm in New York, Gus Hawkins in Los Angeles (followed a couple of years later by Maxine Waters), and Parren Mitchell in Maryland.

There was a lot going on over the span of a few years.

The Democrats were both credited and blamed for these transformative changes in our politics and culture. The Republicans stepped in, stoking the fear of change among the white "silent majority" voters. Richard Nixon, seemingly resurrected from political oblivion, benefitted from a new Republican "Southern strategy" that played to white Southerners' racism to turn them away from the Democratic Party. Nixon also benefitted from Hubert Humphrey's reluctance to criticize Johnson's Vietnam policy and eked out a narrow victory in the 1968 presidential election.

Something else that few people know about informed the Republican Party.

Lewis F. Powell Jr., a corporate lawyer who sat on the boards of eleven major companies, wrote a confidential memo in 1971. His missive, sent to the director of the US Chamber of Commerce, called for corporate America to get more involved in shaping our political landscape. Before the "corporations are people" movement, there was the "Powell Memorandum," which laid the foundation for present-day politics: big-money donors and corporate interests having more influence than the electorate. Powell called for the surveillance of and elimination of "left-wing elements." He wrote of censoring textbooks and television content, and monitoring left-wing activity on college campuses. Just weeks later, President Nixon nominated Powell for the Supreme Court, which he joined in January 1972, replacing the late Hugo Black, a liberal.

Increasingly, since Powell's memorandum, our society has followed the path advocated by the proponents of a market system that subsidizes corporations and CEOs instead of working families, and that assigns the rewards of risk to corporate executives and investors and the costs of risk to wage earners and society as a whole.

We have accepted policies that have undermined organized labor, shifted tax burdens to the poor, and protected high-income interests as if these are essential outgrowths of the American ethos. Our economic policies have not accounted for the human impact of these decisions.

The strategy reflected in the Powell Memorandum shaped the modern-day Republican Party. It was the blueprint used by Ronald

Reagan, and it's the manifesto put forward by Wisconsin congressman Paul Ryan and the current crop of Republicans.

What happened to the Republican Party? It has been hijacked by folks who practice the politics of divisiveness toward people of color, immigrants, women, and the LGBT community. It has been hijacked by corporate interests, and interests that are more concerned about protecting private gain than about advancing the entire nation. The party of Lincoln was founded with the intention of preserving the Union, of keeping America together. Today's Republican Party seems to have adopted the opposite philosophy.

14

WHAT'S THE MATTER WITH CONGRESS?

When people ask me why Congress is dysfunctional, my response is that democracy is an open and messy process. Well-organized groups, interests, and parties constantly vie for power and influence over national priorities and how money gets spent. Well-organized groups within our democracy can either move an agenda forward or block action on issues. Right now, the most well-organized group in the Congress, the Republicans, is openly dedicated to blocking the agenda of President Obama and the Democrats.

The situation is made worse by how the filibuster has evolved in the US Senate, essentially giving veto power to its Republican minority. Hence, several initiatives have ground to a halt. We saw a powerful example of this recently when a minority of senators blocked progress on background checks for guns. The rest of us, who need Congress and government to work, must figure out how to get things moving forward again. The Congress is engaged in major debates about our future, such as gun safety, immigration, jobs, and the economy. We need to have the discussions and move forward.

In some ways, today's Congress is more civilized and functional than in the past. Washington politicians used to duel to the death over a mere insult. In 1804 Aaron Burr killed Alexander Hamilton in a duel, shooting him through the liver. In 1838 Congressman William Graves of Kentucky killed Jonathan Cilley of Maine on the Marlboro Road in Maryland. (Graves and Cilley couldn't actually duel within the DC city limits because Congress had banned the practice there. Apparently Congress could at least agree on proper locations for dueling.) The Graves-Cilley conflict was the last congressional duel, thankfully. Nowadays we argue a lot, but at least everyone walks away.

Many people who claim that Congress—and by extension, government—is dysfunctional are trying to imply that representative government can't work for regular people. Actually, Congress and government work well in many areas most of the time, which is something the public often takes for granted. We drink government-inspected water and eat government-inspected meat, all according to laws passed by Congress. When natural disasters hit our communities, public-sector emergency workers are there to help, and Congress appropriates money to help Americans after disasters. People commute to work on public transit, and trucks drive to market on public roads. Millions of Americans receive their Social Security checks on time. When these services don't happen perfectly, we say that this is unacceptable. But we generally don't acknowledge how many things work daily in every community across America. The narrative that government and Congress are dysfunctional ultimately erodes the confidence of citizens, and it opens the door for privatization and outsourcing. It becomes a self-fulfilling prophecy. In fact, while reform is necessary, a functioning democracy is well within the grasp of the American people. We do have work to do, and it should happen now.

Big money has a corrosive effect on our democracy. Legislation enacted into law too often reflects the priorities of the wealthiest Americans and the corporations. For example, the skewed tax code requires wage earners to pay as much as 39.6 percent but allows financiers to pay only 20 percent. There are dozens of examples of preferential treatment for the wealthy in federal legislation. Remember how Mitt Romney paid less than 14 percent in income taxes in 2010 on earnings of more than $20 million? He paid a much lower rate of income tax than the vast majority of families of modest means. This is just one small example of how the tax code benefits the richest Americans. Now, of course, there has been some notable legislation to help America's middle class, working class, and poor, particularly under the speakership of Congresswoman Nancy Pelosi and President Obama, such as the Lilly Ledbetter Fair Pay Act, the Credit Card Bill of Rights (also known as the Credit Card Accountability Act), the Dodd-Frank Wall Street Reform and Consumer Protection Act, and the Patient Protection and Affordable Care Act. Great working-people's legislation from the past includes Social Security, Medicare, Medicaid, and there's much more.

But today Congress appears stuck. In fact, the 113th Congress may go down in history as one of the least productive ever. One example illustrates the point. On May 16, 2013, the Republican majority in the House of Representatives held its thirty-seventh attempt in about two years to eliminate or weaken the Affordable

Care Act—or, as they love to call it, "Obamacare." The Democratic-led Senate and the president are working to implement health care reform and bring health insurance to millions of people. So why do the Republicans continue to try to repeal the law? Congress is mired in a strong disagreement about health care. It is fair to ask why and more importantly, what can we do about it?

America is at a crucial crossroads. Since 2000, we have seen major and significant steps forward in terms of inclusion: a black president, Muslim elected officials, openly gay senators, the power of the Latino vote. At the same time, we have seen an intensified backlash from the conservative wing of Republicans in the form of the Tea Party. Will America continue to be more inclusive, or will we stagnate?

We are witnessing a devastating increase in income inequality. For example, according to Hedrick Smith, author of *Who Stole the American Dream?*, yawning chasms separate Americans today in terms of wealth and income. According to Smith, "While the middle class stagnated, the ultra-rich (the top 0.01 percent) jumped from an annual average income of $4 million in 1979 to $24.3 million in 2006—*a 600 percent gain per family*. The super-rich (the top 1 percent) gained so much that they captured 23.4 percent of the national economic pie in 2007, more than 2½ times their share in 1979." The question may not be, Why is Congress dysfunctional? but, rather, Why doesn't Congress operate in the interest of the vast majority of Americans? Whose interest does Congress promote?

Unfortunately, the challenge before all Americans is not just the vast income and wealth inequality but also the political power that accompanies it. Princeton University researchers Larry Bartels and Martin Gilens have studied the relationship between what members of Congress do and what their constituents of different economic situations would have them do. What they found is, sadly, not surprising. It turns out that wealthier Americans are more likely to be heard and heeded than the rest of us. Citing Bartels's and Gilens's research, Jacob Hacker and Paul Pierson write in *Winner-Take-All Politics: How Washington Made the Rich Richer— and Turned Its Back on the Middle Class*, "Bartels looked at how closely aligned with voters U.S. senators were on key votes in the late 1980s and early 1990s. It turns out there is a pretty high degree of congruence between senators' positions and the opinions of their constituents . . . in the top third of the income distribution. For constituents in the middle third of the income distribution, the correspondence is much weaker, and for those in the bottom third, it is actually negative." In other words, Congress generally yields to the wealthy, is indifferent to the middle class, and actually opposes the desires of the poor. This problem of the hyperconcentration of wealth coupled with concentration of political power is the real dysfunction, not necessarily the debating and the disagreements in Congress.

The divisive attitude displayed by some in government is fueled by sensationalism in the media and nurtured by unlimited political spending by corporations and billionaires, but it can't survive without support among the voters. I firmly believe that we can work together to breathe a more generous and pragmatic spirit into our politics.

The obstacles are great, but we can move Congress, and our democracy, forward.

When my fellow Minnesota representative Michele Bachmann (who has announced her retirement at the end of her term) went on a McCarthy-esque tear against Muslims, stating that the government had been infiltrated by the Muslim Brotherhood and that citizens like me were in league with terrorist organizations, many lambasted her, including members of her own party such as Senator John McCain of Arizona and Ohio representative John Boehner, the Speaker of the House since 2011. But then she tweeted that she had received more than $1 million in donations. She was rewarded for saying outrageous things about Muslims.

During President Obama's 2009 speech on health care reform, Representative Joe Wilson of South Carolina, in a show of disrespect and lack of decorum, yelled out, "You lie!" He was initially embarrassed by his outburst and was set to apologize—until the campaign donations started pouring in. He took in more than $1 million in the days following the outburst. Some people with money supported his disrespect for the president of the United States and decided to reward his bad behavior.

When I appeared on Sean Hannity's TV show on the Fox News Channel to discuss the sequester in March 2013, he called President Obama "President Panic" and implied that the president wasn't telling the truth about the significant harm that would result from the sequester. Hannity showed a video clip with spooky music playing during the president's speech regarding the negative effects of the sequester. I took offense to the way that Hannity presented the president's words and called him a "yellow journalist."

I am not proud of how I reacted, and I wouldn't do it again. But over the next several days, a number of small donations came into my campaign because people liked the way that I had confronted Hannity.

)))➡

The media often does a great job of presenting the issues, but its focus on ratings, on breaking and running with stories, is also part of the problem. Some in the media fan the flames, giving platforms and audiences to provocateurs who strive to reinforce division rather than find truth and common ground. In some cases, the media is responsible for keeping the drama going.

For example, the birther issue, questioning whether President Obama was born in America—a nonissue, easily verified and dismissed—was allowed to persist. The media hung on every word uttered by Donald Trump and covered birther rallies. "Well, it was news, so they had to cover it," some would say. I grew up in an era when journalists knew the difference between news and propaganda. They had a responsibility to report the *truth*, not just allow any baseless inflammatory opinion to make the news.

The legitimacy of government is rooted in the consent of the people who are governed. And how do they give their consent? Through voting, through being on juries, through civic participation. But how can you truly consent if you don't have the knowledge?

We need *informed* consent.

Some media outlets are not disseminating the news but are replacing news with opinion and entertainment. Others focus on reporting about personalities and "the horse race" in politics, presenting "both sides" of any question with no effort to sort fact from falsehood. Too few focus on giving voters the information they need to make up their own minds.

During the 2012 election cycle, Republican presidential nominee Mitt Romney proposed defunding the Public Broadcasting Service (PBS). I was opposed to this proposal, as all Americans should have been. PBS provides one of the best outlets where we can get news and information that's accurate. And he wanted to get rid of it?

The existence of PBS and National Public Radio (NPR) is

crucial for having informed citizens. They provide an important alternative. Some people may not want to tune in because they're not "entertaining" enough, and the right wing claims that they have a liberal bias (I disagree). But it's necessary. Without PBS and NPR, and other fact-based outlets, we would be worse off.

The Constitution says that Congress should make no law abridging the freedom of the press. Congress also says you have a right to a lawyer if you're charged with a crime. But what do we do if people can't afford one? We give them a lawyer. If we aren't getting a free press, I believe the government should at least support public broadcasting.

When I was growing up, Walter Cronkite was the standard-bearer of news. From 1962 to 1981, he anchored the *CBS Evening News*, and when he told you something, you trusted it. You believed it. He was a journalist. And he was the epitome of fair and balanced. There was only one crack in his professional armor, which came the day he announced, "President Kennedy died at one o'clock Central Standard Time, two o'clock Eastern Standard Time, some thirty-eight minutes ago." It was the only time we caught a glimpse into what he might have been thinking or feeling about a national event. Walter Cronkite was a true newsman.

Today we have Glenn Beck and Rush Limbaugh. They highlight the issues that bring ratings, which are also the issues that divide us the most.

Some in America's economic elite support this agenda of national division. The Occupy Wall Street movement raised this issue by focusing on the vast disparities between the wealthiest 1 percent and everyone else: the 99 percent. The Occupy organizers pointed out that income inequality is the most damaging division in America today. We now have a corporate, conservative elite who remain staunchly opposed to paying their fair share. They complain about Social Security and food stamps but don't want anyone to touch their tax breaks, which cost our government and economy a huge amount of money.

The corporate elite are not held accountable for their actions. They often fund these anti–middle-class agendas. They are the ones sending jobs overseas and offshoring their assets and dodging taxes. The financial institutions that caused the Great Recession are now sitting on record cash accounts without having been prosecuted for their actions—while millions of Americans lost their homes and their nest eggs.

This point highlights another reason why the will of the voters is often not fully reflected in the actions of Congress. Too many major policy decisions are driven by special-interest money. Large corporations fund associations and groups that hire lobbyists to push their agenda. They also fund political organizations that contribute to political campaigns. The problem of money in politics has gotten worse since the 2010 *Citizens United v. Federal Election Commission* Supreme Court decision, which opened the floodgates for unreported and unaccountable corporate money to flow into advertising during campaigns.

In the current debate about the deficit, Republicans have maintained a hard line against tax increases of any kind. They protect indefensible tax breaks for oil companies, hedge fund managers, offshore cash holdings, and even corporate jets. I sit on the House Financial Services Committee, and Republican members are trying to roll back consumer protections in the Dodd-Frank financial reform legislation. We see corporate interests pushing back constantly on the enforcement of clean air and water regulations by the US Environmental Protection Agency (EPA). They strive to reduce regular citizens' ability to be heard in government, and government's ability to serve the interests of the middle class, working people, and the poor.

In some respects, a number of those in Congress function like athletes who get sponsors. You have a bunch of athletes (members of Congress), and each one is supported by sponsors (donors and supporters). Each athlete tends to attract sponsors who share his or her agenda. You don't necessarily have to win, but you have to work for the agenda. This is how the sponsors influence the debate. There are a few congresspeople who practice a pernicious version of this formula. You don't have to be great at what you do, but if you get media attention, you can get the backers you need. There is another model where members work effectively behind the scenes for their sponsors and insert special-interest language into bills as they move through the process.

The problem of big money and politics is complex and institutional. The idea of a quid pro quo is overly simplistic, and the influence of big money is much more pervasive than the idea of a single vote for a donation. In fact, this simple version isn't what happens. Large donors have more access to members, and donors support politicians who they expect will support their agenda. The late senator Paul Wellstone, who taught political science before he went to Congress, would illustrate this point with a joke:

"I'm proud to say I've never accepted a dime in contributions from the tobacco lobby!" he'd proclaim. Then he'd add, "Of course, they haven't offered any, either."

We all have to raise money, myself included. No member of the US Congress can ignore the need to generate campaign funding. It's one of the aspects of being in Congress that I dislike the most. The time I spend making fund-raising calls and attending fund-raising events is time I can't spend serving the people directly. But if I don't raise the money, I can't mount a proper campaign, and then, if I lose, I won't be able to serve my district. It's a catch-22.

I'm fortunate, however. My campaign depends on thousands of small donations. The people who support my campaign also support my vision and share in my ideas about how to make this country better. I'm for social justice and equality, labor, and building up the working class and the middle class. I'm thankful that there are plenty of people willing to donate who are for the same things.

We need genuine campaign finance reform. I support putting an upper limit on the amount of donations any member can receive from an individual. This approach could level the playing field between the richest person and someone with an average income. If the candidate agreed to certain spending limits, his or her campaign could be eligible for a government subsidy. I would like to see a specific time limit on campaigning. No campaign ads or postings before the time allotted. There should be publicly supported access to media for all viable candidates for federal office. We, as Americans, own the airwaves. Media companies could donate time during election season to make sure that the voting public can learn about the issues and the candidates.

We should return to being able to raise money from individuals—real people, not corporations. It will take a massive organizing effort to reduce the influence of big money in our politics. But we must reverse the 5–4 *Citizens United* ruling, which effectively allows unlimited corporate spending during political campaigns. And we should limit the amount that the superwealthy can give to political organizations. Unlimited political spending, much of it anonymous, inevitably skews our democratic process.

Think about it. If ExxonMobil and other pro-oil organizations support your campaign with the maximum contribution year after year, how likely is it that you're going to advocate to regulate the oil companies or reduce their tax breaks? If you're taking money from, say, casino magnate Sheldon Adelson, who funded Newt Gingrich's 2012 presidential campaign and later put his money behind Mitt Romney, is it likely that you will help regulate the gaming industry? You won't see many of the conservatives in Congress opposing *Citizens United*. Why? Because many of their pet issues benefit as a result of the law.

))))►

For the people, by the people? Of course, that's the plan. But it hasn't been working very well lately. Over time, though, we do get it right. The United States was once a slaveholding country, and then blacks were second-class citizens for another hundred years. Change took a Herculean effort in the streets, in the courts, and in politics. It's not perfect, but it's much better. I believe that we can free our politics from the excessive influence of corporate money in the same way. Regular folks can still be heard in our government, but only if we get together, work hard, and never stop organizing.

One reason why I ran for cochair of the Congressional Progressive Caucus (CPC) was to connect working Americans with members of Congress who want to partner with them. The CPC is a group of seventy-six members of Congress dedicated to the simple idea that democracy must work for working families. When I started as cochair, along with Arizona congressman Raúl Grijalva, we set out an agenda designed to advocate for the middle class, working people, and the poor. The Progressive Caucus agenda, called the Progressive Promise, is based on four simple ideas: economic justice, civil and human rights, peace at home and around the world, and environmental sustainability. We fight for Social Security, Medicare, and Medicaid. We scrutinize efforts to privatize government. We stand against racial and religious profiling, and we argue that good relations between nations is the best security. We believe that diplomacy and development are significantly underused tools to manage international relationships. The CPC is reaching out to the progressive community throughout the country to build effective partnerships with grassroots organizations. We need committed progressive leaders in the Congress who can advance legislation, and we also need a fired-up base of people who can organize on the issues. Progressive activists can focus on educating, mobilizing, and organizing. We need one another, and the CPC is on a mission—in partnership with the grassroots movement—to restore the American dream.

One thing that is interesting about the Congress (and something that most Americans don't know as they witness the public arguments between Democrats and Republicans within our governing body) is that, individually, members of Congress get along with one another. Despite passionate debates, the conflicts that play out on C-SPAN are generally not personal. In fact, the atmosphere is mostly congenial. For example, Republican congressman Sean Duffy of Wisconsin (and formerly of MTV's *The Real World* fame) and I both have a large number of new immigrants in our districts. We recently teamed up to try to streamline banking regulations that could help our constituents send money to their families abroad. Congressman Duffy is no shrinking violet and probably inspires Tea Party cheers when he's going after "job-killing regulations." But he and I work together.

There are members who have taken stands against Muslims, and yet I can still hold a conversation with them. In fact, it is essential that I maintain a relationship in which I can speak to them about anti-Muslim bigotry. Michele Bachmann is cordial when we see each other. In fact, she can be charming in person. Long Island congressman Peter King and I are friendly when we see each other in the halls of Congress even though he has advocated spying on Muslim congregations in our country. I have taken the time to explain to him why this is against our national values and alienates law-abiding American citizens.

I strongly disagree with Representative Steve King from Iowa's Fifth District, who is virulently against immigration reform. But we get along fine. When I exercise in the congressional gym early in the morning, I often run into Paul Ryan and his crew doing P90X. We all get along in person: Republicans and Democrats, liberals and conservatives.

At the end of the day, Congress will be fixed by We the People, and people all over America are striking out to demand a share of prosperity and a responsive government. People all across the country are demanding a fair economy, election reform, and even media accountability. Low-wage workers are on the move, and they are not waiting on Congress but are taking back their country and their democratic rights.

In the spring of 2013, low-wage and fast-food workers showed that despite logjams in Congress, people can still organize and improve their lives. These workers would benefit from Congress raising the minimum wage, but they aren't waiting for Congress to act. They are organizing as few people could have imagined. I am impressed with the attitude of the fast-food workers who are striking in cities all across the country. First it was in New York City on April 4, 2013, followed by Chicago, Milwaukee, St. Louis, and Detroit, where employers brought in replacement workers who immediately went on strike as well. It's exciting because these workers, who are of all colors, all cultures, and all faiths, are united by the desire to earn a livable wage. These workers prepare the meals we eat every day all over America, and they do it for as little as $7.25, or even $4.25, an hour. When they go on strike, they are risking everything because they need these jobs, low paying as they are. But they also need a future for their families, and they are demanding better pay.

These workers know that the corporations they work for are making ample profits, and the executives atop these fast-food companies are paid exorbitantly. All they want is a fair share.

So what's the matter with Congress? Nothing that wide-awake and active Americans can't fix.

15

HOT DISH: A NEW AMERICA

If the 2008 and 2012 elections showed us anything, they demonstrated that America's demographics are changing and influencing our politics. No longer is race simply a matter of black and white. We have large voting blocs of Hispanics, Asians, young people, and the lesbian, gay, bisexual, and transgender community. For too long, we talked about the black vote or the white vote, but America is a more diverse melting pot than ever before. Over the next decade, several states will become majority minority—meaning more black and brown than white. But that will mean nothing without empowerment. South Africa had a majority minority population during apartheid. With the push for voter suppression, particularly in brown and black districts, we must struggle to stop efforts to disenfranchise these growing demographics.

I'm excited by the diversity within America. I love seeing new people emerge on the political landscape: folks from India, Cuba, people who are Muslim and Sikh, people who are openly gay. Because that means America has truly matured into a nation for the people and by the people. A nation where people are elected for their character, not the color of their skin, their sexual orientation, or their creed.

I come from a state where this philosophy is the norm. My congressional district is 75 percent white. I am the first person of color—any color other than white—to represent the Fifth District. But the people sent me to Congress because we share the same values and vision.

In Minnesota, we have a favorite food called hot dish, which is almost a rite of passage. I got my first taste in 1987. I had just started law school, and one of my student buddies invited me over for dinner. It was a potluck sort of thing, and everyone brought a dish.

Someone brought hot dish. It's a casserole with a mushroom soup base, to which you add either tuna or chicken. There's usually some kind of noodle or Minnesota wild rice, and it's always topped with corn flakes or Tater Tots. Hot dish's seasoning and ingredients are often determined by the cook's culture. The basic concept is universal.

Many people call the United States a great melting pot. What we have is not a melting of cultures and languages, races and creeds, but, rather, a hot dish of differences that, when brought together, can make something truly delicious and fulfilling—when it works.

And for the most part, our hot dish does work, although there are entrenched differences in cultural norms that will persist. For instance, I get Muslims who come up to me and ask, "Brother Keith, how can you be in favor of gay marriage?"

I'm in favor of civil rights for all. I'm in favor of freedom. I believe that Americans have every right to expect that their government will treat them fairly and equally.

16

My Faith

When my daughter was eleven, she decided that she wanted to wear the hijab and dress in traditional Muslim clothing. At the time, she was hanging with a group of girls who were wearing traditional clothing, and she wanted to wear it too. I never discouraged her, nor did I encourage her. While she certainly was a practicing Muslim girl, I knew that she was wearing the hijab more to fit in socially than as some expression of her faith.

Three years later, she started high school, where only a few girls wore traditional Muslim clothing, and guess what? She stopped wearing it. I never made a big deal about it either way. I don't think that wearing the hijab makes anyone more pious. I think telling the truth makes you pious. I think that being charitable, merciful, generous, and standing up for the rights of the powerless makes you pious. But wearing something on the outside is just that for me: show.

For me, faith is a personal connection with the divine. However you express that is your choice. I don't believe in judging how people choose to worship or if they choose to worship.

If I were Jewish, I would probably be a reform Jew. If I were Christian, I would be one of those come-as-you-are nondenominational Christians. Faith is not about my expressing what I believe so that the world can see that I'm faithful. I don't believe in following a strict set of rules to prove my love for God or to prove my faith.

The tenets that I follow within Islam, I do to please God, not man. There are basic things you must do to follow Islam. You must first declare that there is no god but God. You need to fast during Ramadan. You should go on the hajj—if you can afford to. And you should pray five times a day.

If you are putting love into the world and you're fulfilling the basic requirements of the faith, you're fine. I doubt that wearing a particular style of clothing, facial hair, or symbol brings you any closer to God. However, it does identify you as a member of a particular group, and maybe that's what some people are looking for. Much of what is commonly associated with Islam is, in fact, a cultural expression.

I've been to Saudi Arabia several times. It is one of the most traditional of the Muslim nations. There are religious rules, or fatwa, on everything from banning women from driving, to upholding traditional women's clothing, to banning unmarried men and women from working together.

I had a friend from Egypt who had come to the United States and become a leader in our community. Not long after moving to Saudi Arabia with his wife and kids, he died in a car accident.

Under Saudi law, his wife could not settle his affairs. When I asked her about it, she told me that she had to wait for her son to turn eighteen to sign the necessary documents to settle her husband's estate. Their son was a teenager at the time, so she would have to wait a few years.

"They won't let me sign because I'm a woman," she told me.

That "law" has no religious relevance. Actually, the notion that women should be second-class citizens is antithetical to the teachings and life of Muhammad. In fact, if you study the Prophet's life, you will find that women were prominent and dominant figures.

When Muhammad first received a revelation from God through the angel Jibril, or Gabriel, he was very shaken. He went home and sought the comfort of someone who loved him: his wife, Khadija. She was a wealthy woman who owned caravans that would travel to Syria to buy and sell goods. Muhammad worked for her, and she saw him as a trustworthy young man. He made a lot of money for her, and she suggested that they get married. He was twenty-five at the time. She was forty.

Khadija was one of Muhammad's closest confidants. And while polygamy was more the norm, she was his only wife until her death at the age of sixty-four. She was there when God called the Prophet. And he went to her to help him sort out whether the message he had received was indeed from God.

Khadija went to her cousin, Waraqah Ibn Nawfal, a Christian, for answers. She said, "Muhammad received this message, and he's not sure if it's from God." Her cousin confirmed that Muhammad was receiving divine revelation. Khadija was very important during this transitional period in Muhammad's life. Women in Islam are functioning, operating players in the story of Islam. Khadija, the first convert to Islam, was a primary advisor to Muhammad. And it was Aisha, one of the wives Muhammad married after Khadija died, who played a major role in revealing and spreading his teachings.

Islam teaches that men and women are *equal* before God. So why do we have these draconian laws subjugating women in some Islamic nations? Because people confuse faith with custom, laws, and politics.

))⯈

Without any doubt, there are people who claim to follow Islam who want to hurt America and Americans. That's not a matter of dispute.

Osama bin Laden's stated reason for attacking the United States was that America had set up camp on Arabian soil. He claimed he wanted to get this Christian country off Islamic land. That was his justification. His battle wasn't inspired or supported by the Quran.

Those who attacked the United States on September 11, 2001, were also not acting based on their faith. They were not following the teachings of Muhammad. I don't care what they said. Shouting "*Allah akbar*" ("God is great") does not sanction criminal terroristic behavior. Just yelling God's name does not make one righteous or the representative of others' faith.

There are people who blow up women's health centers and kill doctors who work there, and they say they're doing so because of their Christian beliefs. But nowhere in the Bible does Jesus ever say that's acceptable.

Somehow we understand that Timothy McVeigh, who blew up the Alfred P. Murrah Federal Building in Oklahoma City in 1995, might have identified himself as a Christian, but his actions are not an indictment of all Christians or Christianity. But with Islam, an action committed by a Muslim in the name of Islam becomes an indictment of the entire religion and those who follow it.

Faisal Shahzad, the naturalized American citizen from Pakistan who intended to set off a van full of explosives in New York's Times Square in 2010, wasn't acting according to faith. That was an act of terrorism; he was acting based on a political ideology. The Quran does not sanction what he was doing.

When US Army psychiatrist Major Nidal Malik Hasan went on a rampage at Fort Hood, Texas, and killed thirteen people in 2009, my first impulse was horror and sadness for the victims and their families. My second impulse was that there would be a backlash against innocent Muslims.

Nothing in the Quran says a Muslim should hurt people who are not Muslim.

The Quran is not a history book. It doesn't read chronologically. It doesn't tell a story in the same way that the Bible is full of stories. It's more a collection of God's words to Jabril, who then repeated them to Muhammad.

Muhammad was very careful to distinguish what God said from what Muhammad himself said. Because Muslims believe that the Quran is from God, it is sometimes used to justify unjustifiable actions, just like the Bible is. We've seen this occur throughout history: from the Crusades, to the Reconquista, to the Salem witch trials, and to the present. People have used their religion to persecute, murder, and commit genocide. But to label an entire religion as responsible is wrong.

The Quran says to fight against those who fight against you. But it also says that you should be inclined toward peace because Allah likes peace. So the notion that Islam is a radical, violent religion doesn't hold water. Violence is not preached in the Quran. And violence was never the nature of Muhammad.

))))➤

I sat before the House Homeland Security Committee at the hearing commissioned by Congressman Peter King. The room was packed. Representative King had convened the hearing to discuss what he called the radicalization of Muslim extremists in America. The debate was sparked over the building of a mosque near Ground Zero in New York City, and it picked at a scab that was still healing, and played into the backlash against Muslims and Islam in our nation since 9/11.

It was the ten-year anniversary of 9/11, and I had had enough. I'd had enough of hearing the stories of discrimination against American citizens because of their Islamic faith. I'd had enough of labeling and branding people who choose to follow and serve Allah. And I'd had enough of Americans not being treated as Americans simply because of their ethnicity or faith.

I had been making the media rounds, talking about McCarthyism and drawing parallels to the internment of Japanese Americans during World War II. I called on people to stand against these hearings.

I believed, and I still believe, that this great nation of ours and the people in it can rise above prejudice and stereotypes. I approached Representative King to appeal to his conscience. I talked to him about the hearings and asked him to cancel them. He refused but said that he would allow me to testify.

My testimony addressed several points, including the issues of racial profiling. I talked about the importance of building partnerships between the Muslim community and law enforcement, with an example from my hometown of Minneapolis. At the end of my testimony, as I recounted one of the stories I had been told over the past few years, I became overwhelmed with emotion. The story

I shared that day was of Mohammad Salman Hamdani. I started talking about how this twenty-three-year-old man had so much hope and promise in this country. I talked about how Mohammad, like my son and so many of our sons, loved *Star Wars* and played football—American football. Mohammad was from Pakistan, a country where soccer dominates. But Mohammad played on the offensive line for his high school football team in Queens, wearing number 79. Like so many young Americans, Mohammad wanted to pursue his passions. And he was working toward his dream.

Mohammad Salman Hamdani wanted to be a cop. He was working part time as an EMT worker and was a first responder for the New York Police Department. And he was there on 9/11. As people were running for their lives, he ran into the building to save lives. Mohammad was a real American hero.

But the *New York Post* labeled him a terrorist. Why? Because his name was Mohammad? Because he hailed from Pakistan? Without checking its facts or asking just a few questions, the paper jumped to a conclusion and besmirched the life of a young man who should have been praised and lauded, not vilified.

I spoke with Mohammad's mom on the days leading up to the King hearings. She talked about the hurt and the pain she'd endured as she had to bury her son and shield her family and his memory from the terrorist label that some irresponsible news outlet slapped on him. She was forced to mourn twice for her son.

I carried that pain with me to the microphone that day, and it lodged in my throat as I attempted to put a human face, a human experience, to the thousands of devastating stories I had been told.

To have Mohammad Salman Hamdani turned into a terrorist and his family harassed and interrogated was wrong.

Unfortunately, the Hamdani experience isn't unique. Across the country in the aftermath of 9/11, hundreds of Americans—

Muslims and those who just "look Muslim"—were assaulted, examined, detained, interrogated, and labeled simply because of their faith. And I thought about them all, and how, for these Americans, their life, liberty, and pursuit of happiness were being stripped away and sullied by ignorance and bigotry.

My throat began to tighten, and I started choking up as I spoke. Then I felt the tears. It was as if my body just opened a floodgate of emotion, and I had no control. I was actually embarrassed by my emotional display. But no matter how hard I tried, I couldn't stop. I didn't want to stop speaking. I knew if I stopped and tried to collect myself, that would add to the drama that was clearly unfolding. So I soldiered through. I just kept talking until I got to the last words:

"Mohammad Salman Hamdani was a fellow American who gave his life for other Americans. His life should not be identified as just a member of an ethnic group or just a member of a religion, but as an American who gave everything for his fellow Americans."

Afterward, some people praised me for showing my emotions like that. I didn't *show* anything. They surfaced on their own. You don't circulate your own blood. Your body just does that. Sometimes your emotions are the same way. In that situation, it kind of bubbled up. That was the only way I could describe it.

As I reflect on why I choked up, I can say that it was an accumulation of sadness from hearing so many stories like Mohammad's and knowing that no American should be treated like that. The anti-Muslim hysteria was getting worse, and I feared that there would be a point when we couldn't turn back. I wanted to let America know that we could, that we *must*, do better.

I couldn't believe that we were having what amounted to a "witch hunt" hearing in this day and time. Hadn't we learned anything from our history? Hadn't we grown up enough to be able to finally embrace all Americans, no matter their color or creed? I was dismayed that Peter King would hold hearings targeting a particular religious group and feed into the nonsense. Islam didn't attack the United States on 9/11. Some crazy extremists who happened to claim Islam as their religion attacked America. Islam didn't attack America, just as Christianity didn't attack America when Timothy McVeigh killed 168 men, women, and children six years earlier.

Can you imagine a hearing on "Christian radicalization" or "Jewish radicalization" in America? It's unthinkable. But it's okay to target Muslims? I told Representative King, "If you're going to have such a hearing, you must include every religious group." He didn't agree.

Following the hearings, I didn't anticipate the kind of attention I received. I mean, my first run for Congress in 2006 had brought quite a bit of unexpected attention, but this was different. I was now being held up as a spokesperson for the Islamic faith, and I was not comfortable with that. Not at all. My faith was rarely something I wore publicly. I've never led a Friday congregational prayer in my entire life. I've never delivered a Friday sermon. I've never even given religious advice. I rarely pray in public. I'm not that guy.

I don't see myself as a religious leader. I practice my faith the way that millions of other Americans practice their faith: personally. The relationship between me and God is just that: between me and God. So I never wanted to be put in a position of being seen as some sort of Islamic leader.

I *am*, however, a secular leader.

I ran for Congress to improve the everyday lives of people in my district and my country, not to be a spokesperson for a particular faith. But I do understand that, as the first Muslim ever elected to Congress, I would be asked to step outside my comfort zone a bit more than I wanted. And that hearing was one of those times.

))))➤

My first year in office, I traveled widely throughout the country. Often Muslim people would tell me personal stories about the bias they'd faced. They would tell me about their daughter having her hijab pulled off and being called a towel head or a sand nigger. There were countless stories of Muslims being pulled off planes simply because they fit a description or because of their name.

There were positive stories, too. But many more were of personal pain, of people being insulted and in some cases persecuted.

Someone told me of tensions at work; of having coworkers say, "Hey, you're not going to blow up the place, are you?" These were hurtful experiences that Muslims were having just living their everyday lives.

In addition, the attacks on mosques and groups wanting to open a mosque were getting out of hand. Imagine a group enduring backlash for opening a Jewish temple or a Baptist church. No one would picket or protest.

But all of that comes to Muslims in America.

During my run for a third term in 2012, I faced an opponent, Gary Boisclair, who described himself as a Democrat–Tea Party candidate. He ran an ad that was not just offensive but borderline libelous. In it, he referred to my decision to swear in on the Quran for my ceremonial swearing-in.

"The Quran says Christians and Jews are infidels," he said.

He then added that according to the Quran, "Christians are blasphemers and should have their hands and feet cut off and . . . be crucified and killed."

Boisclair ended the ad by saying, "Do you really want someone representing you who swears his oath on a Quran, a book that undermines our Constitution and says you should be killed? I'm Gary Boisclair, and I approve this message."

This kind of rhetoric demeans our politics and our entire community. In fact, the overwhelming majority of people in my congressional district completely rejected this rhetoric. Boisclair was completely outside of the values of Minnesotans.

I was disappointed when my colleague Michele Bachmann played on people's irrational fears regarding Muslims. She, along with four other House Republicans, attacked former Secretary of State Hillary Clinton's aide Huma Abedin (who also happens to be the wife of former New York congressman Anthony Weiner) as being a Muslim operative.

I asked her to provide evidence for her allegations, and she responded with a sixteen-page letter that merely regurgitated her accusations and continued to attempt to divide Americans with totally unfounded allegations.

While some Americans were taking this opportunity to ostracize other citizens, the vast majority of people in this country understood that in that moment, we needed to stand together. There were plenty of Christians, Buddhists, Sikhs, and Jews who came forward and said, "We're not going to let this turn into some anti-Muslim thing."

President George Bush got up and spoke some healing words. My memory of the early period after 9/11 is of Americans coming together. The phrase "United we stand" was popular then, emblazoned on T-shirts, hats, flags, and signs in storefronts and in the windows of homes.

It felt like the country, as a whole, meant it.

President Bush visited a mosque during those days following

the attack. Ironically, President Obama has not been to a mosque in the United States during his presidency. I have invited him, and I think he's made a mistake by never going. If he felt that he would receive negative commentary for visiting a mosque, he needed to ask himself this question: Were those people who would hold it against him—the same people who question his birth certificate and who already think he's a Muslim—going to vote for him anyway?

He will never win that vote. He never had it and never will. Rather than appease people who despise him, President Obama should show support for those who support him. Or he should demonstrate to the nation that millions of Muslim Americans are embraced in the American family.

In the immediate aftermath of 9/11, most Americans were supportive and understood that American Muslims are American and didn't have anything to do with bin Laden and Al Qaeda. The nasty attitudes didn't appear until later.

Over the next few years, the FBI questioned eighty-nine thousand young Muslim immigrant men in this country. Agents would pull the list of all men who'd emigrated from the Middle East, go down that list, and pay them a visit.

People were calling me, petrified. People were being deported based on frivolous findings and trumped-up charges. The agents were asking questions that wouldn't sniff out a terrorist. Remember, those terrorists who attacked the country on 9/11 were doing their best to "fit in." They were hanging out in nightclubs, and dressing and living as the average American would live.

I had a friend who emigrated from Sudan. He received a visit from the FBI, and he remembers being asked how often he attended the mosque. He was asked what the imam said during his sermon and how often he prayed. What does this have to do with his immigration status?

Law enforcement officials confused devoutness with radicalization. Actually, the more devout someone is, the more that person would tend to trust God and be more peaceful. A devout Muslim believes that God will handle all.

The targeting of Muslim American citizens seems like the treatment of Japanese Americans during World War II. Now everyone believes that our treatment of Japanese Americans at that time was wrong. Despite this comparison, there is still way too much Muslim bashing. Bloggers such as Pam Geller and Robert Spencer, and "consultants" like Steve Emerson and Frank Gaffney—there's a whole gaggle of operators who have made a lucrative cottage industry around stirring up fear and hatred toward Muslims.

It is un-American to single out or persecute any American because of his or her faith.

I am a congressman who is Muslim. I am also black. I also happen to be from Detroit. I also happen to be a father of four.

I don't want to have to defend or support anything just because I happen to be Muslim. We shouldn't ask adherents of any faith to do so. I love America, and I love my God, and those two things are not opposed. In fact, my love of my God allows me to see all human beings as worthy.

In 1799 the American statesman Patrick Henry made a public speech on the heels of a debate over states' rights versus the rule of law. It was a debate similar to the ones we are having today over who shall have power in this nation. It was a debate over whether this new nation would come together and be strong or whether we'd fight one another and destroy ourselves from within.

I believe we are at a similar crossroads. At the crux of this debate are issues that some of the founding fathers believed could threaten our republic over time: race, religion, and political ideology. Their foresight is why the founding documents are so brilliant, allowing our country to evolve and mature.

I'm reminded of Patrick Henry's words from that day in March, when he denounced both the Kentucky Resolution and the Virginia Resolution:

"Let us trust God, and our better judgment to set us right hereafter. United we stand, divided we fall. Let us not split into factions which must destroy that union upon which our existence hangs."

Patrick Henry never delivered another speech. In fact, he collapsed after uttering those words and died a few months later. But the sentiment resonates today.

I believe in those words, and I believe that America will see her best days ahead of her.

17

HAJJ

In December 2008 I traveled from my hometown of Minneapolis to Medina, Saudi Arabia. It was the fulfillment of a dream. In 1982, when I took the *shahada*, declaring my faith, the one thing I knew I had to do was attend the hajj. Twenty-six years later, I was going.

As I stepped out of the car and walked into the Minneapolis–Saint Paul International Airport, I was struck by what this trip really meant. This was going to be life changing—a pivotal moment. I expected transformation and transcendence, which is what the pilgrimage is about. There would be about three million other Muslims there, doing the same thing. I couldn't imagine it, nor could I wait to experience it.

I wanted to see firsthand what Malcolm X wrote in his autobiography: "During the past eleven days here in the Muslim world,

I have eaten from the same plate, drunk from the same glass, and slept on the same rug—while praying to the same God—with fellow Muslims, whose eyes were the bluest of blue, whose hair was the blondest of blond, and whose skin was the whitest of white. And in the words and in the deeds of the white Muslims, I felt the same sincerity that I felt among the black African Muslims of Nigeria, Sudan, and Ghana."

I didn't think I would have the epiphany that Malcolm X experienced in regard to race. My experiences have allowed me to see all races as one. But with the sheer numbers of fellow pilgrims, I expected to be overwhelmed.

The first destination on my hajj journey was Medina, the second holiest city in Islam. Originally, Medina was known as Yathrib, but when the tribes occupying the city invited Muhammad to lead them, the name changed to Madinat al-Nabi, or "City of the Prophet." Medina is where Prophet Muhammad is entombed, and where the companions of Prophet Muhammad are buried in a cemetery known as Jannatul Baqi, which means "garden of heaven." I walked around the historic cemetery, and reflected on my life and my death. Nothing like a cemetery to consider finality and judgment. Medina is also the site of the first mosques in Islam. I sat for hours in Masjid al-Nabawi. My favorite spot was on the roof. I loved being up there in the early morning, around the time of the first prayer of the day, known as *Fajr*. It was calm and serene. I felt *presence*. I prayed, read, and sat up there as I contemplated purpose and meaning. I even slept sometimes. I thought about myself as a public servant, as a parent, and as a creature of the divine. It was moving, and I still remember it well. I read passages in the Quran, and I read a biography of Prophet Muhammad entitled *The Sealed Nectar* by Sheikh Safi-ur-Rahman al-Mubarkpuri. I read other things too. My time in Medina was the most relaxing moment of my adult life. I was so relaxed that my regular clothes started to feel confining. So I put on a *thobe*, which is a long gown commonly worn by men in the Middle East. I stood out less too, since most everyone was wearing one. A friend of mine, Minu, gave me a Bangladesh-style one, which was more colorful with a shorter top.

While in Medina, I also connected with my friend Asad and other pilgrims from Minnesota. By the time we were ready to travel to Mecca, I had grown attached to my days of reflection in Medina. I didn't want to leave, but it was time to perform hajj.

The path of the hajj is the bridge that connects to the life of Abraham, the father of monotheism. It is a series of rituals commemorating and reenacting the history of our faith, starting with Abraham. It involves his discovery of the Oneness of God, through reason and faith, but it touches on the lives of his wife and son, Hajar and Ishmael.

The pilgrim walks the same steps that Abraham took to monotheism. For those who believe in God—however we get there—*that* should be the prevailing mind-set. My experience while on the hajj reminded me of how much we have in common with one another on a human level, and it allowed me to reach across cultures, lands, and ideologies to make true human connections.

Part of the ritual is to wear two sheets, as you would at death. Women wear white and don't cover their faces. There are no burkas worn on the hajj. Then everyone circumambulates the Kaaba, a sanctuary at the center of the Sacred Mosque, which, according to tradition, was rebuilt by Abraham himself. We circle it seven times. Seven, in the spiritual sense, represents the infinite; therefore, walking around the Kaaba seven times is a symbolic representation that we are infinitely revolving around the One, the focus of our lives.

The sheer number and diversity of people doing this all at the same time was unnerving. I can't quite describe the feeling. It was both exhilarating and inspiring.

The next ritual is *Sa'ee*, which symbolizes the story of Hagar, one of Abraham's wives. This is where Abraham walks Hagar out to the desert and leaves her there with their baby, Ishmael. While in the desert, Hagar runs from mound to mound seeking help. All the while, she is praying, "Where is my help?" When she thinks that she and her baby will die, a well springs up at Ishmael's feet: the well of Zamzam.

The pilgrims reenact the search for water, and then we all drink from the well of Zamzam. This ritual especially touched me because it celebrates the spiritual truth that when you are put to the test, your strength and salvation can come only from God.

As I was walking between the mounds, I thought of a story that Martin Luther King Jr. once shared. It was at the beginning of the civil rights movement, and his life had already been threatened on numerous occasions. One night he received a phone call, and the person on the other end told him that if he didn't stop what he was doing, they would burn down his house and kill his wife and children. He said he had a hard time shaking this particular threat. Among the many, it struck a nerve in him, and he couldn't let it go. King realized he was completely alone and that there was no one who could help him. He said he prayed and received an answer: "Martin Luther, stand up for righteousness, stand up for justice, stand up for truth, and I will be with you."

I related to this very much. During my run for Congress, I was subject to personal attacks. While not physical, they were hurtful and damaging to me. I read a lot of King's writings during this time. I listened to his speeches. And through his words and commitment, I was able to put what I was going through—which was nothing compared with his trials—into perspective.

And that one story about how he turned to God and received an answer was poignant as I walked the path and drank from the well of Zamzam.

After my hajj, I returned to the king's residence, which was not where he actually lived but where he received guests. There was a reception for sixty to seventy dignitaries from all over the world—from Indonesia to Iran, Palestine to Pakistan, China to Chad. The North Carolina state legislator Larry Shaw was also there.

I was sitting on a prayer rug in a room full of dignitaries, and across from me was a member of the Iranian parliament. We were drinking cardamom tea. I introduced myself and said, "May Allah accept your hajj." He nodded and said something similar. The conversation was short and respectful. He seemed interested in my point of view. I felt that after thirty years of no dialogue between Iran and the United States, we needed a vehicle for communication, and I expressed that to him. He agreed. There was never any follow-up, but I remain convinced that dialogue is an indispensable part of a working relationship. It is odd that in the minds of some, dialogue has been construed as acquiescence or agreement. It's not. It's an exchange of views. That's it. But it reduces the likelihood of mistakes and misunderstanding. How can that be bad?

There is tremendous tension between the United States and Iran. At the time, no member of the US Congress had been to Iran since 1979, when a mob of Muslim students, angry over America's longtime support of its deposed shah, stormed the US Embassy in Tehran and took five dozen Americans hostage. I also knew that no member of the Iranian parliament had been to America. And there were no meetings at a neutral site during that time. But here I was talking with an Iranian member of parliament, discussing the conflicts between our nations and ways in which we could come together to talk. And while I remain steadfast in my belief that no nation, including Iran, should seek to acquire nuclear weapons, and that nations that have them should reduce them, I was able to express it without acrimony or discord. In reality, of course, neither of us was in a position to change the climate in our respective countries. But for that half hour, I knew it was possible. All I know is that we need to have more dialogue and less inflammatory rhetoric.

Iran is an ancient civilization with a strong cultural orientation toward innovation and cultural refinement. Persian culture gave us the thirteenth-century poet Jalāl ad-Dīn ar-Rūmī, the algorithm, and the first codified declaration of human rights, by King Cyrus the Great. The successor to the shah, Ayatollah Khomeini, and his religious state are a relatively recent development, emerging from fundamentalist thinking—born partially of the current leaders' resentment of the civilization's history of domination by the west. The current leaders also believe that their version of religious understanding should be the basis for governing Iran. But it is important to bear in mind Iran's roots in rationality. Of course, some of the powerful people leading Iran today do not want dialogue with the West. If that dialogue developed, their population might be more open to interacting with the rest of the world. We should continue trying to engage Iran and the Iranian people, and signal our respect for its culture and the intelligence of its people by distinguishing between the population and the government. Aggression on our part feeds the Iranian government's narrative that the West is out to dominate Iran. It also justifies, in the eyes of the Iranian regime, its repression of dissidents.

I was one of only eleven members of the House who voted against HR 1905, a bill that would have prohibited government employees from contacting anyone associated with the Iranian government. Some members of the Jewish community in my congressional district expressed concern that my vote might indicate a lessened commitment to the United States' alliance with Israel. My response then and now is that more diplomacy is exactly what we need to ensure the security of all concerned in the region, including Israel.

This bill was combined with economic sanctions against Iran. I have my doubts about whether sanctions work. The extreme elements that control countries like Iran are not short on resources and are concerned predominantly with maintaining an ironclad grip on power. Our sanctions only increase their power by weakening the country's middle class and moderate elements. Bill HR 1905 gave more power to the extreme elements, while restricting diplomacy.

Sanctions can play a role in transforming a government, but without a robust diplomatic engagement, I don't believe they work effectively. In South Africa, they worked because there was an active movement opposing the government there. There was broad international consensus. But they didn't work in Iraq because there was no serious transformative movement inside the country, and there was no real "exit" for the Hussein regime. Under apartheid, the South African government knew that if it relented on its segregation policy, the world would back off. It did, culminating in the release of Nelson Mandela, and then the world welcomed South Africa back to a role among nations. There has to be a realistic path out of sanctions. If the United States asserts that regime change is the only acceptable outcome, then we should not be surprised if there isn't cooperation. America wants to prevent Iran from weaponizing nuclear technology; Iran wants access to banking channels, medical technology, and ultimately, normalization. There is plenty of room for dialogue, and I support efforts toward dialogue and a diplomatic solution. The real change in Iran will happen from within, not from without. We have implemented sanctions against Cuba for more than fifty years, and our efforts have not brought that country closer to becoming a free democratic society.

Throughout history, those who want perpetual conflict over land and resources have painted their goals as serving some exclusive religious or ethnic groups. Religious and ethnic passions can fan the flames of a conflict in which extreme minorities have become invested. What is the terrorist organization Hamas without the Palestinian conflict? We should not accept definitions of conflict that are framed by the most extreme points of view.

When I was appointed to the House Committee on Foreign Relations in early 2009, I had an opportunity to visit Gaza, a strip of land twenty-five miles long and a few miles wide, which is home to 1.7 million Palestinian people. In 2007 Hamas had seized control of the district from the Palestinian Authority and began launching rockets into Israel. In December 2008, Israel responded by invading Gaza. When I was considering making the trip, a member of the US Department of State told me that I was foolhardy.

My planned trip was stalled because I had no way to get there; I couldn't get any help from the State Department. But Andrew Whitley, director of the New York Office of the United Nations Relief and Works Agency for Palestine Refugees in the Near East (UNRWA), told me that he would host me. This conversation took place as the war in Gaza was raging. It was after the November 2008 election but before President Obama took office.

I arrived in Gaza in February, during the Israeli blockade that permitted only limited supplies to enter the district. I was accompanied by former representative Brian Baird from Washington State. I was making a presentation at a conference in Doha, Qatar. The plan was to go from Doha to Amman, Jordan, where we would meet with UNRWA representatives. We then drove from Amman to Jerusalem. As I passed over the Allenby Bridge, which connects the West Bank and Jordan over the Jordan River, I thought about the old African American spiritual "Michael, Row Your Boat Ashore":

Jordan's river is deep and wide
Meet my mother on the other side
Jordan's river is chilly and cold
Chills the body, but not the soul

Crossing the Jordan, I noticed how small it was. I was expecting a wider river. When I asked my guides why the river was so narrow, they said it was because the Israelis dam it to preserve water for themselves. This is one of many ongoing conflicts in the Middle East. Every land conflict is accompanied by an access-to-water conflict.

In Jerusalem, we met with Christian Palestinians and discussed the Gaza situation. We were told about the difficulty of getting people out of the district for medical treatment. Then we went to Augusta Victoria Hospital, a Lutheran-run hospital for Palestinians. We learned how hard it was to get people past the checkpoints. In Israel, if you're a Palestinian doctor, it may take a couple of hours to get to a patient.

On this trip, we also visited Sderot, an Israeli town that frequently falls victim to rocket fire from Hamas. I saw playgrounds with bomb shelters nearby and spoke to people about the impact of the constant conflict on families and children. I was struck by the common themes of the stories of children growing up in a war zone—for both Palestinian and Israeli children.

Then we arrived in Gaza. We went through the Erez Crossing. I was amazed by how little time it took for us to get through. They processed us, and we entered quickly compared with the European aid workers who were waiting for hours. Once in, it looked like a war zone—worse than I had seen in Afghanistan. UNRWA personnel picked us up and drove down a dusty road where we saw infrastructure damaged in previous wars and the vestiges of new wars with damaged *new* infrastructure. We were moved by the suffering we observed among the children of Gaza, both as a direct result of war and the shortages of food and medical supplies resulting from the Israeli blockade.

During this trip, I developed my opposition to the blockades by Israel, because I saw their impact on the daily lives of regular Palestinians. The blockade only reinforced Hamas's grip on power in Gaza. The only way to get many essential supplies to Gaza was through tunnels dug under Gaza's border with Egypt. Gangsters, who supplied money to Hamas, controlled the tunnels. Through them, Hamas controlled much of the economic life of the district. Seeing that firsthand gave me the information to ask then Secretary of State Hillary Clinton about our support for the blockade, which was the first time an alternative view was acknowledged by our government.

We have to speak from what we know, not what we hear. Often, the only way to know what's happening on the ground is to have elected officials visit countries, meet people, and talk to them. We have to see both sides.

If we continue to view world conflicts as defined by extreme viewpoints, we don't develop opportunities for diplomacy. If we accepted the promise of diplomacy and combined it with an increase in foreign aid—from 0.2 percent to 1.0 percent of our gross domestic product—we might have a better chance to overcome the forces that are committed to the status quo. That is because diplomacy benefits the majority, while military approaches benefit those in power and those who sell weapons.

We need an appropriate-sized military to protect our country, but we also need to work diplomatically and encourage democracy whenever we can. We never could have enabled the Arab Spring by military force, whereas through diplomacy we can encourage and provide motivation for people around the world to demand and fight for their own freedom.

My trip to Mecca provided a profound perspective on this. Not only did I have a spiritual experience but I also got a practical experience. I got to see people—some from these very nations that we consider our enemies—as people. I got to see men and women with the same dreams, hopes, and aspirations that we have. And I understood that if we could reach the people and sidestep the governments, we could have the kind of world that we can all be proud of.

18

An Ounce of Prevention

On September 11, 2011, the tenth anniversary of 9/11, we held an observance in Minnesota. We were standing on the steps of the state capitol, singing songs and honoring our first responders. I stood there thinking, *Ten years later, how have we responded? Two wars, a doubling of our military budget. We've seen an increase in anti-Islamic hatred. We've prevented a number of new terrorist attempts but have we really made ourselves a safer people?*

Maybe we need to understand what safety means. There was an impulse in the aftermath of 9/11 to ask the question "Why do they hate us?" That was a gut-level emotional response and probably not the right question. The word *they* is too broad, because only a very small minority of radical individuals perpetrate terrorist acts. But to take a step back, we would serve ourselves better to ask, "Who are 'they,' and how and why do they recruit others to their cause?"

We tend to look externally for the answers. Some in power assumed that the proper response was to double our military spending and plunge into war. We know that we can bomb a training camp. But going to war without a clear understanding of how to win or how to exit is akin to throwing water on a grease fire. We needed to smother this fire. But how do you smother it when you don't really know why it burns? How do we deny terrorists access to their power base?

The truth is, there were a number of things we could have done. There are a number of things we should do as a nation.

We should have engaged with all our international partners, and not just a few; perhaps convened an international conference on how to undermine terrorist outfits and regimes.

We should reenergize our effort to bring peace between the Israelis and the Palestinians—an effort that Secretary of State John Kerry began again in 2013. We needed to intensify the peace process and make it the center of our policy. As an ally to Israel and the Palestinians, we should have leaned harder on then Egyptian president Hosni Mubarak and the Saudis, and told them that we would not support their oppression of their own people.

In addition, we should do more to develop sources of renewable energy right here in America so that we would be less dependent on imported oil. We should speak more in the United Nations and organize for human rights. Repression breeds resistance. That resistance isn't always democratic and peaceful; sometimes it's violent and intolerant.

There are more things we could have done.

In *The Looming Tower: Al-Qaeda and the Road to 9/11*, Pulitzer

Prize–winning author Lawrence Wright notes that bin Laden knew his terrorist network couldn't go toe-to-toe with the United States militarily. But what it *could* do was to draw us into the kind of fight we couldn't win; one in which we would end up involving people who had nothing to do with the initial attack. Al Qaeda was hoping that we would hurt civilians, which it could then use as a recruiting tool. "See, they droned you, they killed your family, that Great Satan. Join us!"

Some of our actions, like the military occupations in Iraq and Afghanistan, gave the terrorists more recruiting arguments—a dilemma that US soldiers have had to deal with.

We spent trillions of dollars in Iraq and Afghanistan on this "war on terror," and what did we get in return? Over six thousand Americans dead and tens of thousands wounded. Hundreds of thousands of civilians killed and wounded, millions made homeless. How much of this carnage and tragedy could have been avoided if we had focused on bringing our true enemies to justice?

It's time we start thinking about how to move forward.

I think that the United States is now in a place of reflection, where we can take a moment and truly ask ourselves if we acted properly following 9/11—especially as it relates to invading Iraq and staying in Afghanistan as long as we did.

We must have the courage to admit that Iraq was a colossal failure. The justification to invade Iraq was 100 percent wrong. Yes, we got rid of Saddam Hussein, but he had nothing to do with 9/11. Was he a bad guy? Extremely. But we work with bad guys every day. Where do we draw the line? I don't see us going into Russia and getting rid of Vladimir Putin. I don't see us getting rid of the leaders of China. Both Russia and China have committed human rights atrocities. North Korea brutally oppresses its people and actually is developing weapons of mass destruction and threatening its neighbors with war. Should we invade that country and replace its government?

Invading Iraq was wrong. It wasted more than 150,000 Iraqi lives and displaced millions, and nearly 4,500 American lives were lost there. That war also heavily damaged seven thousand years of human history. Iraq was the birthplace of civilization, and the destruction of historic places and the looting of museums took away something precious the world can never get back. And for what? Are we any safer? Are our gas prices any lower?

I don't believe we handled the war in Afghanistan properly either. If there was a justification to attack Afghanistan—and there was certainly justification to attack training camps—there was no justification for a twelve-year occupation. The Afghan people didn't attack us on 9/11, Al Qaeda and terrorists who trained in Afghanistan did.

If a criminal invades your home, law enforcement should capture the criminal. But should it also burn down the building where he lived or, worse, the whole neighborhood? We allowed ourselves to lose track of the goal. We should have focused our resources on eliminating Al Qaeda while doing as little damage as possible to the Afghan population. Instead, we invaded Iraq.

I've been heartened by President Obama's recent commitment to rethink the policy of drone attacks. I was concerned about the program under George Bush, and I had grown even more concerned under President Obama because he accelerated the drone program. However, blaming Obama isn't the issue; creating a transparent policy that reflects international standards of human rights is. The drone strike program has outpaced rules of accountability and transparency. We need public, transparent rules that make sure we prioritize protecting civilians.

We should target only the people who are planning immediate attacks on the United States. If we do otherwise, the simple reality is that we might solve our problem in the short term, but we will exacerbate it in the long run. If people think of us as the ones who fly silently over their countries, killing with impunity, we will have a more serious long-term problem.

I have a lot of Pakistani friends. The drone attacks are taking place far from Pakistan's major cities, in the tribal areas, which are similar to Native American reservations. Most Pakistanis have no experience with the strikes because they live in the urban areas. Even so, our drone policy has had a negative impact on how they see us.

I first went to Pakistan on a congressional delegation in 2009, with the House Democracy Partnership. This is a bipartisan congressional commission established in 2005 to interact with emerging democracies. During that trip, the Pakistani people were all excited about this first Muslim in the US Congress. They were incredibly kind and hospitable. And everyone wanted to talk to me and hear my thoughts on various topics.

When I returned to Pakistan in 2011, however, the climate was remarkably different. Usually we talk to heads of state, but this time we interacted with members of parliament. We worked on budgets, how the committees worked, ethics rules, constituent services, things like that. People were significantly more hostile to me than two years earlier. They were asking me very tough questions such as: "Do you support the president's drone program, *brother*? Do you know how many people have been killed?" "Why is your government violating Pakistani sovereignty?" I appeared on television, being grilled on a news channel. "Why does the US not listen to us?" I was asked. "They listen to India and not us."

The Pakistani people told me that the United States used to be loved in Pakistan. They talked about how Pakistanis worked with us to fight the Soviets when the USSR invaded Afghanistan beginning in late 1979 but the US dropped them when the Soviets were defeated. They asked me if I thought that we should be able to come into their country and make war. We're supposed to be allies.

I didn't have a lot of answers.

But I do know that we had an opportunity *before* Afghanistan became a hotbed of terrorism to take some preventive actions. I believe we must invest in failed states. Afghanistan was a failed state, which is why Al Qaeda was able to set up shop there.

In 1989 the Afghan people finally drove out the Soviets with US aid funneled through Pakistan. Then we walked away while the country fell into chaos and was taken over by the Taliban. After we invested the money to defeat the Russians, we didn't follow up to make sure that Afghanistan could stand on its own. We spent billions to defeat the Soviets but didn't spend millions to stabilize the country.

We were highly motivated to defeat an enemy but not motivated to build up a new friend. It's their country, who cares? Once Afghanistan was no longer important in our global chess game with the Soviets, we didn't care about it. We needed to win peace and stability, not just the military conflict.

After Al Qaeda attacked us from bases in Afghanistan, we invaded and occupied the country, pouring billions of dollars into trying to rebuild that nation. We would have been better served if we'd organized the international community to invest a fraction of those resources to keep the country from falling into chaos in the first place.

))))➡

Somalia is in a similar situation today. Al Qaeda is there. Al Shabaab, a group of heavily armed fundamentalists similar to the Taliban, is there.

My district has the largest Somali population in the United States. What is happening in that country should be an issue here. The United States could have worked harder with the international community to stabilize Somalia before Al Qaeda moved in.

About twenty years ago, Somalia plunged into chaos. There were different factions who tried to claim leadership, and it became a warlord nation. Somalia has major oil reserves, it has beautiful beaches and massive coastlines, including the Red Sea and the Indian Ocean. But there are unthinkable horrors going on amid this beauty.

The reason Somalia can't get back on its feet is because the state is weak, and some interests want to keep it weak. Why would anyone want Somalia to get strong? They can cross the border now and take what they want. Why get into a trading relationship when you can just take what you want? If I'm a Somali warlord, why would I want to give up my power to a legitimate government?

Somalia has been in chaos. Al Shabaab has killed thousands of Somalis and attacked Uganda. It has kidnapped and killed Western tourists who were on safari in Kenya. Worst of all, Al Shabaab prevented international aid from reaching Somalis starving as a result of a horrible famine. A quarter million died, half of them under five years of age.

Somali pirates were attacking cruise ships. Now just floating a boat through the Strait of Malacca, you have to pay a higher insurance premium because of piracy.

Before the emergence of the pirates, France and Italy used to dump medical waste in Somali waters, and it would wash up on the coast. Young men from Somalia got in a boat and said, "We're not going to let them do this!" Then it progressed to "We're going to take a tax off of these people." It went from protection of their space to real criminal activity. Why didn't someone step in and help before it got out of hand?

Somalia occupies a strategic place at the Horn of Africa, on the continent's east coast, where the Gulf of Aden provides access to the Red Sea and the Suez Canal, and to Saudi Arabia, Yemen, Egypt, Sudan, and Israel. If given a choice, a young person in Somalia would most definitely prefer to work for and fight for his or her country than join a terrorist organization. But if that terrorist organization is making it possible for a young man to feed his family, he will join that side. It's not about ideology as much as it is about survival. Our recent support of African Union (a collection of African states that come together on a regional basis to address economic, security, resources, and other issues) peacekeepers and international economic aid have helped stabilize the country, but we must maintain this priority. A peaceful Somalia will be a great benefit to its neighbors and to the United States.

I visited Mogadishu, Somalia, in February 2013. My personal presence in Somalia was the fulfillment of a campaign promise to my Somali constituents, and it was an opportunity for me to gain some firsthand perspective on the situation. Friends and family, as well as some people in the US State Department, cautioned me about the danger there. I even had to promise not to leave the airport. But I had to go.

You can say you care, and you can mean it. Or you can say you care and not mean it. But you can't fake showing up. You're either there or you're not. I had to be there, and I am so glad that I went.

Now I can report that Somalia is not as dangerous anymore. It's time to invest and help the country rebuild. A plane carrying the late congressman Donald Payne, a Democrat from New Jersey, came under mortar fire as he was departing Mogadishu in 2009. No member of the US House had been there since.

When I went, all was well. And I pray that it stays that way. The people of Somalia deserve peace.

))))➤

I've also been to Dadaab in Kenya, the largest refugee camp for Somalis fleeing the atrocities there, and currently the largest refugee camp in the world. It was designed to hold ninety thousand people but now holds a *half million*. Somalia is perceived to be so dangerous that its people were racing across the border to get out, but maybe they can finally think about going home again. It's very dry and dusty. Water is very limited. There is no infrastructure. When I visited, there were three doctors to care for some three hundred thousand people.

I spoke with one of the doctors, a twenty-seven-year-old Kenyan woman from Mombasa, just out of medical school. She told me she was so overwhelmed that she couldn't deliver babies; she handled only the high-risk pregnancies. The young woman had trained some of the refugees to act as midwives. She was dealing with severe malnutrition, HIV/AIDS, and malaria. Disease was rampant. Crime was rampant too—everything from stealing water jugs to rape.

But even in this environment, there were amazing expressions of human solidarity. I saw people making the best of their situations. One of the reasons I went to this camp was to deliver books from a nonprofit organization in my district called Books for Africa. BFA has shipped over one million books to Africa since it began. I had been told by people in my district that in addition to basic needs—food, water, clothing—folks were really asking for books.

There was a little library, more of a makeshift tent, at the center of the camp. And the books they had were worn. "Used" would be an understatement. But kids were in there reading, and parents and other adults were reading to kids.

That was remarkable to me. Even more remarkable was the hospitality I found as I walked around the camp. People were so kind and polite. These people barely had enough food or water, but they offered me tea. It blew me away. How can we sit by and watch people die and do nothing? We're America.

As I was leaving, word got around that I was a congressman from Minnesota, and refugees began coming up to me and handing me letters for their family members who lived in my district. I was more than happy to deliver those messages. And I felt bad about leaving. The people there had so much they wanted to share with their families in America. They had so much hope.

It is senseless that we, as a nation, are ignoring this crisis.

I've been to Gaza, Afghanistan, and Iraq. And I will go to Somalia again. If mothers, grandmothers, and babies are living there every day, I can certainly go to see what's going on.

We must do something about Al Shabaab. These guys are maniacs. They're killers. They do things such as blowing up a café in Kampala, Uganda, where people were watching World Cup soccer games. They are so violent that they have driven hundreds of thousands of Somalis to flee to Kenya. Al Shabaab is more and more on the defensive, but the world can't afford to give the organization a chance to regroup, as it has in the past. We keep killing bad guys, but bad conditions create new bad guys. You got a few bucks, and you've got yourself an Al Shabaab soldier. We must do more with our friends in Africa, Europe, and the rest of the world to help build a nation that can take care of itself. Even Britain has held an international conference on Somalia.

What have we done?

We encouraged Ethiopia to invade Somalia in 2006 in an effort to curb the power of Islamic parties. By doing so, we gave the most extreme nationalists credibility they would never have had otherwise, and contributed to the growth of the terrorist groups.

Here's what we can do: we need to step up efforts by the international community to bring safety to the Somali people and get the economy moving again, and we must take a leading role in that effort. Somalis are very industrious. All we'd need to do is help to get them on their feet. Just making it possible for planes to land there safely would be a huge help.

A lot of Americans think, *Why should we help them when we can't even help ourselves?* We are willing to devote $10 billion a week to fight in Afghanistan, but we won't invest one one-thousandth of that sum to get wells and schools established there or anyplace else, for that matter.

The average American family is far better off if we spend a little in improving the lives of others abroad rather than spending trillions on wars. Spending a little more in development and aid will allow us to keep more of our money here.

Pop quiz: How much of the United States federal budget goes to foreign aid? It's about 1 percent. Israel receives $2.4 billion, Egypt gets $1.5 billion, and our old buddy Russia receives $1.3 billion. The entire foreign aid budget is about one-twentieth of what we spend on the military.

Surely there's a little bit more in our budget to help poor nations in ways that will undermine the growth of terrorism and create allies in strategic places in the world. Surely we can find value in doing some preventive maintenance?

19

DEMOCRACY *IS* THE SOLUTION

Our nation must engage with the world and make sure we live by the values that we profess.

When I hear people from the Middle East complain about America, their complaints are often rooted in choices that we've made in favor of stability rather than our values of democracy. We preach liberty and justice for all, and yet we have aligned ourselves with dictators such as Hosni Mubarak and even Saddam Hussein. (Yes, throughout much of the 1980s, Saddam was an ally of ours at the same time that he was oppressing his people. Why was he our ally? Because Iraq was mired in an eight-year war against our enemy Iran.) Anyone living under those regimes and understanding our partnership with these dictators would wonder why the United States supported these regimes. And some people would understandably have hard feelings about this. But, in fact, most people around the world look to American democracy as a beacon of hope.

It was President John F. Kennedy who said, "Those who make peaceful revolution impossible will make violent revolution inevitable." In backing Mubarak, we made peaceful revolution more difficult, if not impossible. Why did we back Mubarak? Doing so supported US strategy in the Middle East and established an ally for us. In 1978, when Egypt was still led by Anwar el-Sadat, we supported that country in order to advance the Camp David Accords and a peace agreement, but American foreign aid didn't go to the Egyptian people. We provided funds to the military to ensure peace. That was shortsighted. If the Egyptian people act up, who's going to put them down? The military. So in essence, we funded their oppression.

On January 25, 2011, when more than fifty thousand Egyptians packed Cairo's Tahrir Square—and in the subsequent days, when those numbers swelled to one hundred thousand, and then to three hundred thousand—the Egyptian military shot tear gas canisters into the crowd. The words "Made in the USA" were written on those canisters.

How do you think the protesters, fighting for liberty, fighting against the yoke of a dictator, viewed America when they saw those canisters? We didn't actively oppress the people of Egypt, Pakistan, or Iraq. But we did support their dictators and funded the military that maintained those dictators. We made a trade-off: stability for human rights. Through our support for Mubarak, we didn't uphold the principles we espouse—the very principles upon which our great nation was founded.

Free Democratic countries tend to be led by the popular will. Historically, we have had a mixed record on supporting the popular will. Sometimes we have supported free elections and human rights, sometimes we have not. Sometimes we would rather deal with a country like Egypt via one person, like Mubarak. In Iraq, we went from supporting Hussein to invading Iraq to overthrow him, and we supported the development of a constitution and elections. In Egypt, we cared about *our* agenda, and we believed that Mubarak could deliver it. But he couldn't. Eventually we supported the antidictatorship activists in Egypt and in Libya.

Egypt and countries like it are not so simple, not so black and white. We cannot just deal with someone like Mubarak and expect that the things we want to see happen in the Middle East will come to pass. We have found it to be quite the opposite. Countries such as Egypt are as politically complex as the United States is.

In America we have the Tea Party at one end of the spectrum and the Occupy movement at the other end. But when we think of the Middle East, we tend to regard it as one big party, one mindset, one culture. However, I think our views are broadening due to the movements of the Arab Spring.

The stereotype is that the Middle East is all Arab and Muslim. However, Turks also live in the Middle East. Most are Muslim, but they aren't Arab. They don't have the same culture or language as Arabs. You also have Coptic Christians in Egypt, and Maronite Christians and Orthodox Christians in Lebanon. You have a group called the Mandaeans, mostly in Iraq and Iran, who follow John the Baptist.

The head of the Coptic Church works on a cooperative basis with the Egyptian government. In fact, there are Coptic Christians in the Muslim Brotherhood. Yet, visiting there in 2012, I heard firsthand about attacks on Christians by Salafist extremists, fundamentalists who subscribe to a "pure" form of Islam.

The Middle East has many ethnicities, including Kurds, Persians, Tajiks, Uzbeks, Pashtuns, and others. You have people in Syria who look as Caucasian as someone from Sweden. You have Jews throughout the Middle East. And 20 percent of people in Israel are Muslim Arabs and about 2 percent are Christians. The religious decisions in Israel are made by the most orthodox authorities. A reform rabbi in America cannot perform a wedding in Israel. But a majority of Israelis are not conservative religious Jews.

It's very complex.

In Saudi Arabia, they practice Wahhabism, a form of Islam that's extremely austere and culturally conservative. Although it's a very dynamic society with great oil wealth, a few aspects look similar to other Middle Eastern countries: a lack of democracy, a high percentage of youths, and high unemployment—meaning those young people don't have enough to do.

Egypt and Jordan subsist on foreign aid, but most of the economies are extractive. Saudi Arabia and the other Persian Gulf countries have oil, but the wealth from it is not trickling down to the masses. Libya produces a lot of oil—2 percent of the world's supply and some of its best, sweet crude. It made Muammar Gaddafi fabulously rich. Libya also has a population of 6.5 million people who don't see much benefit. So you have a few with a lot of money and the multitude who are poor.

We need to evaluate our relationships with these countries. Our relationships need to be more multidimensional and less superficial. We need to invest in more academic exchanges. We have only 150 Fulbright scholarships to help Iraqi students study in the United States. We should have 1,500. America has the wherewithal to fund these exchanges. When Fulbright scholars return to countries where their rights are limited, they're going to bring knowledge of the United States and our values that will prove invaluable in building future relationships. We should provide educational and cultural exchanges and at the same time pressure governments to uphold standards of justice and human rights.

We should offer conditional foreign aid. No one should have to live in this world without a basic standard of justice. We should tell these countries, "This is American taxpayers' money, and if you want some of it, you have to demonstrate that you have fair elections, freedom of speech, and that you don't persecute your minority groups. Only when you meet those criteria will you get our money."

What about the Muslim Brotherhood? I hear that question all the time. It has existed for decades, The United States has avoided dealing directly with the Muslim Brotherhood in Egypt because of the alliance with Mubarak, who insisted that the group was connected to terrorism. We gave his regime money, training, military cooperation, and equipment while it imprisoned and tortured members of the Brotherhood.

The Muslim Brotherhood was founded in 1928 by a preacher named Hassan al-Banna. But it gained a following a generation later under the leadership of Sayyid Qutb, an Egyptian. He came to the United States on a scholarship and earned a master's degree at Colorado State College of Education from 1948 to 1950. Although he wrote many books and articles on Islam, even an article about America—in which he criticized us for our racism, jazz, and intermingling of the sexes, among many things—Qutb didn't return to Egypt as an ideologue or religious zealot.

He was tortured in Egyptian jails and became more radical in his views. Even more radical offshoots of his movement would greatly influence Osama bin Laden, and that's where the ideology behind Al Qaeda was born, in opposition to Arab dictators. In origin, it was an anticolonial group that decided the only way to deal with Arab dictators was to use violence and terrorism.

But that philosophy simply doesn't work. It doesn't lead to real or lasting change. In 1981 these Egyptian Salafist extremists assassinated Egyptian president el-Sadat, but nothing changed in Egyptian society. If anything, the regime became even more repressive. Nonviolent protesters in Egypt accomplished in eighteen days what the terrorist groups couldn't do in three decades: they overthrew a dictator and established the groundwork for democratic government. The United States should support movements like this. We should promote the Peace Corps in places such as Jordan and Morocco. We need more points of contact. We should focus our commercial exchanges on small businesses, especially those run by women and other traditionally excluded people, and we should support trade on a small to medium basis. We need to suck the oxygen from violent extremists. We should maintain an excellent relationship with Israel and also have excellent relationships with other countries in the Middle East. There shouldn't be just one democracy in the Middle East. It should be a neighborhood of democracies. Democratic neighbors would be a precious addition to the security and prosperity of the region.

Where we are now in Egypt, the government has used military power to depose the duly elected president. People who opposed the coup went into the streets; hundreds of people were killed. The military jailed the opposition and shut down their media. And the United States government has suspended military aid and military exercises. My position is that United States and Egypt need a new relationship. Egypt can do whatever it wants to do. But we shouldn't be in a relationship with a country that is maintaining flagrant abuse of civil rights. If Egypt restores democracy, we should restore the relationship with them based on what is mutually beneficial. Until then, we should cut all aid. We should maintain an embassy and improve our diplomatic efforts. But we should not fund coup leaders.

Just weeks after the 2011 Egyptian revolution, I traveled to Egypt as part of a congressional delegation. While there, we met with members of parliament. Some of my friends from Egypt arranged for me to speak at the Medical Syndicate, a regular town hall forum.

I walked into a space with about three hundred people. I started talking to them about models for democracy, and the audience was really open in expressing its views. Early on, one guy stood up and started screaming at me: "America is evil! America is bad! America is terrorist!"

I leaned back and waited until he had finished.

"Thank you for your views," I said. "But the bottom line is you have an image that all three hundred twenty million of us are all the same. There were many Americans who were happy to see the Egyptian revolution take place. So you're wrong."

I went on to talk about how our relationship could be stuck in the past—with elites in Egypt and elites in America looking out only for one another—or we could get people to see one another as people.

He calmed down and didn't have anything else to say. And the rest of the crowd seemed genuinely excited and hopeful.

Later that night, we all went to Tahrir Square. A crowd of about five hundred or six hundred Egyptians milled about. Now, we didn't have security. Two guys with our delegation were Egyptian by birth and spoke Arabic. One of them suddenly called out, "Hey, everyone! We have a congressman from the United States right here. Ask anything you want!"

I was a little startled initially, not knowing what the reaction would be. It introduced an element of surprise. All day long, security people had been moving our delegation around in a very precise way. We were in black armored Chevy Suburbans, and when we arrived at a venue, they would tell us to stay in the vehicle until they came around and opened the doors. We were told never to open our own doors and get out. Security would surround us, creating a phalanx when we walked from the car and into a government building. And here I was out in the middle of Tahrir Square among hundreds of Egyptians with just a few buddies of mine.

But I'd said I wanted to see Egypt; I wanted to be among the people. Here I was. I knew if I'd asked for permission, they would have advised against it. Strongly. So I didn't ask. I figured, what was the point of being here if I wasn't going to make a connection with the people? I didn't want to be on one of those junkets where you go to a country, and it's superficial.

On the other hand, I'd wanted to observe; I didn't want to be announced as a congressman. I wasn't expecting to hold court. I could have easily blended in with the folks there.

After my friend announced my presence, one guy yelled back in Arabic, "Do you expect us to believe this guy is really a member of the United States Congress?"

"Yes," Ahmed said. And I confirmed it.

Then someone yelled out, "Why does America support Israel over the rest of the Middle East?"

Someone else asked, "What are we going to do about jobs in Egypt?"

I was bombarded with one question after another. And I stood there, attempting to answer every single one. It was a long night, but I really felt that it was a valuable experience.

The United States is the biggest superpower in the world, and there are a lot of people who give us more blame than we deserve. But they also give us more credit than we deserve. To ask me about jobs in Egypt definitely imbues America with more power than we actually have. They knew that America gave foreign aid to Egypt.

They also knew that *they* weren't seeing any of it and wanted to know why.

There was a man, small in stature, about five foot two. He had six children and wanted to know, If democracy came to Egypt, would he get a job? Someone else wanted to know if Egypt should be an Islamic society or not.

"I'm not here to tell you whether to have an Islamic society or not," I replied. "There must be a basic standard of justice for all humanity. For everyone. I'm not speaking as an American congressman but as a citizen of the world. Everyone must participate in selecting the leadership of your country: women must have a chance for equality, and minorities must also have a say. I don't care what you call it, but everyone must be part of it in order for it to work.

"In America," I continued, "we have a separation of religion and government, and this actually protects religious people. It would be an extreme outrage if someone from the government tried to tell a minister what to say in a church or a mosque or a synagogue. In a nonfree society, political authority would try to tell the religious authority what to say or do."

There was a young girl wearing a hijab. She said, "You guys think we're trying to have a theocracy. We're not. We're calling for our society to be informed by religious values."

There was a lot of open dialogue and exchange of ideas that night. Many in the crowd were surprised to learn that I was a Muslim; they'd never heard of such a thing as a Muslim in American government. But it did help build a bridge and break down some barriers.

All they wanted was to be heard. All they wanted was to matter.

20

PROFILES IN LEADERSHIP

My 2012 run for Congress was my fourth campaign. It was as amazing as the last three in many ways. One learning experience was a debate in which I called my opponent a scumbag. My opponent stepped beyond the bounds of what is appropriate when he targeted my family and took a swipe at my relationship with my ex-wife and my children. I reacted badly with the name calling.

I apologized for it, and it was heartfelt. Nothing a political opponent does justifies such a reaction. His behavior was irrelevant to my response. I can't follow the "If he plays nice, then I'll play nice" construct. That means my behavior is contingent on what he does. That's not what leaders do. This unfortunate occasion reminded me of my duty to serve the people and to never allow personal attacks to steer me away from that goal.

I contemplated the essence of leadership, and the qualities I admire in some of my favorite leaders, to remind myself what it is I can and should be doing in my role as a representative of the people.

Leaders are complex people, with flaws and failings. But what makes a good leader is understanding that what he does is greater than who he is.

The date was January 30, 1956. Martin Luther King Jr. was speaking at a meeting at the First Baptist Church on Perry Street in Montgomery, Alabama. The pastor was King's confidant Ralph Abernathy, and the church was just blocks away from King's own, Dexter Avenue Baptist Church.

During the night, word came in that King's house had been firebombed. He rushed back to find a mob outside his smoldering home. The fire had been put out inside, but outside, angry blacks, brandishing guns and knives, were being held back by a barricade of white police officers.

It was a powder keg, ready to explode.

King, after making sure that his wife and ten-week-old baby girl, Yolanda, were safe, went onto his porch and quelled the angry mob. He assured them that he and his family were fine, and he reminded them of all the work they had accomplished and why they were on this mission.

"I want it to be known the length and breadth of this land that if I am stopped, this movement will not stop. If I am stopped, our work will not stop. For what we are doing is right. What we are doing is just. And God is with us."

Most people wouldn't have blamed King if he got angry or even if he indulged in a little bravado about not being afraid. He didn't do any of that. Not only did he defuse a moment that could have ended in many deaths and injuries and potentially derailed the movement, but his calming leadership propelled those angry people to go home and take action in another way.

For thirteen months after Rosa Parks was ordered to give up her seat to a white male passenger, more than seventeen thousand black folks boycotted the buses in Montgomery, Alabama, bringing the system of segregation on public transportation to its knees. On December 17, 1956, the Supreme Court upheld a lower court's decision that segregated buses were unconstitutional under the Fourteenth Amendment. Three days later Dr. King boarded a bus in front of his home and sat at the front, next to a white man.

Leadership—real leadership—never loses sight of the big picture. King had a plan and a vision, and even the personal attack on his home was not going to derail that plan and vision.

I toured King's Montgomery house in 2012. It's now a historic landmark. They walked us through the room where the bomb landed. It was chilling to think about Coretta and little Yolanda coming so close to being killed. As I walked through the tiny home, I thought about how much was at stake for King personally. And I wondered if he ever considered quitting.

I know that in his position, I'd surely have contemplated walking away. I also know that even if King thought about doing so, he never let on. He persevered despite enduring threats, arrests, and actual attacks.

In one of his speeches, King told of having received a threatening phone call. "If you're not out of town in three days, nigger," the voice snarled, "we're going to blow your head off and burn down your house!"

He knew they meant it. But he refused to quit. He refused to quit even when his own people turned against him. And while people love to honor King, name streets after him, build monuments honoring him, and have a national holiday in his name, the reality is that during the height of the movement and his leadership, King had as much opposition from blacks who saw him as "soft," especially in the wake of the emergence of the more radical black power movement, as he had opposition from the government— which identified him as a threat—and from white racists.

Martin Luther King Jr. is one of my favorite leaders.

He was awarded the Nobel Peace Prize in 1964. The Civil Rights Act passed the same year, followed by the Voting Rights Act in 1965—all propelled by him. By the age of just thirty-five, Martin Luther King had changed the landscape of America, legally and socially. And he did this against seemingly insurmountable odds. The country was against him. The country didn't want to change.

MLK was never naïve. He was never under the impression that we are going to love people away from racism. He always maintained that America was sick and that the racists were diseased. He called them out and stood firm against the hatred.

Many of the leaders of the country were gunning for him. FBI director J. Edgar Hoover called MLK the most notorious liar in the world—after he received the Nobel Prize. And Bobby Kennedy—yes, *that* Bobby Kennedy—as the country's attorney general, granted written approval for wiretaps on King's phones.

Instead of lying low after making all of those civil rights gains, King turned his attention to the Vietnam War and US foreign policy. And then they really turned on him. They turned on him bad. Even civil rights leaders felt that King should stick to civil rights. But he didn't stop there. King went into Appalachia, where poor white people lived, and tried to organize them. He was starting a "poor people's movement" that included everyone. He was letting them know that "black people," or immigrants, or "those people," weren't the problem. It was similar to the arguments of today with the Occupy Wall Street movement and the 1 percent versus the 99 percent.

King was really an outcast. They called him a Communist, a plagiarist, everything but a child of God. But he was an amazing leader because he kept going despite the opposition.

To be a great leader, you have to overcome great odds. What was harder to overcome than Jim Crow and its racial dictatorship, in a nation dedicated to liberty and justice for all? The status of black people stood as an accusation of hypocrisy to white America unless someone solved it. White Americans could not really live in a society based on freedom while black Americans lived in misery and oppression. And while poor whites lived a poor quality of life and didn't even know why—thinking it was blacks, Mexicans, or gay people—when it was really people at the top of the food chain who were the oppressors.

MLK faced the problem head on. He strove to give America a chance to be what it claimed to be. He gave the nation a great gift by demanding that it live consistently with what it said it represented. But he did it at great personal sacrifice. His whole family made the sacrifice. Coretta stood by him to the end despite his personal infidelities.

But MLK gave the ultimate sacrifice: his life.

He had divine visitations. MLK had a special connection to the Creator. I remember his final speech, delivered on April 3, 1968, in which he said, "Like anybody, I would like to live a long life. Longevity has its place. But I'm not concerned about that now. I just want to do God's will . . ."

Imagine sensing, *knowing*, that your life hangs in the balance, and you continue anyway. King knew he wouldn't make it. He even went on to say, on that night before his death, "I've seen the Promised Land. I may not get there with you, but I want you to know tonight that we as a people will get to the Promised Land. "

He spoke without a single note. He wasn't reading from anything prepared. And when King finished, he peeled away from the microphone and sat back down, looking exhausted. Spent. It was nothing short of amazing.

It would have been easy for him to do all he did if he'd been some sort of angelic figure. But King was just a man. He met the moment that history put him into. How many could have done that?

He was head of the Montgomery Improvement Association (MIA) at the age of twenty-five. Older members of the community didn't give him that position because he was an amazing guy. They didn't know he was amazing at the time. No one noteworthy wanted the position. They didn't want to lead it, because if it didn't succeed, they didn't want to be blamed for the failure. There was too much on the line. So they decided to let the new kid do it. If it didn't work out, he could go back to his hometown of Atlanta and still be okay. His daddy had a big church there, and he could settle right in.

But King didn't fail. He met the challenge and then some.

While MLK was a great leader, he wasn't a perfect leader. He wasn't a perfect man.

MLK had girlfriends. This is very hard for some people to handle. He smoked a lot of cigarettes, drank whiskey. He cussed. And among the young people, they called him "Da Lawd." They did so because they considered him too sanctimonious and a little pompous.

Great leaders are not perfect people. They are human beings

who, faced with making crucial decisions or tough choices, do the right thing because it's the right thing to do.

))))➤

Another of my favorite leaders is Abraham Lincoln. He, too, was flawed and complicated.

Lincoln has drawn criticism for seeming to be indecisive or politically expedient on the issue of slavery. In fact, in his inaugural speech, Lincoln spent a lot of time assuring the South that he wasn't going to end slavery. What was that about?

Here's what that's about: when you're a leader, you cannot ignore parts of your constituency, even if you know they're not going to vote for you. What Lincoln did was not pandering. He'd sworn to uphold a Constitution that recognized slavery. I believe that, at the time, he truly felt he could heal this nation without ending slavery. In fact, abolishing slavery was never high on his list of priorities.

So when he made that commitment, he intended to honor it. The South, however, refused to capitulate, so Lincoln had to do what he had to do. But his goal was to be president of the *United* States, and that meant honoring and considering the desires and the goals of even those Americans who would never vote for him. That's true leadership.

And when you consider the Emancipation Proclamation, it did not end slavery. It ended slavery only in the rebel states. The states that were loyal to the Union—Maryland, Delaware, New Jersey, parts of Tennessee, and so on—got to keep their slaves right up to the passing of the Thirteenth Amendment, which ended slavery for all.

Lincoln ended slavery in the South as a tactic to preserve the Union. It wasn't some sanctimonious or even acrimonious act. Lincoln never publicly gave in to anger. He would say to the South, "We're not enemies, but friends." He did all he could to keep the South in the fold. But its leaders wouldn't stay.

He didn't run headlong into war. Lincoln preferred peace. But once again, a good leader, a true leader, never backs away from what must be done. Not only did Lincoln preserve the Union, he ultimately ended slavery by seizing the opportunity late in the war to move the Thirteenth Amendment through Congress.

Lincoln was also a visionary leader who helped to pass the transcontinental railroad bill. This, too, was highly controversial at the time. And the railroad ultimately got built—through the near-slave labor of Chinese and other workers.

But our leaders, good leaders, are not pristine and perfect. Not even Lincoln, who was willing to spill buckets of blood and cost the lives of thousands in his pursuit of progress. But the historical record doesn't contain anything that suggests he was motivated by anger and ego. Many of his decisions went against his core principles, perhaps. But he considered the greater good.

The greater good . . .

))➤

I've tried to imagine what it must be like to sit in a jail cell for twenty-seven years simply for fighting for justice and equality. Twenty-seven years is more than half of my life right now. I could not imagine actually being able to leave that jail cell if only I'd agree to give up that fight for equality and not taking the chance at some point, not buckling, bending, or giving up.

Nelson Mandela never wavered. Not in twenty-seven years.

Not until apartheid ended in South Africa. All he had to say was, "I'll be quiet. I won't cause any more trouble," and they would have let him walk free. But he refused.

Mandela is certainly among my favorite leaders.

Yes, it seems like I'm cherry-picking the easy ones. But I have to tell you, Mandela was also a complex man. He had all kinds of problems, all sorts of flaws, but he transcended them to lead a nation out of darkness into a new light.

When Mandela finally got out of prison in 1990, he didn't come out bitter and angry. He never gave in to racialized revenge. He said, "No, we will be *one* South Africa, black and white and colored." It is because of Mandela that South Africa was able to not just heal but also grow and thrive.

South Africa is an inclusive democracy today because of the legacy laid down by Mandela, who went on to serve as president of South Africa from 1994 to 1999. He's such an empowering figure.

Mandela taught all the possibilities of overcoming tremendous obstacles with amazing grace, being really clear about what was at stake.

Some of the best leaders are those who don't necessarily show up in history books—these are the people who do great works, not looking for recognition or accolades. They simply roll up their sleeves until the work is done.

)))➤

Ella Baker is another leader whom I greatly admire. She is relatively unknown, but without her work there may not have been a civil rights movement. She was one of the major organizing forces behind the Student Nonviolent Coordinating Committee (SNCC) and the Southern Christian Leadership Conference.

She was the national director of the Young Negroes Cooperative League, a 1930s group dedicated to economic empowerment within the black community. She was close friends with John Henrik Clarke, who introduced African studies to US academia, and Pauli Murray, the civil rights and feminist leader, and she worked alongside W. E. B. Du Bois, Thurgood Marshall, and A. Philip Randolph, and mentored the likes of Rosa Parks, Martin Luther King Jr., and Stokely Carmichael.

Ella Baker didn't need to be at the front of the band; she preferred to be the instructor, making sure the band played well. She was the planner and organizer of the movement. She devoted her life to civil rights. Growing up on a farm, she was inspired by her grandmother—a defiant former slave—and other activists in her family.

She went to Shaw University in the 1920s, a period when women were just getting the right to vote, and very few (especially black women) were getting a college education. She graduated magna cum laude. While there, she organized students to challenge unfair school practices.

Ella Baker used the power of the pen, writing for newspapers such as the *Negro National News*, and fought to free the Scottsboro Boys, nine young, poor black men who were hitching a ride on a freight train between Chattanooga and Memphis, Tennessee, when they were accused of raping two white women. Despite the fact that the women recanted their story, these boys were imprisoned for many years for a crime they did not commit. Their case was an iconic example of the poor treatment of blacks and the second-class citizenship that many were languished in. There was a rally of support to free the Scottsboro Boys, and Ella Baker was at the forefront of that movement. She also taught for the Workers

Education Project (WEP) of the Works Progress Administration (WPA). Here was this educated woman, getting her hands dirty working on labor matters.

I'm a student of civil rights history, and I was curious about the SNCC while I was in college. At Wayne State, I was excited about getting our school to divest from South Africa, and that's when I read about Ella Baker. Who *was* this woman? Of course, I'd read about Rosa Parks and Fannie Lou Hamer. But what I discovered about Ella Baker was simply amazing. If you took her out of the mix, many of the strides made during the late 1950s, 1960s, and 1970s might not have happened at all. She did critical organizing for the NAACP in the forties, and helped create the SCLC. She called together a conference at Shaw, and out of that came SNCC and its great leaders: John Lewis, Julian Bond, Stokely Carmichael. A lot of white kids took her work and started Students for a Democratic Society (SDS) based on models she'd laid down and her ideas about political engagement.

Ella Baker knew that not just black people needed a better deal. She believed that we suffered from a lack of democracy. She didn't like messianic leaders. Ella Baker knew that real change would never be sustained through one leader. It was all about the organization, and it was about everyone participating.

There was Ella Baker behind the scenes, and there was MLK at the forefront. Some say he kind of fell into history. That's not really true. It is true that he was pushed to the forefront of the movement, but he had such amazing gifts that galvanized his place in history. Ella Baker prepared the way for him to step into history. There were thousands and thousands of people struggling and fighting that fight. Martin Luther King Jr. was the symbolic leader. Ella Baker understood that MLK was a man, a human being, and that human beings are born, they live a life, and they die. If you base a movement on a leader and that person either makes a mistake or dies, then where are you? Her philosophy was to stick to the principles that would get us there.

Ella Baker was a thinker and an activist and never got the attention she deserved. A lot of women have been integral to many movements. But because they were the workhorses and not the show horses, the world may never know their names.

))))➤

To me, leaders may fear failure, but they don't let that fear stop them from doing what's right. MLK wasn't going to stop despite the death threats. Bombs weren't going to stop him. Even his fellow ministers going against him didn't deter him. In his "Letter from the Birmingham Jail," written on April 16, 1963, King brilliantly schooled his Christian opposition. He basically asked them how they could tell him to wait for freedom. He told them very eloquently that they needed to step up and live their Christian faith and stop being afraid.

Great leaders don't take the easy way out.

The easiest thing for Lincoln would have been to let the South keep slavery and do what it wanted. Lincoln had faced a lot of tough decisions that caused him great pain. He suffered from depression. He lost a couple of children, and his wife had health issues.

Great leaders may have all kinds of professional and personal problems, yet they manage to keep their eye on some transcendent goal and have a sense of how to get there. Great leaders have tremendous passion and are great listeners.

Great leaders are both made and born. Ella Baker once said,

"The movement made Martin. Martin didn't make the movement."

King was brilliant and confident and talented. There were a lot of people with those same qualities who, if put in that same situation, couldn't have done what he did. Sometimes stepping into such a situation reveals greatness.

Being in office, particularly if you're trying to accomplish something really good, is a character-building experience. You can get to be better or worse, but you cannot stay the same. Being the target of unrelenting hostility does something to you. It has to.

I think Barack Obama is a very passionate man. I think he throws himself into what he does. You show me a great leader, and I'll show you a person who cares desperately.

John F. Kennedy was a great leader. He wasn't in office long, but he was a phenomenal leader of this country. The work is always bigger than the true leader. It's always about the bigger issues: human rights, democracy, equality, freedom, preserving the union, eliminating slavery. Leaders set their sights higher and beyond their present situation.

All of us are challenged every day, and we can do the easy thing, the safe thing. But if we pursue a higher sense of purpose, then we too can achieve great and remarkable things.

If MLK's goal had been to amass a million dollars, he could have done that easily. He entered college at the age of fifteen. He was brilliant. He could have made a lot of money, and the world might never have known him. The country needed someone to make the movement live up to its mission.

Purpose is such an important component. It's like an engine. It's a yardstick. It's a magnet. Purposeful people draw others to them.

These leaders teach us all that if you want to lead a successful life—to meet your goals and justify your existence—you must have a purpose.

Purpose organizes your life. It helps you decide what you're going to do. It allows you to say yes and no. My prayer is that everyone finds his or her purpose.

Epilogue

SWEET LAND OF LIBERTY

We are in a battle for our national soul. As America marches into this new era, we must decide who we are and what we stand for. We have to look in our individual mirrors and determine whether we will embrace the words written in our Constitution, such as "We the People" and "to form a more perfect Union," or whether we want to toss it all away for selfish goals and ambitions. Will we allow apathy, distraction, and a lack of passion to carry us to our weakest point? Will we work to ensure the blessings of liberty for all, or will we allow the blessings to be reserved only for the fortunate few as our country moves toward plutocracy?

Are we going to come together, united? Or are we going to fall together, divided?

Will we be a nation that looks out for those who can't look out for themselves? Or will we simply say, "I got mine; don't look to me for help"?

Where do you see this nation in twenty, fifty, one hundred years? And what will be your contribution to its future?

I'm reminded of that quote from Hubert Humphrey in which he talks about "the moral test of government." I wanted to pass that test.

I ran for Congress in the spirit of Hubert Humphrey. I ran for Congress because I believe in the words written in the Declaration of Independence, I believe in our Constitution, and I believe in America. Instead of standing on the sidelines complaining about the things I thought needed changing, fixing, or highlighting, I decided to get in the game and be part of the solution, not part of the complaining.

During the 2012 election cycle, there was a lot of attention around the issue of voter suppression. There were more than two dozen states circulating voter-ID and voter-qualification laws. Minnesota was one of those states. The Republican-led legislature, headed by Mary Kiffmeyer, managed to get a voter-qualification law on the ballot. If it passed, it would be part of the Minnesota state constitution.

Under our US Constitution, voter qualification is determined by the states. That's why if you have a felony in Florida, you can never vote, but if you commit a felony in Vermont, not only can you vote but also you can vote while serving your time. Each state can determine the way it wants to handle voting.

When I heard about the voter ID being proposed in my state, I was disappointed. The governor had already vetoed a proposal that very year. So its proponents figured they would take it to the people. At first, the notion had overwhelming support. A leading poll showed that 80 percent of Minnesotans were in favor of the

Republican plan. It seemed reasonable, and people didn't immediately see the obstacle it would place in front of many voters. Just because something is popular doesn't make it right.

My reelection campaign would be dedicated to defeating this amendment despite the odds. Defeating this antidemocratic photo-ID amendment became our priority—not getting reelected. When my team went out canvassing, knocking on doors, and campaigning, their mission was to educate people about the proposed voter-identification law. And they were to urge people to vote no on this bill.

Why was it important? Because too many people died to eliminate these kinds of laws, and we had to do our best not to see their sacrifices diminished by the adoption of new voter restrictions.

In 1965, before the passage of the Voting Rights Act, there were all kinds of voter-identification laws designed to disenfranchise voters—mostly in the South. All kinds of tactics were employed to keep black people from voting, including intimidation, poll taxes, and tests. And even for those blacks who did vote, there was very little freedom of choice. There were no candidates whose platforms served them and no bills or laws being proposed in their favor. So if they voted, they were voting mostly for people whose agenda was to oppress them. Sure, blacks had the right to vote, but that right could not be exercised in any meaningful way.

On the surface, the proposed amendment seemed reasonable. No one likes to see voter fraud. But seemingly well-meaning laws can have very insidious outcomes. The purpose of our voting system is to allow qualified citizens an opportunity to participate. Millions of qualified voters do not have a government-issued photo ID, particularly young people, the elderly, the urban poor, and the disabled.

This law didn't come about because there was an actual problem with fraud, with people voting more than once. Actually, we have a problem getting people to vote *once*. Minnesota has the highest turnout in the country, and we get only around 76 percent. I've devoted each of my campaigns to the goal of increasing voter turnout in Minnesota's Fifth District, and we've increased the percentage of eligible voters going to the polls in each election cycle, compared to the election four years previously.

There has never been even one documented case of imposter voting in Minnesota, and, if it was happening, it wouldn't be hard to find. This push was simply about voter suppression. More than thirty states were offering up these laws, and I, and thousands of other Minnesotans, refused to let Minnesota be one of those to pass it.

All I could think about was James Chaney, Andrew Goodman, and Michael Schwerner threatened, beaten, shot, and buried in 1964. They lost their lives fighting for all folks to have the right to vote freely. We owed it to their memories to make sure that we didn't turn back the clock on this issue.

We had to fight the good fight in honor of people like Viola Liuzzo. Chaney, Goodman, and Schwerner are the most noted of those who lost their lives in this battle for human and civil rights. But Viola Liuzzo was just as impactful. I learned about Viola while in college. She was from Detroit, so naturally I gravitated to her story. She was a white woman, married to a Detroit Teamster. She was a mother. She was active in her community, fighting for civil rights. After seeing the horrific images of the attacks on people working to secure their rights, she protested on the campus of Wayne State, where she was enrolled part-time, but she decided that she could do more—that she must do more.

So she drove from Detroit to Alabama by herself, which I find absolutely amazing. Think about a woman doing that during that time. Viola Liuzzo got in her 1963 Oldsmobile and drove to Selma, leaving behind her three children and her husband. She called him on the way, explaining why she had to go. She said, "This is everybody's fight."

When she got to Selma, she used that Oldsmobile to drive local marchers and civil rights workers around. While on one of these runs, she was met by a carload of Ku Klux Klan, who tried to run her off the road. They then pulled up beside her and blasted her away, shooting her in the head twice. She died instantly. She was only thirty-nine years old. Less than two weeks after she was buried, a burned cross showed up in front of her home.

We would dishonor the memory of Rosa Parks, Viola Liuzzo, Goodman, Chaney, and Schwerner, the Freedom Riders, and the thousands of unnamed heroes who lost their lives in this fight for justice if we sat back and did nothing. We would have failed that moral test of government about which Humphrey spoke so eloquently.

I was told that fighting against the voter-ID amendment could cost me politically. I didn't care. The more I learned about it, the more I knew I had to keep fighting.

I started to look into this voter-identification movement spreading across the country, and I found that it was being backed and funded by the American Legislative Exchange Council (ALEC). Then I discovered that ALEC had been funded by the billionaire right-wing brothers Charles and David Koch following the 2008 election, when there was massive voter turnout—of primarily young people and minority people—for Barack Obama. Who would be most affected by this voter-ID-bill movement? Young people and minority people. And women. And the elderly. And the disabled.

So what was this really about? Some thirty million people would be discouraged or prevented from voting.

ALEC's thought was that instead of trying to persuade the electorate of its political ideals and actually offering viable solutions to our problems, it would simply suppress the votes of those who would be less likely to vote for its candidates. Effective, perhaps. But very un-American.

I was fundamentally offended that Americans were trying to silence votes of citizens in a country dedicated to representation.

Our history should have made this a nonissue. Before 1965, African Americans were forced to live under Black Codes that they didn't get a chance to vote against. So they had to obey laws that they had no power to change. That's called oppression.

I didn't just have my campaign staff out making the rounds, educating folks and telling them why they should vote no. I organized a series of meetings and invited other legislators—local and national—to help spread the word. I invited the NAACP, environmental leaders, labor leaders. I was having town hall meetings, forums at senior centers, and talks on college campuses every week leading up to the election.

My campaign was far from alone in fighting this amendment, but it's important to note that some leaders in the progressive coalition believed that passage of the voter-ID amendment was a foregone conclusion based on the polling. Other progressive leaders, however, didn't care a whit about the polling results. They pressed on because they knew that no matter the odds, there had to be a fight. SEIU, TakeAction Minnesota, an interfaith coalition of congregations known as Isaiah, the League of Women Voters, and their supporters just never backed down. It was a matter of organizing and faith. Some folks thought it would not be a good use of limited funds, and I believe in being responsible with precious resources. But I also believe in standing up for what you believe. And that is what those early opponents to voter ID did. With that faithful fighting spirit, things began to change.

And slowly the tide began to turn.

Mary Kiffmeyer was claiming that this amendment was going to get pushed through because of overwhelming support. Kiffmeyer, a former Minnesota secretary of state, said when running for the legislature that her first goal in office was to push through these photo-ID bills. Oh yeah: Kiffmeyer is a member of ALEC. Was there a particular agenda there?

I certainly had an agenda: to make sure that not one Minnesotan would be disenfranchised. That everyone who was eligible and wanted to vote could vote.

We put it in our campaign script. Whenever we called voters, my people didn't push President Obama first, and they didn't push my reelection. The first thing they said was, "Please vote no to photo ID."

Republicans in the Minnesota legislature also put a second constitutional amendment on the ballot in 2012: one to ban gay marriage. Their state senate communications director later admitted that it was only done to bring out the Republican base. Dozens of organizations and thousands of people came together in a coalition to oppose the amendment under the banner "Minnesotans United for All Families."

Folks working to defeat both amendments created this slogan: "Minnesota Nice, Vote No Twice."

The marriage equality movement had a lot of support on the ground. They had a major campaign to defeat that divisive, discriminatory amendment. But there was little to no countereffort regarding voter ID before we jumped into the fray. So we decided to work closely together and make sure that people voted no on both fronts.

We got help from Washington to inform the voters about what was really happening. Barbara Arnwine, executive director of the Lawyers' Committee for Civil Rights Under Law, came to Minnesota to train folks how to combat these tactics. We even brought some Minnesotans to DC for a voting-rights training session held by the Congressional Black Caucus; there they received training and information about how to help voters understand how to stand up for their rights.

One year after Kiffmeyer proposed her bill, support tumbled from 80 percent all the way down to 52 percent. On Election Day, when the numbers came in, I was literally holding my breath.

And we won!

We defeated an amendment that had seemed like it would be approved in a cakewalk. Now that we beat voter ID in Minnesota on the ballot, people all around America know that you can win. No longer will the moneyed people behind ALEC and groups like it think that they can just walk in and impose their will on issues such as voter ID. This is why I came to Washington: to make this kind of a difference.

Our job as elected officials is to do what's best for We the People. As Humphrey said, to pass that moral test of government. To make decisions that are for the good of us all—not to do just what's politically expedient.

With our victory in defeating the voter-ID law in Minnesota, I learned that you can accomplish almost anything if you work hard and organize. You can't worry about the odds, or the polls, or what people are saying. You have to be motivated by doing what is right, by the power of the idea, and have the passion and commitment to see it through.

In just a few months, we were able to sway an overwhelmingly popular idea that was insidious, get people to see that it was anti-democratic, and vote their conscience. We did it through organization and education.

We also didn't give up. To date, twenty-six states have adopted some sort of voter-ID law. More are considering doing so. Minnesota was the first (and, to date, the only) state to say no.

That victory encouraged me to continue what we started here. It also told me that our democracy works. Our democracy is not something to be taken for granted. You have to fight for it. You have to commit yourself to working for it—for the long haul.

Pundits and some in the mass media will have you quit before you start. You may think that someone knows something more than you do. But in your gut, you know when something is wrong. You should never sit by and do nothing while wrong prevails.

We have to see politics as a moment in time. If we lose in one minute, we can win in the next.

People in power pushed the voter restrictions because they intended to maintain their grip on power. They wanted to be able to pass any kind of law they wanted, and in order to do that, they needed their people in office. That's how power works sometimes. And if people go to sleep and aren't vigilant, it's to the distinct advantage of those holding the power.

My job—my mission—is to do what I can to help build our more perfect union. That requires action. Collective action. I have learned that with action and organization around a righteous cause, you can make a difference.

A historic difference.

Acknowledgements

All books are collaborations, and *My Country, 'Tis of Thee* is no exception. A great number of people helped to make this book possible. No doubt I am going to miss someone. I apologize in advance. This book would have never been possible without Karen Hunter and Charles Suitt. Charles believed in the project and supported it, and Karen and I worked together to produce the product. We talked, and we wrote—together. It was a pleasure. She listened, helped me to find the right language, and offered critical feedback. I also want to thank Brigitte Smith, Louise Burke, and the entire team at Gallery/Simon & Schuster for helping to make this happen.

Charles and Karen were moved to call me and propose the book project following my testimony at a House Homeland Security Committee hearing called by then-chairman Peter King on the subject of Muslim radicalization. My testimony, which grabbed headlines all over the country, was inspired by the heroic acts of Mohammad Salman Hamdani, a twenty-three-year-old Pakistani immigrant who lost his life trying to save fellow Americans during the World Trade Center attack on 9/11. I acknowledge Hamdani as a catalyst for this book, and all the people who gave their lives that day. May God bless them. Hamdani's mother, Talat Hamdani, shared her precious memories of her brave son, and helped form the inspiration for this book as well.

I thank my family and loved ones, including Karen Monahan.

My mother, Clida Martinez Ellison, is and will always be a central figure in my life. I thank her for everything, including the many times we discussed family history and my upbringing for this project.

My dad, Dr. Leonard Ellison, was also a big help in this regard—as were my four brothers and other family members. Richard Kaspari, with his encyclopedic understanding of US history, and Carla Kjellberg, my friend and unofficial big sister, made invaluable contributions to the text with constant feedback and review.

My friend Hannah Allam, an award-winning journalist, was a source of excellent feedback and perspective. Much thanks to co-workers who shared their views and helped with organization, especially Kari Moe and Dusty Brandenburg.

I am sure I am missing many people who deserve acknowledgement for their contributions. You know who you are. Thank you.

Printed in the United States
By Bookmasters